CREATIVE DRAMA
IN THE CLASSROOM
GRADES 4-6

TEACHER'S RESOURCE BOOK FOR THEATRE ARTS

JUNE COTTRELL

Western Michigan University

NTC NATIONAL TEXTBOOK COMPANY • Lincolnwood, Illinois

Dedicated to those children of all ages, especially Laurie,
Christopher, Craig, Sue Anne, Nathan and Matthew, who have inspired
me to keep my "child" alive and well; and to the many classroom
teachers and their children who have so generously shared creative
drama with me through the years.

The author and publisher would like to thank the
following for their contribution to the development of this
book: Professor John Warren Stewig, Ph.D., School of
Education, University of Wisconsin-Milwaukee; Joanne
Jeffers, Teacher of Gifted and Talented, Harlem
Elementary School, Baytown, Texas; and Ann Jensen,
Highland Park High School, Dallas.

The photographs in this text were provided by the
following:

Cover:	James L. Shaffer©, Dubuque, Iowa
Chapter 1:	James L. Shaffer
Chapter 2:	Karen Christoffersen, National Textbook Company
Chapter 3:	James L. Shaffer
Chapter 4:	Karen Christoffersen
Chapter 5:	Karen Christoffersen
Chapter 6:	James L. Shaffer
Chapter 7:	James L. Shaffer
Chapter 8:	Ellis Herwig, Marilyn Gartman Agency, Inc.

Contents

Chapter 6 Integrating Drama with Content Areas

Chapter 7 Creative Drama and Mass Entertainment

Chapter 8   Writing Workable Plans — 221

Preface

Creative Drama in the Classroom Grades 4-6 is a resource book designed to provide classroom teachers, media center specialists, theatre arts teachers, and others with both a theoretical background in creative drama and detailed assistance in doing drama with children in the later elementary/middle school grades. It is the book's purpose to provide teachers, both those who have formal training in theatre arts and those without, with practical ideas and examples of classroom-tested drama experiences based on sound child development theories and pedagogical practices. A companion volume, *Creative Drama in the Classroom Grades 1-3*, is available. It provides material for use with early elementary school children.

Creative Drama in the Classroom Grades 4-6 includes suggestions for providing experiences that can prepare the way for more formal work in theatre for students who wish to do so at the secondary level, while emphasizing that drama in the elementary program should include *all* children in actual participation. This includes the children with special needs and abilities in resource and developmental rooms, as well as those mainstreamed into regular classrooms. In addition, the book offers guidance in helping adults and children select quality experiences as consumers of the theatre arts, including live performance, films and television, with special attention to the role and responsibilities of the child as "audience."

The sequence of activities in this book is planned to parallel the later elementary child's physical, cognitive, emotional, social, and aesthetic development with special concern for the needs of the child who is emerging from childhood and approaching adolescence. The sequence of activities also recognizes that classrooms will include children who have had a substantive background in drama and those who have had little or none at all, at least within the school curriculum. There is an emphasis throughout on a holistic, integrated approach to drama in education.

While the major portion of this book is devoted to practical suggestions for classroom work, it also offers considerable support to the professional educator who strives to create a classroom environment that fosters learner-centered, integrated learning in the broader sense.

Some fortunate children will enter the later grades having participated in drama on a regular basis during the early years. More will have done so on a limited basis or not at all. The later elementary teacher or drama specialist needs to be able to accommodate such diverse backgrounds within a single group, providing very basic experiences and training for some while challenging those who are more advanced and competent. *Creative Drama in the Classroom Grades 4-6* strives to provide practical assistance in meeting such a breadth of needs. Therefore, early work explores body awareness, spatial perception, sensory awareness and recall, creative movement, simple pantomime, and beginning work with vocal expression and dialogue. The sections that follow emphasize more advanced work, including suggestions and examples for small group planning for the dramatization of literature, characterization group improvisation with original dialogue, and situation role-playing for problem-solving. Whether building a foundation or reviewing previously learned skills, the later elementary teacher will want to offer these children drama experiences that suit their maturing abilities, cognitive and social needs, and that are based on content and situations that are of interest to them.

Chapter 1 presents a rationale for including theatre arts education in the later elementary grades. Creative drama is discussed as an art for children, as part of the language arts curriculum, and as a method for teaching and learning in the several content areas. The value of drama for later elementary children is examined in light of contemporary learning theories.

Chapter 2 defines the role of the teacher as drama leader, with suggestions for planning, organizing, and managing drama so as to create a school environment in which both children and drama can thrive. Various instructional strategies are detailed, including leader techniques and the use of storytelling.

Chapter 3 provides a variety of movement and pantomime activities for children with diverse backgrounds and experiences in creative drama. Sensory awareness and recall activities provide a range of ways to involve both beginners and experienced participants in imaginative thinking and creative expression.

Chapter 4 focuses on polishing pantomime and improvisation skills, story dramatization in small groups, and working from the original ideas of the children. A breadth of literary genres are used or suggested as a basis for classroom drama.

Chapter 5 introduces several techniques for the development of characters drawn from literature or invented by the players. Creative drama is used to explore the elements of dramatic structure in literature and in original stories for dramatization. Work with readers theatre and puppetry provides transition experiences in theatre arts prior to moving into more formal work in secondary education.

Chapter 6 focuses on the use of creative drama as a validated approach to teaching and learning in the content areas, including language arts, foreign language study, social studies, science, physical education, and multi-arts expressions. In addition, it includes suggestions for the use of creative drama with mainstreamed children in the regular classroom.

Chapter 7 uses a variety of creative drama techniques to help children better understand television, films, and live performance so that they are prepared to select quality experiences. Special attention is focused on the role of children as consumers of the theatre arts.

Chapter 8 presents suggestions and stratagies for the development of unit plans for drama education, ideas for flow chart planning, writing lesson (teaching) plans and designing useful ways to assess children's growth and progress in drama. This chapter offers a list of verbs that are effective for writing student learning objectives and includes suggestions for a special drama event, a sample lesson plan and a model for designing evaluation instruments.

Six appendixes provide lists of resource materials for use in the classroom, stories to dramatize and an annotated bibliography of literature appropriate to grades 4-6.

An Index of Activities and Ideas, pages 265–270, provides a convenient guide to a variety of experiences that can be used to achieve the theatre arts learning objectives appropriate to the later elementary grade levels.

Throughout the book, several typographic devices are used to promote clear communication between text and reader and to call attention to specific parts of the book. Material that can be directly applied within the classroom—i.e. narratives, poetry, some sequenced activities, etc., is presented in a slightly different typeface than the rest of the book. A special "marker" is used to relate activities/ideas to the learning objectives that appear within this book's scope and sequence chart. The "markers" are presented in large type that runs into the margins of the book and are preceded by a ■.

A significant portion of the book is devoted to the use of creative drama as an approach to teaching and learning in the several content areas. This application recognizes that children learn best when information, concepts, and skills are not learned in isolation but are applied and integrated in such ways that learners can grasp their importance and value. Drama as a teaching methodology does not detract from drama as art. It offers alternative ways to learn that accommodate a variety of preferred learning styles, special interests, needs, and abilities. Furthermore, drama encourages children to learn from and with each other, and as a group art, is especially suited to the increased peer-orientation of later elementary children.

From the perspective of both teachers and children, drama is not just for the few . . . the experienced, the talented, the elite. Of course, additional experiences in theatre arts should be available for those with particular interests and abilities, but all children benefit from classroom drama as an art that extends from the spontaneous dramatic play of early childhood, and that affords a natural, experiential, process-centered way to learn more about themselves and the world. As such, creative drama can be particularly rewarding for our "almost" adolescents, and their teachers, as they are guided in drama to explore and reflect upon a variety of human experiences.

SCOPE AND SEQUENCE OF STUDENT LEARNING OBJECTIVES
Theatre Arts—Grades 4-6

Within each category, concepts, skills, and attitudes appear in developmental order.

■ IMAGINATIVE THINKING/CREATIVE PROBLEM SOLVING

Able to respond to concrete stimuli with an imaginative response.

Demonstrate increased abilities to be intellectual risk-takers.

Able to generate optional ways to think, feel, do, and solve problems.

Use sensory recall and past experiences (real/personal/vicarious/imagined) to guide action/speech/role-playing.

Use a variety of stimuli (concrete and symbolic) to visualize environments and situation.

Able to provide original ideas for translating literature into drama.

Can provide original ideas for group improvisations.

■ MOVEMENT AND PANTOMIME

Use whole body and body parts to imitate actions.

Listen and translate words and sounds into appropriate movement and pantomime.

Able to use body, facial expression, and gestures to interpret ideas and feelings through movement and pantomime.

Can respond to rhythm and melody with representational and interpretive movement.

Can establish a sense of place, time, and mood through pantomime.

Able to refine pantomime skills using disciplined movement, pause and concentration to clearly communicate ideas, feelings, relationships.

Use movement and pantomime to project thoughts and feelings of a character.

Identify specific attributes of character by observation of body actions, gestures, and facial expression.

■ SPATIAL AWARENESS

Work effectively in different sizes and kinds of space.

Can share space in both parallel work and interactively with another.

Use space in aesthetically pleasing ways when engaged in interpretive movement.

Demonstrate how space is used and shared to help define characters and relationships between and among characters.

■ SENSORY AWARENESS AND RECALL

Demonstrate use of senses, separately and in combination to motivate movement, pantomime, imitative sounds and speech.

Demonstrate abilities to use senses separately or combined as motivation for imaginative thinking and expression.

Able to use sensory recall to imagine and create properties, environments, and events.

Use sensory recall to generate spontaneous speech and sincere emotions.

Utilize sensory recall to establish a dominant mood in story dramatization.

Able to use sensory recall to show ideas and feelings of invented characters.

■ VERBALIZATION

Can provide imitative sounds to accompany movement and pantomime.

Use voice expressively in choric work and storytelling.

Use the voice to express a wide range of emotions.

Create appropriate verbal responses in situational role-playing.

Can improvise dialogue in pairs and small groups.

Add extensive amounts of improvised dialogue to the dramatization of literature or original stories.

Provide appropriate "voice" for invented characters in story dramatization, puppet and shadow plays, etc.

Able to use the voice effectively in scripted work when reading aloud (solo and readers theatre), scripted puppet plays.

■ DRAMATIC STRUCTURE

Can analyze a story in terms of who, what, where, when, and why.

Can create the beginning of a story that establishes and communicates time and place.

Can include a variety of kinds of conflicts in story dramatization.

Able to identify a dominant mood.

Can compare and contrast episodic and progressive action plots.

Can identify climax in literary and/or theatrical offerings.

Able to predict endings from textual cues.

Can create multiple resolutions to a conflict and demonstrate optional endings in story dramatization.

■ CHARACTERIZATION

Use actions, gestures, and facial expression to imitate a role.

Able to identify different kinds of characters . . . flat, round, stereotypes, static, dynamic.

Can identify what motivates a character in a literary offering.

Can compare and contrast the point-of-view of different characters.

Able to create a believable character by inventing physical, emotional, and social attributes.

Can translate ideas about a character into action, gestures, facial expression and speech.

■ STORY DRAMATIZATION

Can dramatize a literary selection using pantomime and some improvised speech.

Able to invent and contribute to an original story working from a variety of motivational materials.

Apply understanding of dramatic structure to the development of original stories.

Create unique individual characters when participating in crowd scenes.

Able to manipulate the elements of a story (characters, conflict, setting, mood) to create a new story.

Can dramatize a story using different forms such as live action, puppetry, shadow plays, readers theatre, etc.

■ INTRAPERSONAL/INTERPERSONAL DEVELOPMENT

Demonstrate self-esteem by sharing ideas and feelings during drama work.

Demonstrate self-esteem and respect for others by a lack of exhibitionism.

Listen respectfully to ideas of others, both peers and teacher.

Demonstrate a willingness to use the body to express ideas and feelings.

Demonstrate personal risk-taking by a willingness to explore new ideas and try new things.

Able to work with others in a mature and cooperative way.

Able to contribute constructively to evaluation of group work.

Contribute constructive and insightful evaluation of own work.

■ AESTHETIC DEVELOPMENT

Demonstrate attentive, respectful listening to stories and other materials.

Demonstrate respect for the ideas and feelings of others during planning, playing, and assessment.

Model appropriate audience behaviors as part of a group watching film or other media presentations.

Model appropriate audience etiquette when viewing live performance.

Can compare and contrast various theatre arts forms . . . film, television, and live performance.

Can articulate strengths and weaknesses of a particular offering as assessed against specific criteria covered in class discussions.

Able to describe own preferences and support personal choices with some rationale.

CHAPTER 1

Creative Drama as an Educational Tool

Creative drama is an art for children in which they involve their whole selves in experiential learning that requires imaginative thinking and creative expression. Through movement and pantomime, improvisation, role-playing and characterization, and more, children explore what it means to be a human being. Whether the content of the drama is based in reality or pure fantasy, children engaged in drama make discoveries about themselves and the world. Creative drama is an extension of the spontaneous drama of childhood, and classroom experiences can build on a process already familiar to most children and through which they have been exploring and discovering most of their lives. The progression from the make-believe play of preschoolers, through the creative drama of elementary students, and into formal theatre arts education in secondary schools can be compared to the building of competencies, skills, and critical appreciation in all of the fine or performing arts.

As an educator, you would not want to see a student "frozen" in time and talents in art or music or creative writing, and so the educational system provides continuous opportunities for students to grow and develop their knowledge and skills in these areas of artistic and creative expression. Drama in the classroom ought to be treated similarly. Like participation in other arts, participation in drama offers special kinds of opportunities for children to grow as whole human beings, able to think, feel, and express in special ways. The omission of a full range of opportunities in the theatre arts in K-12 education would deprive students of the valuable experiences unique to drama.

USING INFORMAL DRAMA IN GRADES 4-6

As emerging adolescents, students in grades 4-6 often feel confused and fragmented, quite grown-up in some ways and very young in others. They are in transition: physically, cognitively, emotionally, and socially. They are often unsure about their own bodies, which seem to change faster than their perceptions of them; some are already taking on the characteristics of puberty while others of similar age still look like "little kids."

■ SUPPORTING THE NEED FOR DRAMA

Classroom experiences in drama, with opportunities to deal with body awareness and expression, can provide a format for exploring self-perceptions and attitudes about self and others. In addition, drama often engages students in activities in which they can practice coordination and grace in comfortable, nonthreatening ways. Because drama is a group art, everyone is invited to take part. Those who wish to solo or assume special roles are generally free to do so, and others can be just as much a part of the action without drawing extra attention to themselves. When the classroom or drama teacher creates an environment based on trust, respect, and mutual support, both drama and students benefit. Even the most inhibited, self-conscious preadolescent may find herself or himself sensitively and gently drawn into the experience and remain to explore and grapple with dimensions of that self in constructive ways.

Healthy children at this age are often very physical, and drama invites them to channel some of those energies into physical expression that is neither competitive nor aggressive. It offers an alternative to both sports and roughhousing as a way of directing energies and disciplining the body. And every student can be successful whether or not he or she has special aptitudes or physical prowess. For example, the child who can pantomime, in slow motion, the professional athlete accomplishing some remarkable feat, has also disciplined her or his own body and accomplished something physically challenging. Both the experience and the feelings that accompany such success are fulfilling for the preadolescent.

Later elementary children are also cognitively in a state of transition. Sometimes they function as concrete operational thinkers, able to do many quite sophisticated cognitive functions provided there are ample opportunities to experiment, try-on, and manipulate materials. Like younger students, they benefit from experiential, hands-on learning, and drama is one way to provide this. Other times, they operate in a more perceptual way similar to that of younger children. By the time they reach sixth grade, some students begin to function very much as adult thinkers; they are able to think in terms of cause-and-effect, to hypothesize and predict outcomes based on evidence at hand. Drama can provide opportunities to practice this kind of thinking (for example, to predict an ending to a story or create multiple endings all of which could be possible based upon what has gone before). Drama activities can be designed to accommodate (within the same group and lesson) students who are functioning at these several levels and can provide unusual ways to practice and apply newly emerging modes of thought.

■ PROVIDING HOLISTIC LEARNING

Drama encourages students to keep both hemispheres of the brain actively involved in the learning process, even in such a left-hemisphere world as the classroom. This is not only reinforcing to children who prefer to learn in a more holistic, imaging, and spatial way, but challenges those who are more linear, logical, and verbal to become better at visualizing and synthesizing. Why settle for nourishing half a brain when you can engage students in learning activities that draw on a breadth of functions rather than a few? Many of the suggestions in chapter 6 (Integrating Drama with Content Areas) incorporate a holistic, bi-modal approach to learning a range of subject matter.

■ MEETING DEVELOPMENTAL NEEDS

Today's children seem to be growing up faster than ever before. And although this may be perceived as a cliché of each successive generation of adults, there seems ample evidence to suggest that we may be experiencing a crisis situation with regard to childhood. Neil Postman, in *The Disappearance of Childhood* (1982), examines what he feels is a critical situation for children, both now and in the future. Postman, a media ecologist, places much blame on the electronic media. Whatever the reasons (and there are probably several), many later elementary students exhibit attitudes and behaviors formerly associated with the junior high age. Physically and socially, they often strive to be more like teenagers than their actual years. This often results in trauma, feelings of inadequacy, confusion, and conflict with adults. Trying on roles in characterization, dramatizing literature that offers insights into human experiences, and engaging in situation role-playing (socio-drama) are just some of the kinds of drama work that help these children better understand themselves and others. A traditional view of theatre as catharsis is also not inappropriate to the rationale for drama in the later grades.

■ USING DRAMA AS METHODOLOGY

Those who recognize the benefits but still feel that doing drama with fourth-, fifth-, and sixth-grade students may be taking precious time from the important content areas, should remember that like all theatre, drama always has a content; it is about something. Much can be learned from each engagement in drama. Drama allows students to assimilate and accommodate knowledge in a different way than other methods do. Further, as a performing art, drama utilizes skills, particularly communication skills, and provides a natural format in which such skills can be practiced and polished. And, by definition, drama affords the participants diverse avenues in which to explore and express feelings, to question and challenge perspectives (their own and others), and to search for understanding of the large problems of human existence. Appropriately incorporated into the curriculum, drama with later elementary students need not reduce class time needed for learning: indeed, it multiplies possibilities for teaching in ways that reinforce learning that sticks. That there may also be pleasure and excitement in the learning is generally regarded by teachers and students as a plus.

PREPARING FOR FORMAL WORK

When drama "works" for children, some will want to develop greater knowledge and expertise in theatre arts (just as some do in music and the visual arts). The types of drama activities best suited to grades 4-6 can often provide both transition and beginning work in formal theatre. Students who have regularly participated in creative drama throughout their elementary years should be better prepared to participate in theatre productions later on and to appreciate and enjoy theatre as older youth and adults. They become the performers, directors, and technicians of the professional theatre and patrons of the theatre as well.

■ PREPARING FOR FORMAL THEATRE

Transition experiences in informal drama can include such work as analyzing a story to discover its dramatic structure, utilizing more sophisticated criteria than previously applied. Beginning work in real characterization in which students attempt to build believable characters of multiple dimensions allows them to better develop roles in formal work and makes them better able to build characters from the inside out. As players, they become astute in discovering what motivates their characters. Improvisation work lets students put characters and plot together to tell their own stories, using increased understanding of character interaction in order to generate original dialogue. Fourth-, fifth-, and sixth-grade students want to help pick the stories they are going to dramatize, which means they gain an in-depth exploration of the material—in terms of both literary and human value.

In addition to the creative drama work, related art forms help prepare students for formal theatre experiences. Reading literature aloud with attention to analysis of the literary works in order to more accurately share an author's meaning is excellent preparation for later work with scripted materials. Readers theatre productions, puppet plays using simple scripts, and individual performances of literary pieces around a central theme are discussed in detail in chapter 5 (Toward More Advanced Work). These activities, often integrated with other content area work, bring students along in a natural progression that fits their changing needs, interests, and aptitudes.

RELATING CREATIVE DRAMA TO LANGUAGE ARTS

Drama in grades 4-6 plays a dual role in curriculum: as a performing art and as part of the entire range of language arts. The curriculum for later elementary students expands to include more work in the social studies, mathematics, and science. This makes the use of drama for reinforcing concepts and skills in listening, speaking, writing, and reading take on an even stronger role than it does for early elementary students. The content for the drama can be drawn from other subject areas and used as the vehicle for integrating and applying language arts concepts and skills to the teaching of history, geography, and the natural sciences.

■ ENHANCING LANGUAGE LEARNING

It may seem especially difficult to find time and ways to attend to ongoing work in the areas of speaking and listening. Good communication skills, both oral and written, continue to be designated as paramount to success in both academe and the workplace. Mastery of strong communication skills is too important to be left to chance, and teachers of grades 4-6 must find unique ways to give students all that they need without sacrificing other important work.

Oral language skills

These are some ways in which creative drama can contribute to the oral curriculum in grades 4-6; suggestions for implementation appear in chapter 6.

1. Continued work with movement and pantomime reinforces the important role of nonverbal communication, particularly in communicating the feelings behind the words. Increased concern for congruency between the verbal and nonverbal message systems can be explored through drama work that combines movement and speech.

2. Drama lessons can include a good deal of work in pairs, allowing students to engage in dyadic communication and to experientially discover the transactional nature of interpersonal communication: how speakers and listeners are interdependent and must adapt their individual behaviors if meaning is to be shared and effective communication take place. (Improvised dialogue, especially in pair work, is one of the most successful strategies you can use to practice active listening.)

3. Planning and debriefing sessions in drama require participants to engage in higher levels of thinking such as creative, synthesizing thinking and critical, evaluative thinking. Later elementary students are beginning to move into cognitive stages that permit adultlike thought. Classroom activities that challenge and encourage cause-and-effect thinking, hypothesizing, critical analysis, and synthesizing can directly contribute to more advanced oral and written communication. Only mature thinking can result in sophisticated speaking and writing.

4. Students in grades 4-6 often prefer to work in small groups in drama as befits their growing desires to work with peers, using adults as resource rather than directive persons. Drama can experientially provide insights into how people can function in groups to accomplish tasks and participate in democratic decision making and problem solving.

5. Work with imitative sound and improvised dialogue helps students experiment with verbal expression and recognize the human voice as a remarkable instrument able to communicate powerful ideas and feelings through tone, volume and rate as well as language.

6. Expressing ideas and feelings with clarity, accuracy, and style can be practiced through a wide variety of drama activities.

7. Students may use role-playing and work in developing more rounded characters to engage one another in empathic listening. This is an important kind of listening that is very difficult to "teach," but can be *experienced* by trying on the point-of view of another. Developing the

ability to be an empathic listener is more possible as a student grows out of an egocentric orientation, and drama is an effective means for practicing listening techniques.

8. Improvisations based on original ideas of a group and the informal dramatization of literature both rely on the players to develop their own use of space to establish and show relationships between and among characters. Unlike work in formal theatre, where the director blocks (designates where actors stand and how they move in relationship to one another), in creative drama students must place themselves in relationship to each other in ways that communicate such qualities as status and closeness of relationships.

9. Situation role-playing (sometime called socio-drama) utilizes drama concepts and skills to deal with problems encountered in real life, particularly problems that involve managing interpersonal conflict and making appropriate personal choices. These activities are especially of value to the personal and interpersonal needs of later elementary students.

10. Participation in a variety of exercises and dramatizations causes students to practice the full range of communication functions as identified by the Speech Communication Association's National Project on Speech Communication Competencies, reported in *Developing Communication Competence in Children* (Allen & Brown, eds., 1976): to inform, to control, to imagine, to express feelings, and to engage in the ritual communication of the culture.

11. Drama work integrated with mass media can contribute to students' competencies as listeners to media. It also reinforces the idea that "listening" involves visual as well as aural perception.

Literacy

Drama can play an important role in the literacy components of the language arts curriculum. The following are some ways in which drama can contribute to the writing, reading, and literature programs in grades 4-6:

1. Players can apply their creative drama abilities to the exploration of the elements of a story (exposition, development, conflict, climax, denouement, setting, character motivation, and so forth), when choosing literature to dramatize and in creating original improvisation. While younger children engaged in simple story dramatization are experientially discovering the elements of the story through participation but are not competent to analyze the structure in even a limited way, students in grades 4–6 are capable of applying to their drama new information gained from literature study. Though such analysis is done at a very basic level, where students have the opportunity to actually *apply* their analytical skills, they can begin to handle more difficult concepts. The work provides the concrete basis for discussion.

2. As students become more abstract thinkers, they enjoy creative movement and pantomime work because it lets them explore and demonstrate their own interpretations of poetry by physically responding to the moods, emotions, and rhythms of the poem. Unlike younger children whose interpretations are more often at the denotative level of meaning, these students can often discover ways to show deeper levels of meaning.

3. It is important to find a variety of ways to keep students excited about reading once they have become competent silent readers. Story dramatization affords a special way to make literature come alive, including types of stories that students might otherwise label as dull or too complex (stories from mythology and longer narrative poetry, for instance).

4. Creating original scenes and plays can help in further understanding of the structure of a story and is useful in both the reading and writing programs.

5. A wide variety of creative drama activities can be used for motivating both expository and creative writing, including work with literary inventions such as metaphor, allit-

eration, onomatopoeia, and experimenting with the power of words. Where younger boys and girls participate in this work at an imitative level (for example, creating sounds in an arrow story or pantomiming the actions while saying a tongue-twister such as "Peter Piper Picked a Peck of Pickled Peppers"), in grades 4-6 students may create their own wordplay to accompany movement or make up metaphors to pantomime.

6. Related art forms such as readers theatre or oral interpretation programs composed of individual readings around a central theme may combine both literacy and oracy. Students can select materials and read from them with appropriate vocal expression that sensitively and vividly communicates the literature to an audience.

7. Putting drama skills to work in preparing and sharing a puppet theatre play with other students, a class develops a special involvement with literature and discovers the role of audience in making appropriate selections and adaptations that will appeal to listeners.

8. As students move toward formal theatre work, experiences in readers theatre and reading plays as part of literature can contribute toward beginning work in selecting and performing from a script.

Creative drama in grades 4-6 performs a dual role within the language arts curriculum: as a discrete component as drama and for engaging students in a variety of work in speaking, listening, writing, reading, and with literature. It can keep students reading aloud with understanding and expression even after they are competent silent readers. Both as art and language art, the integrative potential of drama provides good return on investment for the time spent, and this may be critical when there is so much curriculum to cover in such a short time.

LEARNING THEORIES AND DRAMA

Ideally, drama is part of the teaching/learning program in a continuous way from kindergarten on, but most students do not experience this. Sometimes, in fact, drama plays an important role in the early grades but is not perceived as equally important or of value in the later elementary grades. Even if your fourth-, fifth-, or sixth-grade students have had little or no previous classroom experience in drama, you should consider the role that drama may play in helping them cope with their emerging adolescence. You will find support for drama, not only from theatre and language arts educators, but from cognitive psychology and social learning theory.

Developmental theory

To find the broadest support for the inclusion of drama in the learning program for grades 4-6, look at a broad spectrum of educational and social psychology. Some of the strongest rationale are found in Piagetian psychology because it allows useful applications in actual, everyday classroom work. Therefore, this brief discussion focuses on Piaget's insights into the cognitive development of children in this period of growth, particularly as these can be explored and related to drama.

■ VALIDATING DRAMA WITH RESEARCH

During most of the later elementary years, Piaget categorized cognition as *concrete operational* (*The Language and Thought of the Child*, 1957). During this period, children move away from basing their thinking on how things look (perception), to reasoning about things and events. Although not yet ready to think about thinking, the child can use concrete events and experiences as a basis for figuring things out. This allows the child to deal with more than one aspect of an object or event at one time, a process Piaget called *decentering* because the child no longer simply focuses on one aspect of something while ignoring other variables. For example, while younger children tend to give credence to the actual words they heard, ignoring the nonverbal cues to a great extent, older children can take both verbal and nonverbal messages into consideration in order to discover what you mean. As drama at this level begins to include more opportunities to combine body action and verbalization, children can manipulate those elements to send either congruent or incongruent messages. They are better able to understand the persona of the villain who sweet-talks with words but does so with a glint in the eye and a curl of the lip. As they begin real work in characterization, children become increasingly able to develop characters that are more complete than the one-dimensional roles that populate their earlier work. This contributes to a better understanding of their own behaviors and the communication behaviors of others.

Another characteristic of the concrete operational child is her or his movement from the egocentricity of early childhood to being more other-centered. Piaget suggested that the egocentricity of the child must be challenged if he or she is to become able to look at the world from the point of view of others as well as self. Furthermore, Piaget posited that this lessening of egocenteredness is requisite to increased intellectual growth. Drama can provide a variety of experiences to experientially assist the child in making this transition. The concreteness of the drama suits the cognition of the child, and the opportunities to explore a wide range of perspectives and to put the self in new situations where old solutions to problems do not work contributes significantly to intellectual growth.

By about sixth grade, as students prepare to move into secondary school, many are cognitively functioning much like adults—able to reason both deductively and inductively, to hypothesize, and to deal with a number of variables at one time in solving problems. They can use drama to practice these new cognitive skills. Formal operational thinkers can deal with the abstract, they can conjecture about possibilities—what constitutes social justice, why freedom of thought as permitted in a democracy might be preferred over other ideologies, and so forth. Sixth-graders role-playing the Continental Congress begin to appreciate the several points of view that the delegates represented and the complexity of designing and establishing a country based on new precepts. Dramatic simulation affords a concreteness that is of great value to the emerging propositional thinkers.

Drama for students at the later boundaries of concrete thinking and early formal operations provides experiences in which the participants are encouraged to deal with what could be. For example, original improvisations developed by students working in small groups can explore and try out a multiplicity of new endings to a piece of literature. Based on what has transpired, students discover other possible outcomes in addition to an author's ending. Using either inductive or deductive reasoning skills, they may come up with additional ideas of what could be, or using even more sophisticated thinking, they might take an ending and speculate about its causes.

For all students from grades three and four through grades five and six, whether moving from perceptual to concrete operational thought or entering formal operations, the experiential, inventive nature of drama may assist and challenge new, more advanced ways of processing. The drama experiences provide a safe, nonthreatening format in which students can experiment and assess results. Unlike real-life experimentation, prediction, and invention, drama that involves students in exploring what could be or what might have been poses no threat to their physical or emotional safety or damage to their self-esteem. Such invention, central to increasingly more complex work in drama, is also at the core of all education, as defined by Piaget.

> The goal of education is to create men who are capable of doing new things, not simply repeating what other generations have done—men who are creative, inventive, and discoverers.
>
> (Ripple and Rockcastle, 1964, p. 5)

Right brain–left brain

For additional verification and validation of drama for later elementary students, examine the research and writing of Jerome S. Bruner (*On Knowing: Essays for the Left Hand,* 1962). Others who have paid particular attention to how the functions of the brain contribute to how children learn include Robert E. Ornstein (*The Nature of Human Consciousness,*

1974), Jerome L. Singer and Dorothy Singer, (many articles and books, including J. L. Singer with Ellen Switzer, *Mind-Play*, 1980), Bob Samples (*The Metaphoric Mind*, 1983), and Rita and Kenneth Dunn (*Teaching Students Through Their Individual Learning Styles*, 1978). These authors all confirm that people need many opportunities to learn in different ways.

■ REINFORCING BI-MODAL LEARNING

Traditionally, most classroom learning emphasizes the logical, rational, linear, and verbal functions of the left hemisphere of the brain, yet many children (and adults) learn best when they can employ visualization, intuition, imagination, and metaphoric, and spatial thinking—processes resident in the right hemisphere. Ideally, all students ought to use and strengthen their abilities with all functions, with teachers recognizing that for some learners the emphasis on left-hemisphere learning does not fit their preferred learning style.

The arts, including the theatre arts, offer experiences in which *both* hemispheres play major roles, with a considerable amount of traffic, *both directions*, over the corpus callosum, that remarkable bridge that connects the two halves of the human brain. A beautifully crafted British film *The Enchanted Loom* graphically supports a more holistic, integrated approach to teaching and learning that utilizes contemporary knowledge of how the brain functions; although the film does not deal directly with drama, it makes a strong case for the kind of teaching that would include drama as basic to the curriculum.

DEVELOPING SOCIAL SKILLS THROUGH CREATIVE DRAMA

Participation in drama, a group art form, involves students in special experiences that require social interaction and cooperation in order to succeed. The ensemble nature of creative drama (like ensemble work in music and dance) involves interaction in which competitiveness is seldom desired and winning is rarely a goal. Students can apply drama skills to a lively game of charades or "compete" in slow-motion animal tag, but charades are hardly drama and the "race" is more concerned with pantomime skills than finding a winner.

Drama emphasizes goals different from those of team sports; originality and inventiveness are generally valued over following the rules or coming in first. Flexibility and spontaneity of movement and speech are also highly valued. Risk-taking is as valued in drama as on the playing field, with perhaps more concern for intellectual and emotional risk-taking than physical. The following list of behaviors provides guidelines that let you make sure that drama is not only of value in reaching your teaching goals, but also of value to your students.

1. Each student will respond to motivational stimuli in ways that are individual and authentically her or his own; no child will feel a need to simply imitate or echo the responses of others in order to validate her or his own interpretations.

2. Older students engaged in drama will recognize and show tolerance and appreciation for each person's contribution, when planning, playing, sharing, and assessing their work. They will increase in their abilities to value the points of view of others without sacrificing their own ideas, feelings, and ways of expressing.

3. They will demonstrate an understanding of drama as process rather than product-oriented by showing more concern for the rights of all to participate, including those who seem to have less talent or artistry to contribute. This means that there is a minimum of exhibitionism, and individuals cooperate to enhance the work of the group.

4. Students will demonstrate self-esteem through willingness to share ideas and feelings.

5. Students will progress in their abilities to accept both criticism and praise and be able to offer both with generosity and sensitivity.

6. Students will demonstrate an acceptance of their own bodies by their willingness to communicate ideas and feelings through body movement as well as with language and to do so with naturalness and good humor.

7. Students will be willing to suspend their disbelief and engage in drama situations that draw on fantasy as well as more real world settings, characters, and events.

8. Students will show increased abilities to decenter, to look at several variables and possibilities when engaged in problem solving, invention, and critical analysis.

9. And, by the choices they make, the players will demonstrate increased abilities to recognize that which has intrinsic value and is aesthetically rewarding, particularly as they have increased input into determining the literature, concepts, and situations to be dramatized.

Creative drama with students in grades 4-6 remains the same art form as in the early grades. It relies on the participants' own creativity in response to motivation provided by either the teacher or the group: the players do not work from memorized scripts, everyone has an opportunity to participate, and such technical embellishments as costumes, settings, and make-up are not essential to the experience. The emphasis remains on the participation and the learning process rather than on a product to be shared with an audience. However, it is anticipated that later elementary students will sometimes want to polish a scene, a story dramatization, or a piece of improvised puppet theatre and share with others. This will be especially true as they move toward formal work in theatre arts. They enjoy learning stage terms and using them when discussing a scene; they often want to add theatrical trimmings to a more polished production. The real value remains in the *doing:* in being a part of the process, from the planning through the debriefing that should follow the work and in cooperating with their peers in exploring a variety of human experiences.

Drama provides an excellent forum for encouraging social

growth and development. It also affords a special way to explore a breadth of challenges associated with growing up. The content of the drama as well as the participation can materially assist pre- and early adolescents in coping with the anxieties and pressures that confront them on all sides. This can make drama an outlet for their concerns, a way to explore solutions to real-life problems and to try on many different roles as they search for direction for their own lives. The classroom or drama teacher who guides students in these explorations is often rewarded by getting a glimpse of the quality of the young adult just waiting to blossom forth from the child. Drama experiences can contribute to a positive transition from childhood to youth, helping to make the journey a little easier, more positive, and more exciting.

The Teacher as Drama Leader

The role of the drama leader, whether as drama specialist or classroom teacher, can be compared and contrasted with the responsibilities of the director in formal theatre; there are significant commonalities and even more significant differences. Both roles require an understanding and appreciation for theatre arts education, knowledge of the elements of drama, and an enthusiasm for helping players make a story come alive. However, the play director must acquire a whole range of skills that are quite different from those incumbent upon the drama leader. For example, a play director works from a script (that is ultimately memorized by the actors) in creating a Prompt Book, which furnishes a complete acting and staging version of the play with detailed analysis of the production. The contents of the director's copy of the Prompt Book reveal several of the significant differences between leading creative drama and directing formal theatre to which we just referred: detailed directions for blocking, stage business, floor plans of all settings, property lists, light plots, costume sketches, etc.

Drama leaders do not make these decisions for the players, so they do not make Prompt Books. In creative drama, there is no script to be memorized; movement of players, stage business, and so forth evolve from the creativity and decisions of the players as they develop their characters and decide how they relate and interact with one another, as well as from how the storyline is handled.

Play directors, or special casting directors, hold auditions, make choices, and assign roles. Leaders of creative drama

19

encourage all students to participate and use a variety of techniques to make certain that everyone who wishes to be in the experience has an opportunity to do so. Techniques for involving all who wish to participate are discussed in the framework of the several kinds of drama activities presented in chapters 3-5.

CREATING A DRAMA CLIMATE

It is important to the creation of the *drama climate* that leaders recognize the difference between choosing roles in the formal, auditioning sense as done in formal theatre and the choosing of roles in informal, spontaneous drama. The role of the creative drama leader is one of stimulator, guide, and participator in the learning process, although not necessarily as a participator in the drama *per se*. It is generally the responsibility of the drama teacher to provide the initial stimulation/motivation to engage students in the planning and playing. This often takes the form of some kind of sharing: a story, an experience, a sensory activity, a special piece of music, an interesting property, or an event in which the leader and students have participated, such as taking a field trip or viewing a film together. These are common vehicles for stimulating involvement that lead to discussion, planning, and participation in the actual drama work.

As the planning progresses, the leader serves as a guide to keep things moving and to help all students become and remain involved. In addition, several types of drama work require that the teacher provide guidance during the playing—through the use of questioning strategies, sidecoaching, and debriefing. Sometimes the teacher also needs to participate in a special way; for example, by assuming a role and stepping into the drama to keep the action "up" and the storyline progressing in interesting and useful directions. Whether as motivator, guide, or co-participant, the teacher's role is one of facilitator. The leader judiciously monitors her or his own role so as not to dominate but rather to make it easier for students to be successful, both as drama participants and as people. One of the most important and basic ways in which the drama leader is a facilitator is in establishing and maintaining a classroom climate that is conducive to quality drama experiences for students.

■ FACILITATING SELF-ESTEEM/SELF-RESPONSIBILITY

Creating an environment that is not only suitable but encouraging of drama is a major responsibility of the drama leader. The drama climate requires that there be mutual trust, respect, and an absence of duress. Whether a student chooses not to participate out of shyness, apprehension about what might happen, or a need to be contrary or disagreeable, quality experiences in drama are not possible when you force a student to participate. You better serve the creative process by patiently encouraging such students and giving them opportunities to "sit this one out." You can also assure them that when they can take part in ways that do not spoil the play for others, they are welcome to re-enter the drama, but not until they can be comfortable in the work and self-responsible. Your behavior as drama leader, as well as your words, must clearly communicate the importance of courtesy, trust, and mutual respect.

Fostering respect and maintaining trust

You foster respect by accepting both yourself and your students, by being open to ideas, supportive of feelings, and able to see value in the *process* whether or not the *product* is as successful as you desire. As drama leader, you must be a personal risk-taker who can encourage students to be intellectual and emotional risk-takers as well. You must remain as nonjudgmental as possible, not only because you hold a status role and therefore have special power, but also because you are a role model for your students. The importance of establishing a climate in which risk-taking is maximized cannot be understated. Anyone who has ever worked with a student who is reluctant to take an intellectual or emotional risk, who is afraid to guess at a word, or hazard an opinion, or share an honest feeling, understands all too well how damaging and restricting this can be to academic and personal success.

■ CRITIQUING CHILDREN'S EFFORTS

Closely related to this is an acknowledgment of the special relationship that exists between a student and what he or she creates. *You* may understand that the emphasis in creative drama is on process rather than on a finished product of some kind, but students think that whatever they produce — be it a pantomime game, a story dramatization, an original improvisation, or some other drama activity — is important. It is *theirs;* they have a vested interest in it. When they have risked and shared, created, and respected the work of their peers, the product of all of that struggle must not be taken or treated lightly. Particularly in the art of drama, where the product is neither pen-and-ink nor paint-and-clay but the direct exposure of the self, teachers must not fold, spindle, or mutilate.

Listening actively

The supportive climate provides an environment in which both teacher and students practice active listening. Active listening requires that people attend to what one another are saying, tuning out interference as much as possible. We hear one another out before assessing the validity or value of what we think we heard. We try very hard to monitor our listening in terms of our own biases and prejudices as we listen to the feelings and experiences behind the words as well as to their literal meanings. "The listener who wants to become a facilitator hears the words and responds to the ideas that are communicated by focusing on the personal meaning that accompanies the spoken words" (Wittmer & Myrick, 1974, p. 42). Finally, we provide useful feedback, both verbally and nonverbally.

Because creative drama deals with the *whole* child and is allied with holistic learning, the creative drama leader must take a facilitative approach. "The role of the teacher as a facilitator is diminished by any behaviors that tend to inhibit the children's confidence and trust" (Cottrell, 1975, p. 31). When you value and respect the totality of every child, when you accept and provide for individual interests, needs, and differences as far as possible, you have a classroom environment that not only supports creative drama but *all* learning. This is the kind of space in which both drama and children can thrive.

PLANNING FOR SUCCESS: GOALS AND OBJECTIVES

You can provide a supportive environment for students and drama and still come up short unless you also fulfill other responsibilities of the drama leader. Creativity does not "just happen": quality work in creative drama is not simply populating the right environment with facilitative teachers, enthusiastic and creative children, and stirring all together with generous doses of good literature, ample space, and a variety of motivating ideas. Drama of value requires thoughtful and imaginative planning toward reasonable and worthwhile goals: here the planning of the drama teacher is analogous to the play director's preparation of the Prompt Book. Good theatre is not serendipitous, and neither are rewarding experiences in creative drama.

Preparing teaching goals in drama

Long before the days of academic "accountability," superior teachers have known how to determine students' learning and growth needs. Such teachers are able to translate the information into teaching/learning goals and then select, from a wide repertoire of possibilities, the best ways for achieving the goals to meet both group and individual needs. Where education in the theatre arts takes its rightful place within the curriculum, you need to be able to create learner-oriented teaching goals in that field as well. As with all learning, teaching goals or purposes in theatre education should cover *knowledge* (what children need to know), *skills* (what children need to be able to do), and *attitudes* (views we desire the children develop). Goals for drama education should articulate both the information that students should know related to the drama itself and the goals related to the content of the drama. Creative drama, like formal theatre, is always about something. Consider the following example.

■ PLANNING FOR LEARNING

Students are engaged in small group improvisations based on the arrival of the Pilgrims at Plymouth Rock in 1620. In this integrated drama/social studies lesson, appropriate goals deal with both what the students need to know about the concept of improvisation and the information they need to know about the historical event involved. Thus a set of goals for the lesson includes these:

1. As a consequence of this lesson, students will better understand the concept of improvisation.
2. Participating in the improvisation will help students understand the circumstances and outcomes of the Pilgrims' arrival at Plymouth in 1620.

Other examples of knowledge goals for drama in the later grades are these: students will gain a better understanding of the differences between interpretative movement and pantomime; students will better understand the terms "protagonist" and "antagonist"; students will deepen their appreciation of quality literature; students will better understand the relationship between emotions and nonverbal behaviors.

■ IDENTIFYING SKILLS AND ATTITUDES

Teaching goals should also include skills that you anticipate building as a result of a drama lesson. Again, in addition to drama skills that are part of a statement of goals, there may also be skills related to other areas of learning. Skills goals can be written for any domain: cognitive, affective, physical, or social. A skills goal related to a drama lesson utilizing socio-drama might read this way:

Students will acquire a better understanding of the role of active listening in interpersonal conflict (a knowledge goal) and will acquire improved active listening skills (a skills goal).

A skills goal in the physical domain written for a drama lesson that includes a sequential pantomime game would be this:

Students will develop additional expertise in making pantomime more communicative to other players and/or to an audience.

A skills goal in the social domain could cover such behaviors as developing group skills or improved expertise in working interpersonally in pair work.

When appropriate, teaching goals should incorporate the development of mature or desirable attitudes. These generally deal with either the cognitive, affective, or social domains, including attention to aesthetic growth. An attitude goal related to either the planning or debriefing portions of a drama lesson might read as follows:

Students will progress in their abilities to handle valid criticism from their peers when that criticism is provided with respect and sensitivity.

Here are some other examples:

Students will better understand the need for tolerance of the ideas of others while planning a drama activity.

Students will recognize that exhibitionism negatively affects quality work in drama.

A goal dealing with attitudes related to aesthetic growth might be written as follows:

Students will show greater appreciation for films and television programming of higher aesthetic quality as a result of work in creative drama.

Writing student objectives

Once you have established clearly articulated goals covering the most important aspects of the lesson, you write student objectives to cover those goals. Student objectives are most useful when they describe behaviors that are observable and verifiable. Objectives answer the question, "How do I know my goals for this lesson are being met, and met at my desired level of competency for either the entire group or at various levels to accommodate individual needs and abilities within the group?"

Teacher goals and student objectives should always be highly correlated. All goals should be translated into observable student objectives, and there should not be student objectives that cannot be subsumed within one or more teaching goals.

■ ARTICULATING PERFORMANCE EXPECTATION

Gear student objectives for individual lessons toward the teaching goals you have identified, and then state them with as much specificity of observable behaviors as possible. Note that while such verbs as "know," "understand," "enjoy," "believe," and "listen" are useful and appropriate when writing teaching goals, they are far too ambiguous for describing student objectives. (For example, how do you know when a child is "listening"? For what specific behaviors can you look to confirm "listening"?) Furthermore, there are often many possible ways in which a goal may be reached; several different behaviors may be equally valid and indicative of the degree of achievement desired.

Teaching that tends to ignore holistic, bi-modal learning often limits the ways in which achievement can be measured. Paper-and-pencil seatwork is overused, while experiential learning that involves simulations, discussions, and the arts is underemployed. The use of drama, by contrast, contributes several ways in which goals may be met, behaviors such as these: move, imitate, perform, enter, exit, pantomime, and invent. Chapter 8 (Writing Workable Plans) includes an alphabetized list of 130 verbs that describe behaviors useful in writing student objectives in drama.

There are always additional goals and objectives that you could write, and the value of the lesson is never confined to those goals and objectives that are stated in the plan. It is generally understood that one goal of creative drama is for students to enjoy the experience and each other, "to have fun." This goal, however, would seldom be stated in the plan. It is very difficult to write an objective that reassures that such a goal is being met: such behaviors as laughing, smiling, and sounding happy are often indicative of pleasure in an activity, but highly involved students who are thoroughly enjoying an experience (having fun), may not exhibit those behaviors to any degree. They may, in fact, be very quiet, thoughtful, and engrossed in the work in very serious and sober ways. The dramatization of a serious story can provide as much pleasure in the doing as a humorous one.

Helping students develop positive views of themselves is another ongoing goal of drama that is not stated in every lesson. Again, it is often difficult to isolate specific behaviors that show that the goal is being met (particularly when assessing the results of one specific lesson). This type of goal is more often a progressive one, extending over several weeks or months of drama work, and is best assessed for an individual student on a continuum as noted on a long-range report. (See chapter 8 for suggestions about this kind of assessing and record keeping.)

ORGANIZING AND MANAGING DRAMA ACTIVITIES

Thoughtful, carefully articulated planning of goals and objectives is a necessary first step; however, the best plans in the world come to naught if they do not include workable ideas for dealing with the human factors. Some teachers who would like to use drama in the classroom hesitate to do so because they fear their students will not be able to handle the freedom. This may be particularly worrisome for teachers of grades 4-6 who recognize the role that peer pressure plays with this age group. However, when preparation for drama includes plans for organizing the players in ways that deal realistically with the social maturation and interpersonal competencies of students, then the drama should not only go smoothly but help students become more self-responsible in other contexts as well. One purpose of drama work is to offer opportunities and experiences for helping students develop concepts, skills, and attitudes that advance socialization.

As social beings, a class of later elementary students is seldom a very homogeneous group. They are not like early elementary students just emerging from a highly egocentric orientation and strongly rooted in the family, and they are also not full-fledged adolescents striving for independence from the family. They often possess a confusing mixture of babyishness and maturity. In terms of cognitive development, this age group covers Piaget's concrete operational stage, with the older students (fifth- and sixth-graders) preparing to enter the period of formal operational thinking. In all areas of growth and maturation, they are a bewildering combination, sometimes functioning at one level and sometimes functioning at another.

Two classes at the same grade level sometimes exhibit characteristics at opposite ends of the maturation spectrum. How you organize your students for drama should be responsive to the social and cognitive needs of that particular group, and you, as the classroom teacher, are the best judge of where the group is, what it needs, and how best to meet those needs. Variables to consider would include these: how best to organize students for participation, how to plan time and spatial requirements, and what drama activities will best correlate with those considerations. What are offered here, therefore, are some guidelines that can be adjusted and adapted to accommodate varying needs and goals.

Planning space needs

How time and space are organized and managed can make important differences in terms of how well students can handle the necessary freedom required for drama. Movement, pantomime, and story dramatizations require sufficient space to work creatively yet safely. However, there are many drama activities students can perform at or near their desks. Lack of large, open space should not eliminate a variety of creative drama activities. For example, in-place movement and pantomime can take place at or beside desks; pair work in creating spontaneous dialogue or dyadic (interpersonal) situation role-playing can be done by students simply pulling their chairs together. Relatively small amounts of space can accommodate sequential pantomime games, add-on scenes, and all kinds of small group activities by having only one or two groups working at a time. A number of activities described in chapters 3-6 allow total class involvement but with part of the group providing an audience for others, followed by reversing roles. Students serving as audience may do so as themselves, or they may assume roles. In the latter case, all students remain actively involved in the drama but the amount of space required for the activity is generally less. This type of organization could involve half of the group as enthusiastic spectators in the Roman Colosseum during the games while the rest provide the entertainment, or part of the class as members of Congress listening to several of their colleagues debate an issue, or the townspeople gathered to watch the emperor show off his "new clothes" during a dramatization of that story by Hans Christian Andersen.

Whenever possible, however, it is best to work where there is ample space to move freely. You will want to plan ahead as to what space is to be used in a specific lesson and how to use the space to enhance both the drama and students' understanding of spatial relationships. Initial planning should always include making some decisions about the space to be used. Chapters 3-6 offer specific suggestions for drama ideas that help to build spatial awareness and encourage culturally appropriate uses of space.

Too much space can be as troublesome as too little. Some students cannot be within a large, open space without wanting to race about in it. They equate such space with the kinds of activities possible on the playground or in the gym. Furthermore, the acoustics in gyms and some all-purpose rooms are often quite terrible, and drama work with dialogue (dramatization of stories, situation role-playing, and small group improvisations) suffers as a result. Working with content of a sensitive or introspective nature, as found in some stories and poetry, may be more difficult to do well in this kind of space.

Ideal space outside the classroom is often not available, at least not on a regular basis. If you are going to include creative drama as part of the ongoing curriculum, arrange the best possible space within the regular classroom (if a special drama facility is not provided). If this is not possible, look for a spacious room, other than the gym, that is often available and can be quickly cleared for movement and drama activity. Too much precious time is lost if a great deal of rearranging is always required. In some buildings, the music room or a rather private area within the media or library facility may fit the requirements for drama. Anticipating needs and planning ahead for appropriate space can make the difference between success and a good deal of frustration. Students engaged in an activity in a proper space will be easier to manage and more self-responsible than in an inappropriate space.

Managing time

Creative drama generally requires time for a good deal of student input at all stages: planning, doing, debriefing and assessing, and perhaps playing it again. Whether drama is integrated with a content area or done as a lesson unto itself, you need to plan time to do it well and to allow ample opportunity for assessment at the end. This important debriefing should include assessment of the drama work as well as discussion of the content of the drama. This generally means that, realistically, the total lesson will take more time than you might otherwise anticipate. Yet the wrap-up of the lesson can provide excellent opportunities for students to use their developing abilities to analyze and evaluate. When time may be restricted, it is wiser to plan a sequence of activities so that one or more can be dropped if necessary. Nothing is more frustrating than to have to rush the ending of a story or to not see what every group has invented to share.

Drama can be used to help students discover how to share time with one another. It is useful for you to indicate, ahead of time, just how much time is available for each person or group. Some groups will be more self-responsible than others; it may be necessary to have a signal to remind everyone when time is nearly up. In some activities, particularly in any of the theatre games where viewers may be guessing what it is they are watching, it is useful to decide and announce *before the fact* just how much time and/or how many guesses each person is to be allowed. For example, an exciting creative movement game in which a "detective" leaves the room while the rest of the group surreptitiously mirrors the movements of a secret leader, works best when the detective is limited to both an allowed time and number of guesses (e.g. one minute or three guesses with which to discover the leader).

Assembling materials

Other organizational responsibilities that are initially yours involve deciding what materials will be required and arranging for their availability. It may happen that in their planning, students decide they need something you did not anticipate, but the essentials as determined by your plans should be provided before play begins. Properties to be used for introductory ideas and motivation, stories and poems to be included, music, rhythm instruments, information cards for small group work such as situation role-playing or sequence games are all materials that you should list on your plan and assemble before any playing begins. Many potentially exciting drama lessons have been foiled by the need to interrupt the momentum to hunt for a needed piece of equipment. Thoroughness of the planning makes the difference.

Selecting appropriate activities

You must consider the needs and maturity of your particular students if you are to make appropriate creative drama activity selections. Drama activities that can be organized for parallel play may provide a necessary transition for the younger and/or less mature students in grades 4-6. This type of organization, so effective with early elementary students, allows each student to work independently alongside his or her peers, with a minimum of interaction: in-place pantomime as used for an introductory or warm-up activity prior to more intense work such as story dramatization is a good example of this. Parallel work is rarely lockstep, but should encourage individual interpretation and expression in response to the motivation provided. Several examples of this kind of work are provided in chapters 3-6, with a concentration in chapter 3. (Also see *Creative Drama in the Classroom Grades 1-3*.)

Creative drama is generally considered an ensemble art form; one does not do it alone. As such, it suits the ways in which many students in grades 4-6 prefer to work: it not only allows but encourages group involvement and interaction. Many of the types of drama experiences that students of these ages most enjoy require that participants be organized into small groups, an organization which complements the need of the students to plan and carry out activities with their peers. Choosing drama activities that utilize pair and small group organization can reduce confusion, alleviate self-consciousness, and provide opportunities for students to work with others whom they enjoy. Group work has the additional advantage of giving students practice in cooperation, active listening, group problem-solving, and in developing leadership skills. Pair work, whether engaged in creative movement, pantomime, or the creation of spontaneous dialogue in dyads, provides practice in sharpening both the verbal and nonverbal interpersonal communication skills so important to these emerging adolescents.

Situation role-playing in pairs or small groups lets participants try various ways of dealing with relationships and interpersonal conflict. This is also true of characterization based on literature or developed in original stories, as it involves looking at the world from the points of view of other people. This kind of work is often best organized utilizing pairs and small groups. This format encourages interaction but does not showcase individuals and, therefore, provides a comfortable and nonthreatening environment. The experiential nature of the drama readily accommodates the concrete operational thinker, and the organization fits their social needs and maturation.

As students move into formal operational cognition, drama can offer valuable opportunities to predict and to hypothesize outcomes. Working in pairs and small groups to solve problems, create new endings for stories, develop improvisations, and engage in situation role-playing allows students to experiment with cause-and-effect as this relates to human and nonhuman behaviors.

Matching students for group work

When organizing students into pairs and/or small groups, care should be taken to accommodate their special needs, interests, and abilities wherever possible. Sometimes, allowing them to choose their own partners and organize their own groups is satisfactory; children, like adults, enjoy working and playing with friends. However, drama can provide unique opportunities to break down barriers and integrate the full class into a community. Theatre arts (like other arts) can serve to reduce barriers that exist between the less academically capable and the superior students. If students are grouped by ability in the content areas, they may seldom get to work with others of different aptitudes and abilities. There is no evidence to support that "A" students in reading, math, or science have superior abilities in drama. Indeed, drama may be the means by which students of diverse academic abilities can come to know and enjoy each other. This may produce special rewards for everyone in classrooms where special students have been mainstreamed. (See chapter 6 for a discussion of activities especially useful for special students.)

Parallel, pair work, and small groups are ways of organizing that can provide comfortable and encouraging environments for another special group of students in the classroom: the quiet ones. Whether they are quiet because of cultural divergency, social introversion, or communication apprehension (McCroskey, 1977), these are the students who seldom offer ideas when the full class is interacting and who do not assume leadership roles within the larger group. Placing them in pairs or small groups with others who will be encouraging, supportive, and contributing without dominating can provide an environment that may draw out these students. Putting all quiet students in one group may be self-defeating;

little may be accomplished without the stimulation of their more outgoing peers, just as there will be little input from quiet students placed in a group full of the highly gregarious.

Whether students choose their own groups or are randomly or selectively placed into groups by the teacher, drama work affords the additional bonus of helping students develop group skills simultaneously with the development of the drama. The overriding goal is to organize in such ways that both students and drama flourish. This requires that you allow freedom to invent, explore, and create (without generating nonproductive noise, confusion or antisocial behaviors). Chaos is never conducive to creativity.

Establishing rules

Because we have been concentrating on your role as teacher, most (but not all) of the preceding suggestions have been concerned with decisions that *you* make in planning, organizing, and managing for success. However, almost by definition, creative drama means drawing students into all phases of the experience, from the planning right through to the debriefing and assessing session at the end. Managing creative drama is always more successful when the entire group has had some say in establishing the ground rules for participation.

Many drama leaders find it useful to work with students in establishing some kind of signal that can be used to quickly and efficiently gain everyone's attention. Two quick beats of the tambourine might signal everyone to "freeze" their bodies and voices. Such a signal can be arrived at jointly or by teacher directive, but it is only effective if everyone understands and obeys it. The signal is not simply intended to control overly zealous behavior (although that may be a secondary benefit); more importantly, it gives you instantaneous communication with both small and large groups. Unlike the use of language, this type of signal does not seem to intrude, *and* it projects. Trying to shout over the enthusiastic sounds of several students is a self-defeating behavior and a poor role model.

Properly and judiciously used, such a control device can function to encourage creativity rather than to frustrate it. For example, you might bring students involved in parallel pantomime as they explore a spooky cave to a sudden freeze to enhance the mystery, create suspense, and provide a turning point in the direction of the storyline. It is, however, expedient to work with students in establishing the freeze signal and in practicing with it during the introductory or warm-up work.

Later elementary students should help decide other rules—such as how to deal with obstreperous peers. Reviewing the elements of active, respectful listening is often all that is necessary to remind students that drama cannot proceed when one or more participants are behaving in an irresponsible way. You should also remind yourself that you can sometimes be tolerant of isolated actions that you do not endorse but can live with in minimal doses. The high spirits and enthusiasm of students involved in drama can result in more noise than produced by seatwork; when this can be briefly tolerated, the fact that the groups were not interrupted to be admonished may pay off in the long run. However, the increased movement and noise should be considered when planning and organizing; it should influence decisions about how to group students, when and where to do the drama, and what types of activities should be incorporated in any given session.

Much of the truly creative and rewarding work of the play director of formal theatre takes place when planning and making the Prompt Copy of the script. The decisions made at that point require the utmost in creative thinking: predicting, inventing, visualizing, and synthesizing. This is equally true for the classroom teacher or specialist planning creative drama experiences for elementary school students. When viewed as an opportunity to engage in a good deal of creative thinking, the efforts put into imaginative planning, organizing, and management decisions can be rewarding at the time of invention and when leading the drama. To the extent that you can feel freed rather than locked in by a well-conceived plan, the stage is set for the most successful experiences for everyone.

DEVELOPING AUDIENCE SKILLS

So far in our discussion of the role of the teacher as drama leader, we have emphasized planning and facilitating the actual performance of creative drama. However, when drama work with later elementary students is organized to provide for much small group work, it generally follows that the entire group will often want to see the work of everyone else. This creates a natural opportunity for you to assist students in developing the kinds of mature, supportive yet discriminatory, audience behaviors that you hope to find among adult viewers.

■ SHARING/VIEWING AS DUAL ROLES

Earlier in this chapter, we talked about a special relationship that exists between a student and anything that he or she produces. This includes work in drama. Most students are eager and anxious to share, and most are also eager to see what others have done as well. This means that students serve as audience for one another. One good feature of creative drama is that those who are audience at any given time know that they will be the performers another time. This duality of roles functions to make concrete the "Golden Rule": "do unto others as you would want them to do unto you." Students will need to be reminded of this again and again, not only in drama but in all relationship transactions. Developing, with the class, a set of guidelines for audience behaviors can be a useful first step. Once such a list is established, it may often suffice to simply remind everyone that they have agreed to abide by their own rules.

Being a supportive, mature audience involves much more than simply being quiet, respectful viewers who give attention with eyes and ears. Within the drama sharing, students can experientially observe how an empathic, enthusiastic audience can bring out the best in each. Noting the role that the audience played, and examining this during debriefing, provides on-the-spot examples of where the audience let the players down or spurred them on to better work. Such examples are generally not hard to find, especially when the group has already considered the reciprocity involved in the player-/audience relationship during previous work.

You play a special role in all of this. First and foremost, you provide the role model for students to observe and to emulate. Never become so involved in the other aspects of your role as leader that you fail to give full attention to a scene or event that is being shared. This is not always easy to do, especially when you are helping in some way with music or properties. Sometimes you are more distracting than helpful, particularly if you are constantly advising individual members of the audience about their behavior. If the audience is too disturbing—noisy, rude, or insensitive—then the sharing should be stopped while the guilty ones are dealt with and before proceeding with the scene. Students do not expect their peers to be statues, frozen in their seats; they expect that they will respond as live, responsive human beings who may laugh, wiggle, cheer, and generally indicate that they are enjoying themselves and the drama. More often than not, students will take their cues from you, and you need to provide the best possible help in assisting them to become that mature, supportive audience that can turn even a mediocre offering into one of delight.

USING SPECIAL LEADER STRATEGIES

The structure of drama work with later elementary students, both beginners and those experienced in drama, affords a variety of ways for you to guide and participate in the playing. In the following sections, we examine some of the most useful strategies for work with students in grades 4-6.

Sidecoaching pantomime

Although more widely used with younger players, sidecoaching techniques can be extremely useful as a teacher strategy at this level as well. In sidecoaching, you guide students' thoughts and actions by talking them through an experience of some kind. It is a technique especially suited to movement and pantomime work and with guided fantasy. Your students may need more external stimulation to arouse their imaginations than do their younger counterparts, including sensory suggestions to assist them in forming images in the mind.

■ GUIDING BY NARRATION

In one workable technique, you have all of the students close their eyes and concentrate on visualizing an event, a place, even an abstract pattern of colors and shapes that suggests a mood or action. This visualizing draws on sensory recall and is aided by suggestions from you, using language rich in sensory suggestions to stimulate the imagery.

Use voice-over technique to guide the fantasizing. When you do this well, with just the right amount and kinds of suggestions, you provide an excellent introductory or closing segment to a drama lesson.

Sidecoaching while students are actually participating with movement and pantomime creates the motivation and guidance for a narrative pantomime. This may mean that the students are using parallel structure with each person working in his or her own way in response to the narration. This type of play particularly suits the younger, more egocentric players who are less able to spontaneously interact and cooperate with others; however, there are many interesting applications of this technique with older players as well, particularly with less experienced participants in grades 4-6. The sidecoached narrative pantomime that includes opportunities for interaction provides an excellent transition between the kind of activities that work best with younger students and those that work best with older children.

Sidecoaching with students in grades 4-6 may also provide just the right amount of guidance to keep a pantomimed story dramatization cohesive and moving toward climax and closing. Whenever and however used, it is generally most effective when thoughtfully planned and judiciously offered. Better to work from a piece of edited literature, from your own script, or from notes than to omit an important part of the action or get events out of sequence. Effective sidecoaching demands just the right language, full of strong sensory suggestions and powerful, specific action words. Good sidecoaching always flows. This is true whether it is used to suggest images in the mind as during a guided fantasy or to lead students on pantomimed adventure.

Players should never be in limbo, wondering where they are or what is happening. Offer enough direction, but do not deprive them of their own creativity, individual interpretation, and expression. Do not tell players how they feel; provide the circumstances and create the mood that will elicit appropriate feelings. The use of first or second person and present tense can be used to intensify the sense of drama.

Sidecoaching students through an adventure based on *Captain Scott's Last Expedition* (Dodd, Mead, 1913) might include suggestions as follows:

"The sky is dark, overcast, the Antarctic wind so cruelly cold. It is hard to open our eyes. Where are the tracks we made earlier when we entered this forsaken, frozen end of the earth? We seem to have lost them. Lifting each foot seems a nearly impossible task. This is surely the longest six miles we have covered. It would be good to go on a bit farther, but the cold is too intense. Better to stop here and make camp. (Pause.)

"It is nearly impossible to handle the tent in this bitter wind, and awkward with frozen mitts. We dare not take them off. (Sufficient pause to allow for the action required to set up the tent.) There, the tent is in place and it feels good to just crawl inside out of the full blast of the wind. Now to find the tin of biscuits. We'll need to ration each one carefully if they are to last. Where is the primus lamp? Ah, here it is. It is so hard to light it in this dark, cold world. Turn up the flame a bit more. There, a friendly light burns, not much warmth but enough of a flame to set a cup of snow over to brew a cup of tea.

"Perhaps we can write a few lines in the diary while the water boils. Holding the pen is not easy with nearly frozen fingers. Ah, the water boils. Now for a hot cup of tea and a biscuit. The tea nearly burns our throats; the biscuit is hard, cold, and tough. The hot cup is painful against our swollen lips but the liquid warms us from the inside. (Pause while everyone eats and drinks.)

"Now to tidy up and crawl into our sleeping bags. Perhaps by the morning the weather will improve, but now we need our rest. We close our eyes and hope for sleep. We drift off even as the blizzard howls just inches away."

Notice the flow of the action. It is not just a series of directions but a cohesive narration that stimulates the imagination and directs creative response. Useful sidecoaching functions almost subliminally so that the suggestions of the leader do not seem to intrude, and the players are barely aware of the separation between the narration and their own thoughts.

The more experienced and knowledgeable the players, the more important it is that you offer only what is necessary to keep the action flowing and properly focused. Quality rather than quantity of guidance should be your goal.

Narrating story dramas

Students may enjoy pantomiming a story with you serving as a narrator or storyteller. In contrast to the sidecoached narrative pantomime in which students follow your lead, the players may wish to choose roles and develop their own pantomimed story dramatization with you taking the lead from the action shown and/or the literature on which the drama is based. This generally works best with simple stories or ones that are extremely well known.

If you have guided the discussion and planning, and know just how the story is to be played, it is not difficult to serve as narrator as the action unfolds. Myths, legends, and other folk stories are good choices for this kind of story drama. The narration may work by simply using the story as written or it may require some careful editing to match the action and keep pace with the development of the plot as interpreted by the players. Generally, you would want to keep the narration true to the language of the story or suited to the genre. For example, the narration for many folk and fairy tales most appropriately begins, "Once upon a time, in a land far, far away . . ." and although your role is one of storyteller, you also discretely guide the action by your narration.

Role-playing

Another technique useful in both motivating and managing creative drama is role-playing by the leader. The role should always be one that fits with the theme and with your purposes and goals for the lesson. Such temporary role-taking is often effectively coupled with sidecoaching, to lend extra motivation and guidance.

■ GUIDING BY TEACHER-PARTICIPATION

Generally when you do assume a role in the playing, it is one of a temporary nature. It would also not be one that takes over or dominates the action. One important use of technique is to provide just enough new direction to get a scene moving if the action has stalled. This can happen when the players are having a difficult time resolving a conflict in the story in a way that can bring the scene to a satisfying conclusion. When you can assume an appropriate role, it is best accomplished by briefly stepping into the scene and exiting as soon as possible once the players have resolved the difficulty. Your purpose is not to come in as *deus ex machina* to solve the problem for the players, but rather to facilitate their own creative problem solving.

A class of fourth-graders were working from the book *James and the Giant Peach* (Dahl, Knopf, 1961). They had invented a wonderful scene in which the media had come to shoot a news story about the giant peach and its unusual inhabitants. The players assumed the roles of famous newscasters, camera operators, technicians, journalists from big city newspapers, magazines, and a host of assistants. Everyone had a part and they were having a marvelous time with the scene, at least for awhile. However, in their planning, they had not discussed how to bring the scene to an end, and it played on and on.

The teacher, sensing the difficulty yet not wanting to diminish the strength of the scene, briefly stepped in as one of the disagreeable aunts. She briskly ordered everyone to pack up and get off her property or she would deal with them. Then, wiping her hands on her apron, she retreated to her kitchen for a cup of tea. This gave the students an ending for the scene. With mutters and haste, they packed up their equipment, but not without bidding farewell to the crew of the peach. During the debriefing that followed, they treated the entry and exit of the "aunt" as though it had been a part of the original plan and concentrated on talking about their own roles in the scene. During the next lesson, they remembered to give more attention to how they planned to bring the scene to a satisfactory close.

Planning

Although you have thoughtfully planned the drama lesson, the students should be in on part of the planning. Planning to plan should be built into every drama lesson. This is important with players of all ages, but older boys and girls need to take an ever-increasing role and responsibility. In the drama activity described, based on *James and the Giant Peach*, the entire scene had been planned by the players with the teacher serving as a resource person, discussion leader, and encouraging supporter. No matter what is used to introduce the lesson—a story, a film, a property of some kind—a lively discussion should result. No matter how teacher structured the plan may be, the implementation should be developed cooperatively.

■ USING QUESTIONING STRATEGIES

There are always ideas to explore and suggestions to propose to get everyone motivated and involved; central to this is the use of a wide range of questioning strategies. Successful experiences in drama are built upon exploration and discovery; explorers are questioners.

> The quality of the dramatic experiences will greatly depend on the ability of the teacher to ask the kinds of questions that elicit imaginative thinking and promote involvement. Obviously, questions that can be answered "yes" or "no" will do little to stimulate creative thinking or expression.
>
> (Cottrell, 1975, p. 37)

Creative work of all kinds depends on asking just the right kind of questions, and during the planning stage in drama with fourth-, fifth-, and sixth-graders both players and teachers should contribute. The entire repertoire of questioning strategies should be included, from cognitive recall (memory questions that ask students to accurately remember facts, information, etc.) to questions that require higher levels of thought such as analysis, synthesis, and evaluation (questions that probe ideas, compare and contrast, seek the invention of new solutions, and assess in terms of desired outcomes and established criteria). Some types of questions are often overused and others underused. For example, too many questions simply ask students to recall and repeat information, and too few encourage them to combine what is known in new and different ways. Divergent thought is basic to creativity, and concrete and "almost formal operational" thinkers need to be challenged to use their minds in new and more adultlike ways.

Do not ignore the important role of memory questions. These are often important to the establishment of a common recollection of the plot or event. The use of the five Ws (who, what, where, when, and why) help people internalize what we have heard, read, or experienced so that we can work, in common, from that information. Individual interpretations, invention, and critical analysis, however, come about as we probe possibilities. Invention is essential to planning in drama; interpretation is required in the individual expression during the playing; critical analysis and evaluation is basic to assessing the experience after the playing. Probing possibilities is at the heart of all aspects of the drama experience.

"Tell me about . . .?", "What happened after that?", and "What do you think was meant by . . .?" are questions that get at recall, comprehension, and interpretation. Such questions would also encourage students to "translate"—to put information into their own language. However, a question that asks students to compare and contrast one character with another encourages analysis and critical thinking. So, too, do questions that pose a what-if. Never settle for just the most obvious responses to the what-if questions; the more you probe, the more the ideas flow. It does not matter that some

are silly or illogical; what matters is the freewheeling exploration of possibilities and the opportunity to engage in divergent thinking in ways not always possible in other areas of
curriculum. These types of questions are essential to brainstorming, and that process is an important part of much
planning in creative drama. Judgment of ideas is suspended
until many, many possibilities are offered and then the
group, not the teacher, should decide what they want to use.

The kinds of questions asked, and how they are worded,
greatly influence the quality of the learning that takes place.
This also directs how students perceive you and their relationships with you. The quality of the dialogue between
teacher and students is directly tied to the way questioning is
handled, and this affects the learning climate. In studies
conducted by Mary Budd Rowe (1976), the length of wait-
time after a question was presented to a child was examined.
When the wait-time was extended from one second (the
norm as ascertained by the study) to three seconds, children
elaborated upon their responses. Responses to the short wait-
time averaged seven words; to the three-second wait, responses averaged twenty-eight words. The children seemed
more confident and less apt to reply with "I don't know" or
with no response at all. The longer wait-time also encouraged
children to ask more questions and propose more new ideas.
The longer wait-time during a drama lesson could result in
significantly more ideas and more imaginative ones. The fact
that children are also more willing to elaborate on their answers and to ask more questions should contribute to a live-
lier, more productive planning time and debriefing.

Debriefing

Debriefing, as well as planning, is critical to successful
drama experiences. Well-chosen questions are important if
the group is to do a good job of assessing their work so that
they grow and learn from it. Generally, you would initiate the
discussion during evaluation time and model the kinds of
questioning that keeps the discussion focused on the positive.
"If we played this scene another time, how might we change it
to make it even better?" is an example of a question that

probes possibilities for improvement while reinforcing the value of what has been done.

■ LEARNING FROM SELF-EVALUATION

All of the preceding should suggest that students, as well as the teacher, should be posing questions. The use of the heuristic function of language (*Explorations in the Functions of Language,* Halliday, 1973) is essential to learning. In this function, language is used to probe, question, and explore. Students need to develop sophisticated heuristic skills; they need to know *how* to question, as well as when and with whom. During the planning stages of drama, they should raise issues as well as speculate about meaning, outcomes, and so forth. During the preplaying, the class might generate a list of questions that they would hope to answer through the drama. Or they might construct a set of questions that would provide the basis for assessing and debriefing at the end. They should be encouraged to create a full range of questions, from cognitive recall to analysis and evaluation. Their questions, as well as yours, would be incorporated into the discussion. They become partners with you in assessing how well *your* goals and objectives were met. Particularly with older boys and girls, it is also important to identify *their* goals and objectives. You can do this by looking at the questions they pose in the planning and how they attend to them during the final assessment.

STORYTELLING

The drama teacher is a storyteller; later elementary students should be also. Just as students should provide important parts of the planning and assessing, they can also introduce the lesson with their own storytelling or as they invent and share a story through the playing. As reading aloud as a function of the reading program is reduced, storytelling and the reading aloud of literature takes on an even more important role. Whether the story is shared by you or by the students, the well-told tale provides a model for other storytellers and gives pleasure to all. Through the great oral tradition, or through reading aloud from literature using the language of an author, it is the goal of the storyteller to share something that has affected her or him because of the deep feelings, or the humor, or the pure pleasure derived from the story. Ideally, everyone would all have a large, well-developed repertoire of stories that can be *told;* attaining such a goal means regular, frequent work so that we continually add to our offerings. It would be inconceivable, however, for you to limit your storytelling to only a few highly developed pieces, while building the desired repertoire. Therefore, for classroom purposes, include reading literature aloud, traditional stories told without manuscript, and stories of your own invention. We will consider each of these in our discussion of storytelling. We assume that students as well as teachers can be storytellers.

■ CHOOSING MATERIALS

Not all storytellers tell all types of stories equally well. Each person has to discover for herself or himself the kinds for which he or she is best suited. This does not mean that you never attempt to enlarge your scope or share stories that seem less compatible with your own individual style and abilities. But when building a personal supply, especially when adding to the collection of stories we tell without manuscript, it seems to make sense to put our efforts into the kinds we do best.

There is a resurgence of storytelling in the United States, and regional and national groups have organized to discover and share our traditional folklore. Included in the meetings and festivals sponsored by these associations is a wide range of offerings within the folk tradition: humorous tales, tales of the supernatural, hero stories, and so forth. Among the professional storytellers, there are those who are eclectic in their offerings, doing several types well; others find their special forte and specialize.

As a teacher, you can experiment to find just what suits you best, and you can encourage students to do the same. With this approach, you can urge yourself and your students to try new things, to be risk-takers. A storytelling center in the classroom should include a cassette recorder where student storytellers can experiment, practice, and tape a finished product that can be shared with others. Teachers find it equally useful to work with the tape recorder in developing well-told tales. Teacher tapes also make a fine addition to the storytelling/listening center.

Storytellers, both child and adult, generally are most successful when they really like the material they are sharing, appreciate the human and/or literary values in the story, and, therefore, share it with sincerity, vitality, and enthusiasm. Of course, the choice of the story must also be one that interests and appeals to the listeners, and this is especially true when the story will later be used as a basis for drama. The increased involvement required for drama activities ought to be spent on something truly enjoyed. Let us briefly review some of the characteristics of stories that make good listening and useful foundations for drama work with later elementary students.

■ MEETING STUDENT INTERESTS

If we were to choose one word to describe the kind of stories most enjoyed by later elementary students, it would be "adventure!" Since adventure is almost synonymous with action, many favorite stories are excellent for dramatization or as the basis for a variety of drama activities. Adventures can be told through several of the literary genres: folktales, myths, legends, epics, historical novels, science fiction, high fantasy, and biography. The appendixes at the back of the book offers a variety of action/adventure literature appropriate for storytelling and drama.

Students in grades 4-6 are drawn to stories with bigger than-life heroes with whom they can vicariously identify. They seek models to emulate, fantasize about, and give their allegiance. Stories about sports figures, military heroes, and world-class adventurers (real or imagined, classic or contemporary) appeal to students' needs for both adventure and heroes. Students also enjoy stories about children much like themselves, or a little older, who get involved in great adventures, mysteries, or humorous escapades. They particularly enjoy stories in which young people show outstanding abilities to solve problems, unravel mysteries, or accomplish remarkable feats of strength or courage.

There are so many excellent possibilities from which to choose when seeking materials for storytelling and drama that you may prefer the shorter stories such as the folktales, myths, and legends (or longer works with an episodic structure that can be easily divided into short segments). Stories like Beverly Cleary's adventures of Henry Huggins (*Henry and the Clubhouse*, 1962) or *Call it Courage* (Sperry, 1940) are easily divided into scenes to be played within a drama session. With several of these longer works, each chapter is quite self-contained and can provide the equivalent of the short story for dramatizing. The classic *Homer Price* (McCloskey, 1943) is a good example of this kind of structure; each chapter is a story in itself, and several can provide exciting drama.

■ INTEGRATING STORYTELLING AND CONTENT LEARNING

Often, both the storytelling and the drama are integrated with one or more of the content areas. Although by grades 4-6, social studies and science may be taught as separate, discrete subjects with their own textbooks, stories from literature can continue to add both information and motivation to learn. For example, *The Witch of Blackbird Pond* (Spear, 1958) is an exciting historical novel about the Salem witchcraft trials. It provides excellent reading aloud and exciting scenes to dramatize. This Newberry Award-winning story also provides well-researched information and insights into some unusual events in U.S. history. Another excellent historical novel, *Darkness over the Land* (Stiles, 1966), tells about life in Nazi Germany through the eyes of a young boy. *The Dark Didn't Catch Me* (Thrasher, 1975) makes the Great Depression real to contemporary children as they become involved with young Seely and her family. The sharing aloud of the story, the dramatization, and the discussion that would take place in both the planning and assessing can produce a well-crafted, integrated lesson that can meet goals and objectives in literature, drama, and history. The literature and the drama make the times, events, and people come alive.

■ DEVELOPING STORYTELLING SKILLS

The choice of the story guides you in deciding how best to present it: told in your own language, read aloud in the author's words (either by you or by students), told but with language and flavor drawn from the original (for example, paraphrased but with the suggestion of a regional or ethnic dialect), or memorized. The latter is the most precarious choice unless you have read or told the story so many times that you have committed it to memory. This often happens with a favorite piece that you share again and again. Still, the first few times you share without the manuscript, you may want to have it close at hand. Nothing is more devastating to storytellers and listeners alike than the omission of some important piece of information or a scrambled sequence of events.

Some literature should never be paraphrased: poetry, stories told in verse, and that which depends on the author's exact richness or cleverness of language. Some stories can be told using a combination of techniques, for example, paraphrased but with repeated refrains committed to memory. Magic spells and curses are examples of the kind of repetition found in folk and fairy tales. Contemporary stories may have a clever line that is repeated again and again to make a point or to tie several episodic events together. In the telling, students will want to hear the exact language each time.

■ PREPARING TO SHARE

Whatever the source of its material, storytelling is an intimate art. We are reminded of this by master storyteller Ruth Sawyer (*The Way of the Storyteller,* 1942) who describes storytelling as a sharing of the mind, heart, and spirit. The storyteller must be intimate with the story and able to communicate that intimacy to the listeners. This is not possible without a deep familiarity with the material, including an understanding of the time, place, and circumstances from whence it came. Telling or reading, the storyteller needs to know and understand the story as a whole and in proper sequence. The story shared without manuscript demands that the storyteller remember each event in the order it happened and be able to visualize the setting, characters, and events in the mind's eye. "If the story is to 'come alive' for the listeners, it must first come alive for the storyteller" (Cottrell, 1975, p. 191).

Beyond meticulous preparation, the storyteller need rely on little more than a versatile voice, an expressive face, and a modest amount of carefully chosen gestures. It is sometimes fun to add a bit of special clothing or a property, but embellishments cannot save the poorly told tale. Eyes, hands, voice, and body posture taken all together provide the fibers from which the magic is woven. In turn, the storytelling can provide the fabric from which teacher and students can fashion rewarding work in creative drama.

Because we have been examining, in some detail, the role of the teacher as the life-engendering force for drama in grades 4–6, we have concentrated on the teacher as storyteller. In subsequent chapters, we look at students' development as storytellers as they improvise original scenes and plays or translate literature into their own expression through the drama. We do not overlook, however, other ways in which they may carry on the noble tradition: readers theatre performance, multiple readings of literature (prose and poetry) around a common theme, puppet theatre productions, and the taping of individual stories (original or from literature) to be shared by others in the listening/storytelling center.

Storyteller, motivator, planner, organizer, manager, and sometimes participant, the teacher able to lead children in insightful, exciting experiences in creative drama is often rewarded on a full-time basis. The classroom climate required for drama also provides the kind of environment in which all learning can flourish and where every student has an opportunity to develop her or his own greatest potential, academically and personally.

CHAPTER 3

Teaching Basic Creative Drama Skills

BUILDING ON EARLIER WORK

In a later elementary class there are sometimes several students who have had previous experience in drama; from the first day, they want to dramatize a story or show an idea through movement and pantomime. When drama has been a regular part of their learning and expressing, boys and girls want to do drama just as naturally as they expect to write stories or paint. If few students in your classroom have engaged in creative drama, it is useful to begin with them using methods that you would use with younger students but with content at the interest level of your students. However, it will most often be the case that some students have strong backgrounds in drama and others little or none—a dichotomous situation that requires thoughtful planning in order for you to build on the expertise of the few while providing useful beginning activities for the majority.

Several kinds of activities that will be familiar to the "old hands" can serve to create a bridge between them and the newcomers to classroom drama. Many of these focus on movement and pantomime and can be organized to fit the needs of individual students, both experienced and neophyte.

Pantomime for "old hands" and "newcomers"

The techniques and activities that follow play an important role in drama with students in grades 1-3 but incorporate content and variations to appeal to students in grades 4-6 as well.

In-place pantomime

In-place pantomime can generally be done at or near desks and does not require a rearrangement of furniture to be successful. Everyone works in his or her *self-space* (personal space that is identified by each player extending his or her arms without engaging another).

■ DEFINING SELF-SPACE

In order to get everyone involved and moving at the same time, use a count of ten, followed by the command or signal to "freeze."

■ PANTOMIMING IMITATIVE MOVEMENT

The following are possible actions for a ten-count freeze pantomime with fourth-, fifth-, and sixth-graders: To a count of ten, become . . .

1. a basketball player preparing to take a free-throw shot.
2. an astronaut getting into a space suit in preparation for lift-off.
3. Ben Franklin letting out his kite and feeling the surge of electricity as it is hit by lightning.
4. a driver cranking up an antique car.
5. a businessperson logging in on a personal computer.
6. a scientist focusing a telescope (or microscope) and taking a look through the lens.
7. a fisher casting a large net into the surf and hauling a catch of fish ashore.
8. Atlas adjusting the world on his back.
9. a political refugee climbing a ladder to an attic in order to hide.

The content of the pantomime would be chosen to fit the topic being studied. Often the ten-count freeze is done as a series of four or five related activities.

As a beginning activity in drama and used in conjunction with a unit on mythology, the following sequence could be used:

1. Zeus winding up to hurl a thunderbolt.

2. Hercules lifting huge logs and rocks to dam the streams in order to clean the stables of King Augeas in a single day.

3. Amazon warriors using their bows and arrows.

4. Pygmalion sculpting a magnificent statue in marble or bronze.

Students with more expertise in pantomime will use these activities for polishing and refining their skills. However, with each person working independently, beginners should not feel threatened simply because they lack expertise.

Variations on Simon Says

An activity enjoyed by younger boys and girls, Simon Says is a game that can be upgraded to use as a beginning drama experience in the grades 4-6. For example, the game might require the players to discern, from among the directives, actions done by a particular character in a story being read. If the character did what is requested, the players would pantomime the action; if not, they would freeze.

One variation, used after the class has read *The Adventures of Tom Sawyer*, is called Mark Twain Says. If an action in the story is attributed to the correct character, everyone pantomimes the action. If attributed to the wrong character (or one from a different book), the players freeze.

Other variations might use definitions of words as the basis for a game of Daniel Dictionary Says. The statements may use a variety of movements to be done only when correct information is given; otherwise, players freeze.

For example: Daniel Dictionary Says . . .

1. If a chanticleer is a rooster, flap your wings.
2. If a crab is a kind of crustacean, show your claws.
3. If a hospice is a type of seasoning for food, take a big bite.
4. If a livery is an insect, take a swat at it.
5. If a renegade is an outlaw, draw your six-shooters.

Sidecoached narrative pantomime

You can organize students for this activity in a variety of ways. As with younger students, those just beginning drama work in the later grades would play parallel (independently) with no planned interaction among the players. You provide the narrative and everyone plays the same role and engages in the same activities. You can base the narrative on a piece of literature or invent one. Students can either be themselves in the experience or assume roles. When playing roles, however, there would be little emphasis on "getting into character," at least in early work. The role would be primarily portrayed through the actions, *doing* the kinds of things that a person in that situation would do.

The following is an example of a sidecoached narrative for later elementary students in which everyone plays the "I" in the story. Playing begins with everyone seated on the floor in her or his own space. The first paragraph sets the scene, and players are instructed to close their eyes and let the words create images in their minds (to establish a sense of isolation). As the players begin to move, each should interpret the suggestions for pantomime in her or his own way.

"Sitting by the small fire I have finally coaxed along using the dried palm fronds scattered on the beach and some damp matches I found in my pocket, I think again of the others on the small plane. Did they survive the terrible plunge into the stormy sea? I think of my family who must believe that I have drowned. After so many years of living in the islands, so many trips between my father's home and my grandparents just a few island hops away, I didn't seriously worry about disaster or being washed up on an uninhabited atoll. I always loved those stories of shipwrecked sailors, but Crusoe had his Man Friday and the Swiss Family Robinson had one another. If only I were not so all alone. The smoke from the fire is making me very sleepy, too tired to think, to plan. I'm glad I was able to build a fire: a signal fire. Surely someone will find me if I can only keep my fire going. I know I should be planning for tomorrow but I can't seem to concentrate. I'm so tired and so sleepy. (Pause.)

"That sound, what was that sound? I must have slept, for the sky is turning pink with the first rays of dawn. My fire is out, just white ashes. I meant to keep it going. There is the sound again, and not very far away. Be careful, get up but move very slowly. Someone or something may be watching. I'll keep myself low so I'll be harder to see in the dim light. I'll glide along, stretching my body parallel to the sand. No quick movements and *no* sound.

"Day is quickly coming; the sun is turning everything from pink to gold. Stop! I do hear something. If only my heart weren't pounding so loudly. It makes it hard to listen. There's a dark shape just ahead, below the rise where the trees begin. If I move sideways along the edge of the embankment, I can keep my back to the slope and my eyes scanning all around. There is the sound again, closer but fainter. Keep moving, I must find the source of that sound. Maybe it is watching me, but I must know what it is.

"The shore is no longer cool, smooth sand. I need my hands to help me scramble over piles of shells and tufts of beach grass that sting my bare feet and legs. The long shadows play tricks on my eyes. I stop, crouch down, and take my bearings. The sunrise floods the shore with more light. I look again toward the dark shape ahead. It's a shallow cave, one that must fill with water with the incoming tide. I'm drawn to it. My feet hurt as I quickly crawl over piles of broken shells at the entrance. Surely the sound came from inside.

"The opening is not very high. I bend my head to enter. The sound is very near, just ahead of me in the cave. Scratching, pitiful little sounds. What can it be? It is so dark. I feel my way along the inside wall. The floor is wet. Something long and slimy slipped over my foot. Seaweed, I hope.

"Now I hear the noise more clearly—scratching, mournful, little sounds. I flatten myself against the wall and wonder why I came in here at all. The noises have stopped. I drop down on all fours and inch forward. My hand touches something, something cold and metallic. Maybe it's a trap. No, that's silly. I can touch it with both hands if I really stretch. Yes, it must be a trap, and something is inside. I hear it moving; it's making small, eerie little cries. My heart leaps! Could it be? I forget to be cautious. I grab the metal parts and pull. It's not a trap at all, it's the cage Gramma gave me for Pumpkin.

"Pumpkin! She's inside and she's alive! I can hear her pitiful mews. I try to unlatch the door of her cage, but it's twisted and bent. I tug and now I have the whole cage in my hands. I hurry toward the cave opening. The morning sun hurts my eyes. I look down at

Pumpkin. Now I see that one little foot is caught in the twisted cage. Just a step over the debris at the entrance and we're in the sunlight. Pumpkin and I, we're together in the sunlight. She tries to move toward the gate of the broken cage but she's too weak. I look around for something to pry the gate open and get her free. This large piece of heavy shell may work. I sit down with the cage between my knees. Never mind, I tell her, I'll have you out in no time. I carefully work the shell as a lever. There, the cage is open. Now to carefully free her foot. Easy, Pumpkin. I did it! She's free. I lift her out ever so carefully. Her long orange fur is wet and bedraggled, but her eyes shine big and golden in the sunshine. Good old cat. I cradle her in my arms, and she mews. I feel her purr. Maybe I'll just lean back against the embankment and close my eyes for a second. Suddenly I feel exhausted, my head nods. (Long pause.)

"I try to turn over but I can't. I stretch and open my eyes. What is that smell mingled with the aroma of breakfast? Why, it's Pumpkin, you old cat. You must have spent the night prowling around in the wet grass. So now you're ready for a nap, curled right up on my chest, practically suffocating me while you just snooze away."

In the preceding, there is no attempt to get into character. Each student plays the young person in the narrative. There is no need for players to create dialogue, as the sidecoaching also serves as a monologue that guides the actions of the players. Both experienced and beginning players can comfortably participate, with each free to draw on her or his own skills. As part of a longer lesson, the narrative would have been preceded by several in-place pantomimes related to specific actions in the story—such as walking in-place over a variety of different surfaces, straining to grasp something just beyond reach, and showing with facial expression a series of emotions.

The narrative might be used in conjunction with the reading of Scott O'Dell's *Island of the Blue Dolphins* (1960), about a young girl left alone on an island, or Armstrong Sperry's *Call it Courage* (1940), the story of young Mafatu who is shipwrecked by a furious storm. The narrative adventure may be primarily used to involve students in exploring the feelings of any young person who is confronted with loneliness when separated from family, friends, and familiar companionship.

Sequential pantomime games

Although younger boys and girls enjoy telling a story or reenacting an event through a simple sequential pantomime game, players in grades 4-6 can generally handle more complex materials and produce remarkable dramatizations using this teacher-structured technique. The activity provides good introductory work for beginners yet allows more experienced players to utilize their more highly developed skills. The content for a sequence game can be based on literature or principles, concepts, or information drawn from any of the content areas. Materials work best that depend on an obvious sequential ordering and that provide sufficiently discrete pieces of action that can be used for each segment.

■ "READING" PANTOMIME CUES

Sequence games require that you carefully plan each activity ahead of time and prepare the necessary materials. Each segment must be planned to furnish a cue for which the next player is to watch in order to enter at the appropriate time and do her or his part. The directions must include clear instructions of what each player is to do, and the actions must be sufficiently unique to each segment so that clear cues are always provided. You work from a Master List that describes each segment in sequential order, complete with the number of players who are to be involved in each segment. Students work from individual cards, each of which states what the player is to watch for (the cue) and what he or she is to pantomime. Initial experiences with sequential pantomime games, even for later elementary students, work best when there is a limited amount of interaction within each segment.

The following is an example of the Master List for a sequence game that might be used as a drama lesson or integrated with a science lesson on the space program. This Master List shows cues written in capital letters; actions use both upper- and lowercase type. You might make hand-lettered cards using different colors of ink to identify the different parts: cue, directions, and action segment. Do not number student cards. This discourages students from counting to find their turns rather than watching for cues. The numbers in parentheses on the following list indicate an arbitrary number of players who might all have the identical or similar card.

TO THE MOON: A SEQUENTIAL PANTOMIME GAME

1. (3) YOU BEGIN. You are an astronaut beginning a trip to the moon. You are putting on the proper space clothing to survive the trip in the spaceship. After getting into the suit, put on your space helmet and walk back to your place showing how you would move in such clothing.

2. (3) AFTER YOU SEE THREE ASTRONAUTS SUITING UP FOR SPACE TRAVEL, you become an astronaut. Take the elevator to the top of the launching pad. Get into the spaceship and fasten yourself in your seat. When a voice from Mission Control announces "lift-off," pull back in your seat. Then return to your place.

3. (1) You are stationed at Mission Control. AFTER YOU SEE THREE ASTRONAUTS FASTEN THEMSELVES INTO THEIR CONTOUR SEATS, you begin the countdown from 10 to 0. Then shout "lift-off!" You and the three astronauts return to your places.

4. (3) AFTER THREE ASTRONAUTS ARE LAUNCHED INTO SPACE, you are an astronaut. Move inside the spaceship showing weightlessness. Watch out the window and point with one finger as the first stage of the rocket leaves. Shortly after, nod your head "yes" to show that separation is complete. Return to your place.

5. (3) AFTER YOU SEE THREE ASTRONAUTS MOVING ABOUT WEIGHTLESSLY IN THE SPACESHIP AND FINALLY NODDING THEIR HEADS TO INDICATE SEPARATION FROM THE BOOSTER ROCKETS, you are one of the astronauts. You are hungry. Show how you are eating special space food and drinking through a straw. Then return to your seat.

6. (1) AFTER YOU SEE THREE ASTRONAUTS EATING AND DRINKING INSIDE THE SPACECRAFT, you are stationed at Mission Control. Begin checking instruments and show your alarm that something is wrong. The ship is off course! Work frantically at the console of your computer. Finally, show that things are now "A-OK" by making the appropriate sign with your fingers.

7. (3) AFTER YOU SEE THREE ASTRONAUTS EATING AND DRINKING IN SPACE, you are one of the astronauts. The engineer at Mission Control is frantically working at the computer to correct a wrong course. Float over and fasten yourself into your contour seat. The course has been corrected when the person in Mission Control sends you the "A-OK" sign. You reply with a "thumbs-up" signal. Then all of you return to your places.

8. (1) You are an astronaut. AFTER YOU SEE MISSION CONTROL SIG-
NAL THREE ASTRONAUTS THAT AN OFF-COURSE SITUATION HAS
BEEN CORRECTED BY USING THE "A-OK" SIGNAL TO WHICH THEY
RETURN A "THUMBS-UP," you fasten a safety link to yourself and
go out of the command module to take a space walk. You are
weightless and float around outside the spaceship. Return inside the spaceship, unfasten your tether, and then return to
your place.

9. (1) You are an astronaut. AFTER YOU SEE AN ASTRONAUT COM-
PLETE A WALK IN SPACE, you will be at the controls of the command module. You will orbit the moon while your two compan-
ions are landing on it. Continue to orbit the moon by flying the
command ship around the circle until you see an astronaut
place a flag on the moon. Then you return to your seat.

10. (2) AFTER YOU SEE AN ASTRONAUT TAKING A SPACE WALK, you are
one of the astronauts. Float about the spaceship and then climb
into the lunar module with another astronaut and prepare to
land on the moon. While you are landing the lunar module, the
command pilot will keep orbiting the moon. After you have set
down on the moon's surface, return to your seat.

11. (2) WHEN YOU SEE TWO ASTRONAUTS LAND ON THE MOON IN
THEIR LUNAR MODULE, you and another player are now those
two astronauts. While the command ship continues to orbit
around the circle, carefully climb out of the lunar module and
slowly descend to the surface of the moon. Carry a long-
handled tool and a bag with you. Pick up some rocks with the
tool and put them in the bag. Return to your place.

12. (1) AFTER YOU SEE TWO ASTRONAUTS PICK UP ROCKS FROM THE
MOON'S SURFACE, take a flag from the lunar module and place it
ceremoniously on the surface of the moon. Stand back and
salute the flag. Do everything in slow motion to show that there
is much less gravity on the moon than on earth. Return to your
place.

Although this organization allows for more than one player at a
time in several segments, there may or may not be any interacting.
The experience of the players generally determines both the
amount and quality of any interaction. The first time the game is
played, you may wish to use the Master List as a guide for narration.
In subsequent playings, the entire sequence would be pantomimed
without narration, allowing the players to use only their nonverbal
skills in order to tell the story. Note that this sequence activity

accommodates 24 players without requiring anyone to appear in more than one segment. However, individual scenes could be adjusted to utilize more or fewer participants and still complete the game.

The preceding sequence game would be used *after* students have acquired a good understanding of the actual space flights to the moon; therefore, the game may be integrated with a science lesson. You can design sequential pantomime games to use with a variety of topics from the content areas; they may also be based on literature. Short stories or episodes from longer pieces generally work best, particularly materials that employ a chronological order from beginning to end.

As students become familiar with this format and develop more expertise with pantomime, they enjoy the challenge of more complex scenes with multiple players who spontaneously interact in appropriate ways.

One group of fourth-graders particularly enjoyed a sequential pantomime based on James Daugherty's *Andy and the Lion* (1966). They were very familiar with the story and, therefore, able to easily send and receive the necessary cues. Their familiarity also encouraged them to freely improvise some interaction during several segments. For example, in one scene, Grandfather tells Andy about hunting for lions in Africa. Both "Grandfather" and "Andy" spontaneously interacted as one pantomimed the storytelling with great gusto while the other listened with wide-eyed interest and appropriate facial expressions. In another segment there was a good deal of lively interaction as Andy, the Lion, and Andy's dog worked off one another during a chase around a large rock. When players are experienced with both the format and the content material, a sequential pantomime game can evolve into a smooth-flowing piece of drama.

■ EXPANDING A SEQUENCE GAME

A sequence game is highly teacher-structured. Older boys and girls often like to incorporate more of their own ideas into the drama, perhaps by taking off from the sequence game into small group scenes of their own design.

The third part of *Andy and the Lion* involves a circus. After the students had retold the story via the sequential pantomime game, they decided they wanted to do more with the idea of a circus. They divided into four groups and put on their own three-ring circus, complete with a zany group of clowns. In contrast to the teacher-structured sequential game, the circus was totally planned by the students, with the teacher serving only as a resource person. However, the concentration and attention to detail that was required to do the sequence game carried over into the student planned activities. The total lesson accommodated a wide range of experience and skills which suited a group with a variety of backgrounds in creative drama.

Add-on scenes

Add-on scenes are another structure that can be as simple or complex as the group can handle. Until everyone has sufficient expertise to begin to move into characterization and the invention of improvised dialogue, add-ons are best done with movement and pantomime, where the action carries the scene.

An add-on scene can begin by identifying a situation, for example, "Opening Day at an Exhibit of Priceless Egyptian Treasures." A few people start the scene as they hurry to finish the setting up of this much-awaited exhibit at the museum. As other players think of different yet appropriate things to do, they add on to the scene. Some folks might be tidying the room, making final checks of displays, and so forth. Soon someone indicates that it is time to open the doors to receive the patrons. (If a player does not assume this responsibility, you might briefly enter the scene and let the workers know that "it is time.") This suggests new ways to add to the scene: someone may decide to take tickets; another motions to several customers to gather for a guided tour. Yet another player may enter as a security guard who keeps track of what is happening and cautions guests not to handle the priceless treasures on display.

The scene plays on until it begins to lose momentum, at which time, you may simply signal the group to end the scene.

■ ENLARGING THROUGH ADD-ONS

Early add-on scenes often lack a sense of plot, and students have little concern for a beginning, middle, and ending. There is often no conflict and only minimal attempts at characterization. Students must always have sufficient information and/or experience related to the situation to make it work. The choice of subject also needs to inherently provide a wealth of things to do, or it becomes repetitive and dull as players simply add on by doing similar things to the activities already in progress.

The following are some ideas that often work with later elementary players:

1. Decorating a classroom or gym for a school party. (It helps to choose the occasion: a back-to-school party, the opening of a "Boys and Girls Club," a Valentine's Day party, a surprise birthday party for a famous person, or the welcoming of a celebrity to the school are possibilities.)

2. Holding a car wash for a school fundraiser.

3. Building a clubhouse or treehouse.

4. Being workers and shoppers in a large department store or grocery supermarket.

5. Preparing a royal banquet (used with an appropriate piece of literature).

6. Gathering to meet a special train carrying a famous person or victorious team (one the class supports).

7. Arriving to engage in a variety of activities at any of the following places: an amusement park, a fair, a playground, a health club, a beach or picnic area, a sports event.

8. Arriving as workers to harvest a specific crop (picking apples or oranges, various kinds of garden produce, etc.)

9. Setting up an assembly-line operation to accomplish a specific task such as wrapping packages, processing the mail, cooking and baking, moving construction materials to the proper site.

(The latter could be followed by using pantomime to "build" the desired structure.)

10. Forming a human chain to rescue someone or something stranded on thin ice, in quick sand, up a tree, down a well, or over a mountainside.

Add-on scenes can be drawn from an actual event such as the defense of the Alamo, the completion of the transcontinental railroad, the Great Chicago Fire, bringing in an oil well, the opening of Disneyland, or welcoming home a popular hero or celebrity. Literature provides other excellent sources for add-on ideas, from the classic "whitewashing the fence" scene from *Tom Sawyer* (Twain, 1876) to the "Toddle-bike commercial" scene from *Tales of a Fourth Grade Nothing* (Blume, 1972). Any scene where there are several people doing different but related activities can be used; such a scene might be developed to elaborate upon or extend from a piece of literature. When an add-on is used to enlarge a scene from literature, it should do so without changing the original plot.

Add-on scenes provide interesting situations for pantomime work by both experienced and beginning players. They give each student the freedom to choose how he or she will enter the playing. As the group progresses, they will continue to enjoy this format. Advanced work can also be developed using similar techniques and situations but with the players encouraged to develop strong and believable characters who may or may not engage in spontaneous dialogue. Skillful players may extend an add-on scene into a full-length story with characters, conflict, and a complete dramatic structure.

Creating an environment

Creating an environment is a pantomime activity almost universally favored by both experienced and beginning students in creative drama. It is also an activity that easily integrates with every area of curriculum. For example, with literature, the class may create the setting for a story; with social studies or foreign language study, another time, place, or culture may be created; with science, a special environment in the natural world or the setting for a memorable scientific event. Movement and pantomime skills are challenged as students observe the building of an environment and later try to recall and describe what they saw.

Some cleared space is necessary when creating an environment with pantomime. This becomes the area to be "furnished" in ways that serve to identify a unique and specific place. The rules are simple: having identified the specific environment to be created, each player has an opportunity to put something appropriate into the designated space. Only one item (or cluster of related items) is put in at a time and each player has a turn. Large, bulky, or heavy items may require one or more students to carry and put them into place and a player may, therefore, recruit a helper. Once something is in place, it cannot be ignored or removed. Subsequent items must accommodate what is already there. And finally, after putting an item in place, it is helpful if the "inventor" does something with it in order to differentiate among *imagined* objects that may be similar in size and shape.

Imagine that the class is enjoying *From the Mixed-Up Files of Mrs. E. Frankweiler* (Konigsburg, 1968), an amusing yet provocative story about two children who leave home and take up residence within the Metropolitan Museum of Art. The enormity of their adventure becomes more vivid as students visualize the setting. Mark off a space on the floor to represent an area within the museum. The group may first brainstorm a whole list of possible items that might be in such a place. (The book gives many ideas, but the class would not be limited to only those items mentioned in the book.) As a player "invents" an object or furnishing, it is carried into the room using movement and pantomine and placed in an appropriate spot. Before exiting, the student does something further to give additional credibility to the pantomime. A piece of sculpture might be dusted; a picture hung and straightened; a chair sat upon; a lamp plugged in and lighted; a potted plant watered; a book placed on a table or desk already put there by a previous player, and opened, briefly read, then closed.

Outdoor as well as inside environments may be created and furnished with appropriate items. Children studying the

Bedouins of North Africa might begin by creating an oasis complete with palm trees, a watering hole, a tent into which they place the household items required by a nomadic family, even camels and other animals that travel with the tribe. Successful work is only possible after students have sufficient information gained from their studies. The drama experience can provide an excellent way to review.

In addition to the creation of environments for which students draw on previously studied materials, they may also invent their own places.

One sixth-grade class spent some time furnishing an "ideal classroom." After they declared it complete, they spent some time discussing how they would feel going to school in that space. Originally their room included such extravagances as a soda bar, a rear-projection gigantic TV, a pool table, and a large refrigerator. During their analysis and discussion, they began to question their choices. "Too crowded, too distracting, and with no space for some important classroom activities such as science and drama," were some of their assessments.

Permission to remove items had to be obtained from the person(s) who had put them there (and who then had first choice at creating a replacement item). In a democratic fashion, they voted on the items in question. Their final product was a classroom with innovative features but modified to accommodate and encourage first-rate teaching and learning. They had to weigh the value of each item and make a reasoned decision. The experience not only challenged their pantomime skills, but also their abilities to work in a cooperative, democratic fashion, using their developing cognitive abilities to use cause-and-effect thinking and prediction.

■ ENLARGING FROM INVENTED PLACES

Other invented environments might be used as a basis for creative storybuilding as the class answers questions about 1) where and when this place might exist, 2) who might live there, 3) what the inhabitants would do in this place, and 4) why they would do those things. The addition of tension and conflict provides the ingredients for a scene to be dramatized and/or used as a basis for creative writing.

The class has created and furnished a primitive cabin. The group may then decide if it were built by settlers long ago, is a vacation cabin in a wilderness location, or the contemporary home of someone who lives a primitive life here or in some other part of the world. The class divides into small groups, with each working with the decision of its choice. They further identify who lives there and what the kinds of things they do. If a full-fledged scene is to be developed for drama or group storytelling, they may brainstorm several conflicts that would fit their who, what, where, and when. Each group would select the conflict idea they like best and develop their scene.

If your class includes both experienced and inexperienced players, make certain that each small group has a blend of both. The structure for "creating an environment" activities should permit everyone to feel comfortable in the drama. Those with more expertise often elaborate on their contributions to the creation of the special place; beginners make simpler additions. For everyone, it offers valuable work in nonverbal communication, including a focus on how people use and share space within a clearly defined environment.

Spatial perception and movement

For students who have not engaged in frequent experiences in classroom drama, it is important that beginning activities offer many opportunities to explore how people use and share space (in U.S. culture). Most students in grades 4-6 have discovered several "truths" about space, often because their "transgressions" have been pointed out to them. By now, most understand that space may have ownership, that personal space is finite: it ends where someone else's begins. They have also discovered that there are some implicit rules that govern how they conduct themselves in different kinds of space. Through drama, especially through movement and pantomime work, students can refine their understandings about space and how it functions. They can begin to appreciate the reasons behind the required behaviors: that how they function and relate in space is often as communicative as words.

■ DEVELOPING SPATIAL AWARENESS

Younger boys and girls have a high motility urge, that is, a strong physiological need to move. Although this need has generally dissipated by fourth or fifth grade, emerging adolescents often have a new self-consciousness about their bodies. They sometimes perceive themselves as awkward and clumsy, and their embarrassment with their changing bodies can contribute to a lack of coordination, gracefulness, and self-confidence.

The following series of activities allows later elementary students to comfortably work in a variety of spaces using different ways of organizing. The activities are designed to give insights into how people function interpersonally and move in space and to let students practice the kind of discipline necessary if the body is to be responsive to the mind's commands to operate with coordination and grace.

1. In-place pantomime activities, including those done with the 10-count freeze provide experience in working in self-space. Activities may involve moving with different levels of energy and speed. Remind students that they are to work within their own space and without trespassing into the space of others. Explain, in a positive way, that everyone—big, little, young and old—has an inherent right to her or his own space. "Your space belongs to you and you have the right to invite another into it or not," is one way of introducing this idea.

2. Sidecoached narrative pantomime in which each player moves through the larger space but without interacting with others requires each student to remain aware of the rights of others. Successful experiences in narrative pantomime are not possible unless everyone remembers to be sensitive to one another's spatial needs. Practice in disciplining one's own body movement may be further enhanced as players may be required to move at different levels (crouching down, stretching, bending and twisting), expending varying amounts of energy, and moving with a variety of speeds from rushing to slow motion. Exploring various environments through narrative pantomime, both literature-based or invented by the teacher, can incorporate a range of demands on individual movement control.

3. Having two students combine space with each other and perform similar and different activities within the shared space is one way to move into pair work in drama. "Mirror" activity, done with or without music, is an excellent pair activity to do in shared space and is enjoyed by people of all ages. (One person leads while the other follows; then roles are reversed. Players are cautioned that the goal is to mirror each other as accurately as possible rather than to try to trick their partners. Movement may be free-flowing and interpretive or the leader may pantomime very specific behaviors. The choice is generally related to both teaching purposes and the context in which the game is used.) Inasmuch as this activity invites the players to "put themselves in the shoes of the other," it can provide an opportunity to talk with students about empathy. Spatial awareness, coordination, and grace are central to successful mirroring work.

4. An extension of mirror work can be done as a shadowing activity using the larger space. (Students work in pairs, front to back, rather than facing one another. The lead player initiates the movement and the "shadow" follows behind. The challenge is to work with as much synchronization as possible, remaining alert to spatial relationships between and among the players.) Shadowing is delightful done to music; it can also be integrated with literature or science lessons.

■ SHARING SPACE IN PAIRS

5. In-place pair work may also involve players in work in which each participant does a different activity. This provides a different challenge than the mirroring, for each must accommodate the activity of the other. (For example, one person might pantomime spading a garden area while the partner puts young plants in the freshly prepared earth, or one person might dry dishes while the other puts things away in the cupboard. There are many different but related tasks that might be done with pairs working in shared space.

6. At some point, one pair may combine with another pair so that an even larger space is gained but is now shared among four persons. Instruct players that they are to discover some things that they can do in the larger space, either interactively or by working parallel and independently of each other. If a group begins by working parallel, they should follow that activity by

engaging in something in which everyone must be interactively involved. This often results in the group creating some kind of game: tossing an imaginary ball amongst the players; imaginary jump rope with two players turning the rope and two jumping, together or by turns; a game of leap-frog; or other games or sports that can be played or pantomimed.

7. Finally, two contiguous groups of four may combine so that there are groups of eight. Whereas the double-pairs are often able to agree on activities with very little discussion, groups of eight very often need to take some time to discuss and plan what they will do. The activities often continue to have a game format but are more complex and generally require more rules.

■ ANALYZING SPATIAL PERCEPTIONS

If you have been able to move progressively from individual work in self-space into shared activity in groups of eight all within one session, the total experience can provide the basis for some provocative discussion. Here are some follow-up questions to explore with students as they probe their own perceptions about space and how they function in it.

1. Were there activities that you could do better in self-space than in shared space? Describe several. Why did this seem to be the case?

2. What were the advantages of the double space? The quadrupled space? The combined space of eight individuals? Were there also disadvantages? If so, what were they?

3. Several groups seemed to be able to plan activities to accommodate four people without much talking or planning. When you combine into groups of eight, there seems to be a need to talk and plan. Why do your suppose this was necessary?

4. Can you think of examples in real life when you like to work in your own space? With another person? In small and larger groups? Do some of the same things happen that you experienced in your work using movement and pantomime?

An extension of these activities is described in the Drama and Social Studies section of chapter 6. However, initially you may want to simply engage all of the students in exploring space through movement, practicing individual awareness and control, as you concentrate on discovering insights about how people use, share, and communicate spatially.

Cooperation in the larger space

Sidecoached narrative pantomime is one way to get students working cooperatively in the larger space. Although each player is free to make her or his own interpretation based on the sidecoached suggestions, there is still a good deal of teacher control over the movement. However, as students move into drama work in which they provide much of the basic planning, it becomes increasingly important that they can work cooperatively in the available space with self-discipline. This is particularly true when the entire class works as one cast in order to dramatize a story. Interpretive movement in the larger space, with or without interaction, is an excellent way to encourage students to use the larger space in ways which take advantage of it, share it with others with sensitivity and mutual respect, and practice moving with grace and coordination to express ideas and feelings.

■ MOVING TO MUSIC

The following are suggestions for incorporating interpretive movement into the drama program to provide additional work with body awareness, rhythmic response, and spatial perception.

1. Moving to music of various types, moods, and tempos. Younger boys and girls tend to "interpret" music by responding to it in a very literal way: martial music suggests marching as soldiers or becoming members of a military band. However, students in grades 4-6 should be encouraged to become less literal and more abstract and imaginative in their interpretations. They can be challenged to let the music guide their ideas, feelings, and images. Less experienced or imaginative players may respond more literally than their more accomplished peers; however, everyone would be encouraged to express their own individual ideas and feelings through the movement. For example, martial music may elicit a range of activities from the more literal—such as driving spikes to complete the transcontinental railroad or digging for buried treasure—to such abstract interpretations as a variety of machine-type, high-energy movements. However, they choose to work, everyone is required to

explore the larger space, respond to the tempo and mood of the music, and show consideration for the spatial needs of others. (People who argue that this type of activity is not "drama" may need to be reminded of the important role that dance of all kinds plays in theatre arts. Whether the experience is labelled interpretive dance or whatever, it can be especially beneficial for students as they struggle to develop greater poise, coordination, self-discipline, and confidence in themselves.)

■ MOTIVATING MOVEMENT WITH COLOR

2. Moving through different colored environments. Flooding an area with colored light can turn a familiar place into something quite unusual. Students may have imaginative ideas or ones that are less representational. (For example, exploring a room flooded with golden light may make some students think of a sunny beach, so that they perform the actions of people at the seashore; later elementary students should be encouraged to show through their movements a variety of concepts and feelings stimulated by golden places. Before the playing, the group might brainstorm a list of ideas, everything from positive emotions associated with sunny places to feelings of great wealth and power associated with a world of gold including such opposites as greed and generosity.)

3. Responding to contemporary art. Both paintings and sculpture, particularly those of an abstract nature, can provide excellent motivation for using the body in interpretive ways. Urge students to "show with your body and through movement how the art makes you feel." In-place pantomime might be used to form the body into a shape and position that imitates shapes shown or suggested by the art. To a beat, the players begin to move in ways to extend the concept of the shape and interpret the dynamics of the art through movement. Color as well as shapes and patterns should be considered.

■ COMBINING SENSORY STIMULI

4. Multiple stimulation for interpretive movement. Combining music, color, and forms as the motivation for interpretive movement may produce very imaginative results. This may also result in a greater willingness to branch out and utilize the available space more advantageously. (For example, a recording of Holst's "The Planets" played in a space flooded with blue light should excite children to use their bodies to suggest a

variety of interpretations, everything from celestial phenomena moving in space to underseas exploration or intergalactic
travel. "Appalachian Spring," by Aaron Copland, combined
with a green environment may inspire interpretive movement
suggesting springtime, growing things, birth or rebirth. However, it may also suggest feelings of release from bondage as the
human spirit soars in a fresh, new world.) Brainstorming with
the group may open up possibilities not otherwise imagined.

As each person interprets and moves in her or his own way, the
more imaginative are free to be as inventive and abstract as they
choose. Others are allowed to be very literal, even trite, without
feeling inadequate or second-class. You can utilize interpretive
movement within the drama program in so many ways of such
great value that you should also anticipate providing frequent opportunities for students to engage in movement work. It is tremen-
dously useful to have on hand a variety of musical selections (particularly instrumental works), some safe and easy way to flood an
area with colored light (perhaps a revolving light wheel of the kind
used with aluminum Christmas trees), and a few pieces of exciting
contemporary art (modern art posters and a piece or two of pottery
or sculpture).

The motivation for interpretative movement suggested in
each of the preceding examples was provided by some highly
sensory stimulus. Keeping sensory awareness alive and
strong is essential to growth in drama. This may be especially
important with later elementary students as they move farther and farther from the perceptual/intuitive stages of cognition and depend more and more on language as the primary way of knowing and expressing.

KEEPING SENSORY AWARENESS GROWING

Successful work in creative drama depends on the abilities
of the participants to use their sensory systems to go exploring in order to make discoveries. The improvisational nature
of creative drama requires students to reach inside themselves for most of what they need in order to imagine, invent,
and express. There is no script to follow and no director to
tell them where to stand, how to move, or think, or feel. The

motivation and information necessary to "do drama" must, therefore, primarily come from the child's own experiences, personal and vicarious, real and imagined. Through sensory stimulation, thoughts and feelings are aroused and recalled before they can be expressed through action and/or words. This ability to use sensory recall is basic to the full range of drama work but is fundamental to pantomime, for both beginning and experienced players.

Sensory recall and pantomime

Very simple, beginning work in pantomime depends on sensory awareness and recall. So, too, does the complex and often abstract pantomime of the artist. Marcel Marceau crosses one leg over the other and "leans his elbow on the mantle." We know what he is doing; we see it in his posture, in the distribution of his weight as he balances between the floor and the mantlepiece, and in his angle of inclination. His sensory recall provides him with the mantlepiece—its height, width, and texture. Sensory recall also provides him with the knowledge of how his body interacts with the mantle, the floor, and so forth.

Of course, it is neither our expectation nor our goal that students participating in creative drama will develop great expertise or artistry in pantomime, but if their work is to be adequately communicative and satisfying to both do and observe, they will need continued opportunities and regular practice with sensory recall.

■ STIMULATING IMAGINATION

The following in-place pantomimes focus on each of the senses to provide the necessary motivation and practice. Many may be done at or near seats or desks.

Listening recall

1. Concentrate on recalling a tune that you know very well. Become an orchestra leader or solo performer either leading or playing that piece of music.

2. Recall the sound of someone typing or working at a computer keyboard. Become the person producing those sounds, and demonstrate with pantomime what they are doing.

3. You are lying on the floor reading a book. Suddenly you hear the phone ringing nearby. When you hear it, get up and answer the phone. Show with facial expression whether you are pleased or displeased to have your reading interrupted by the phone call.

4. Imagine that it is very dark and you are trying to grope your way to close and fasten an open window that is rattling in the wind. Let the recalled sound guide your movements.

5. You are walking home from a friend's house just as it is getting dark. You hear footsteps behind you. Listen to the footsteps as they go faster and faster, then slower and slower. Pace your footsteps to those you hear behind you.

Visual recall

1. You are getting into your shirt and discover a very loose button. Find a needle and thread. Use your recollection of threading a needle to put the thread through the needle's eye, etc. When you have everything ready, resew the button.

2. Imagine that you and a friend are playing ping-pong. Watch as your friend serves the ball and return it several times. On the fourth or fifth volley, you miss the ball and watch to see where it rolls behind you.

3. In front of you is the control panel that operates your TV set. Turn it on and adjust the picture to your liking.

4. Using visual recall, reach into your closet and select a favorite outfit to put on. Take each item from your closet and proceed to put on each piece of clothing.

5. Pick up an apple or peach from in front of you. Examine it carefully. Now, pick up a knife and peel the fruit, cut it into several pieces, and enjoy!

Tactile recall

1. Using tactile recall, run some cold water into a basin and splash it over your face. Next, without looking, reach for a towel and dry off.

2. In front of you is a ball of clay or plasticine. Work with it until it is very soft and pliable. Use your hands to fashion a simple pot.

3. Imagine that it is very dark outside and you are trying to find the keyhole in an old-fashioned lock. Feel for it with your key. Insert the key and turn the doorknob to open the door. Grope for a light switch just inside the hall and turn on the light.

4. Recall the feel of soft earth. Begin to dig a hole using a garden tool. Suddenly you feel a large stone; work it out using either your hands or the tool. Show the size, shape, and weight of the rock as you lift it out of the earth. With your hands, refill the hole you made.

5. You are walking barefoot over hot sand, sharp gravel, a rain-slicked sidewalk, or through some thick and oozy mud.

Olfactory recall

1. You are baking cookies for a school bake sale. Keep check of how they are doing using your sense of smell. They begin to burn and you must rescue them before they are ruined.

2. You are lying on your bed reading. You begin to smell something unusual. Using sensory recall, imagine what it is and show whether it is something pleasant or unpleasant that you smell.

3. You open the refrigerator and something inside does not smell very fresh. Keep checking with your nose and eyes until you locate the offensive item.

4. You are walking down the street on a spring day. You smell something fragrant. Use sensory recall to imagine what it is and do something to show the source.

5. Think of the nicest smell that you remember. Use movement or pantomime to show what it is.

Taste recall

1. Recall your favorite food; someone has just put a serving in front of you. Take a bite.

2. Recall a least favorite food; take a bite of that. Next, wash it down with a big drink of water.

3. Pop a piece of bubble gum into your mouth. Notice its taste and

texture. Begin to chew it. When it is soft and pliable, see if you can blow a bubble.

4. You are swimming in the ocean; suddenly a big breaker surprises you and you gulp a large mouthful of salt water.

5. You are thirsty. Open the refrigerator and discover a pitcher of frosty lemonade. You can smell its lemony tartness. Pour a glass and take a big swallow. It wasn't lemonade at all; it was lemon juice!

These simple in-place pantomimes can be expanded into multi-sensory experiences in which players must recall a variety of sensory input. This is a good time to review the properties of an object: weight, shape, texture, temperature, color, and so forth. One useful approach is to guide students through a sequence of steps in which they recreate within the mind a full range of sensory recollections.

The ability to recreate a breadth of sensory images is essential to gaining competence in pantomime, storytelling, and characterization; it is equally of value to the writer. Therefore, many of the preceding and following activities provide excellent prewriting motivation as well as preparation for creative drama.

Sensory recall and guided imagery

Stimulating and guiding sensory recall in drama can be done in a variety of ways. One that utilizes the technique of sidecoaching and also employs both left- and right-hemisphere processing is the *guided fantasy*. However, before trying a full-length visualized experience, it is useful to do some short, highly focused activities in which students practice "seeing pictures in the mind's eye." Think of these short, practice exercises as "tuning" activities like those musicians use to warm up their voices or instruments before performing a longer work.

■ BUILDING VISUALIZING SKILLS

You can adjust the content of the practice experiences up or down to match the age, maturation, and kinds of experiences appropriate to the majority of players. Since your purpose here is to encourage sensory recall, it would be counter-productive to ask students to create images with which they have had little or no experience. This does not mean, however, that they cannot create new images; they can and you must urge them to do so. "New" in this context means something invented by combining in different ways that which is already available to the student.

The following sequence of activities begins with short, highly specific ideas and builds toward longer, more interpretive ones.

1. Encourage students to get comfortable, close their eyes, and clear their minds of all external sounds, sights, and other distractions. Compare this to a movie screen inside their heads upon which they have not yet projected a picture.

2. Most students have played with a kaleidescope. Those who are ready for abstract work enjoy imagining that inside their heads are kaleidescopes full of an almost limitless number of patterns. Through sidecoaching, suggest that students create several patterns, combinations of shapes and colors, until they get one they especially like. (It is not unusual to see some shake their heads each time they change a pattern.)

3. Once a student has produced a pattern of special appeal, it should become the basis for an emerging scene with the player letting the colors, shapes, and patterns stimulate a recollection of a scene. The leader suggests that the scene may be either an indoor or outside scene, busy or pastoral, real-life or fantasy.

4. Less abstract thinkers generally have better success when they are guided to create a more realistic and familiar picture in their minds—their room at home, a favorite place to play or visit, or the schoolroom. Like those playing with more abstract patterns, they may wish to create several different scenes before choosing one for further work.

5. For players working with familiar scenes, suggest that they manipulate the scenes by changing the time of day or season of the year. The idea is to allow students to experientially discover that they are in charge and can create and manipulate their mind-pictures at will.

6. However arrived at, once all players have chosen a scene for extended work, guide them to add sounds, textures, tastes,

odors and movement—as many multisensory details as they wish to add.

7. If they have not already done so, suggest that students put themselves and/or other living things into their scenes. Students particularly enjoy "seeing" themselves in the setting they have created.

Once students are experienced and adept at guided visualization, a remarkable range of creative work can ensue. In chapter 2, we observed that the use of visualization is important to the storyteller and to the listener as well. Indeed, students may first practice such visualization as they listen to the stories of others; later, as storytellers, they are encouraged to image the scenes and characters in their minds as they tell a story. With words, voice, facial expression, and gesture, they help others to see *their* "pictures" as well.

Poetry

Listening to poetry, especially that which is rich in multisensory suggestions, provides an excellent way to practice visualization and sensory recall. As in the practice exercises just described, the combination of language and visualization produces interaction between the hemispheres—a process generally associated with creative thinking. Research reported in *The Gifted Child Quarterly* (Hershey & Kearns, Spring 1979, pp. 71-77) found that regular exposure to guided imagery significantly increased the abilities of intermediate-grade students to think divergently.

■ VISUALIZING FROM POETRY

The following poem illustrates the kind of multisensory material you can use as a basis for visualization. Ask students to close their eyes and let the words create the sights and sounds, tastes, and smells suggested in the poem.

Spring in the City

Spring in the city.
Spring in the city!

It's bright and bold,
It's boisterous and witty.

Not gentle like the spring refrain
That echoes through the country lane.
Here spring must shout, for it competes
With blaring horns and rushing feet.

The children are the first to hear
The call of spring, and soon appear
With jumping ropes and games of jacks,
And trikes and bikes and balls and bats.

Brave girls and boys on roof tops race
To toss their kites in the March wind's face.
Bold bits of colors flying free
Above the slim antennae trees.

And candy shops all yummy and sunny
With marshmallow chicks and chocolate bunnies.
Pink, purple, red, black, orange and green;
Most every kind of jelly bean!

Though only March, store windows say,
"Buy spring clothes" (to wear in May!)
And each displays new fashions bright . . .
Red and blue, and lots of white.

The flower vendor's cart is filled
With mounds of yellow daffodils;
And violets pale and shamrocks green.
Are adding to the springtime theme.

Soon up and down the concrete lanes,
Window boxes will bloom again,
For spring has come to city places,
You see it in the happy faces.

Spring in the city.
Spring in the city!
Bright, bold, blooming,
Spring in the city!

Whether the visualization is followed with choral reading of the poetry, creative writing, art, interpretive movement, or drama, the creative expression should be enhanced by the listeners' active rather than passive role. You should have on hand a rich supply of poetry to guide imaging activities. The collections listed in appendix E offer a wide variety of wonderful possibilities.

■ LONGER VISUALIZATION

Visualizing poetry makes wonderful practice work; as students gain experience and skill in using sensory recall to form mental pictures, they enjoy a "full-length feature." This can be provided via a guided fantasy with opportunities for each person to take small, individual "side trips" into realms of her or his own choosing.

The following activity allows digressions from the main guided adventure. You might play a piece of soft, flowing music in the background to provide continuity, particularly during those longer pauses while students explore and discover on their own.

A WALK IN THE WOODS IN LATE SUMMER

Everyone get very comfortable. Close your eyes if that helps you to concentrate on the suggestions and to more easily see, hear, touch, taste, and smell, using only your past experiences and your imagination. Sometimes on this journey, you will be able to spend some extra time in your own way, for each of you is all alone on this adventure. When we return, there will be a time for sharing, so each person will want to choose something special to remember—a favorite place or a medley of colors, a sound, perhaps a special texture or taste that you explored. You will also want to recall your own special feelings. Don't worry if you have never been to just such a place in real life, for all of you will discover that you have had experiences from which to draw to create a special place in your own imagination. (Pause.)

Are you all ready to take a leisurely walk in a wooded place? (Brief pause.)

It's a perfect Saturday in late summer, a great day to take a long, relaxing stroll in the woods. You are wearing your old clothes, so you can do some exploring. The sun feels almost hot, but you quickly notice how much cooler it becomes as you enter a thick grove of trees. The path is already showing signs of a change of season, for there is a light covering of fallen leaves, leaves that have ripened to shades of yellow and gold and fallen prematurely.

Stop to look beneath some of the fallen leaves. What insects might you find? The undersides of the leaves are wet; notice the damp odor as you kneel to examine the busy world beneath the decaying leaves. Look about. What else is there to see on the floor of the woods? (Pause.)

You move on. Look up and watch the play of sunlight among the green leaves overhead. Listen! Hear the sounds of the woods all around—insects and the call of birds. See how many things you can spot that are contributing to the chorus. (Pause.) Move slowly. Here and there are small flowers in bloom, bits of purple and gold among the green, reds, and browns of the forest floor.

Now the shade is very deep and the woods seem more mysterious. The squawk of a jay startles you; you scan the treetops to find it. Something darts across your path! What was it? (Pause.) Up ahead you see bright sunlight. It is a clearing. At the edge of the clearing is a jungle of bushes and tangled vines. Many tower over your head. It is a medley of colors. As you enter the clearing, the sun is warm on your face. This place is alive with buzzing insects. You spot some wild grape vines. They are a jungle of leaves and twisted trunks. Perhaps there are wild grapes within. Bees buzz around your head as you feel your way into the mass of vines. You can smell the sweet, pungent fragrance of wild grapes. Can you find some? (Pause.) Try some if you like. (Pause.)

When you are ready, come out of the grapevine jungle. Scramble back to the path. The underbrush in the clearing smells dusty from its long summer. Now let's explore the clearing. Long grasses bend beneath your footsteps, sometimes leaving heads of ripe seeds on your jeans. The breeze is stronger here, and you try to catch a milkweed seed as it drifts past you, carried by its own parachute. Listen, there is a new sound. A tiny trickle of a stream flows through this open place. Do you hear it?

Follow your ears to find the stream. You hear something splash into the water. The stream must be nearby. When you discover it, take some time to poke along the bank. See what you can find. (Pause.) Can you tell if the stream is sometimes larger during other seasons of the year? Follow the water a little way, and when you are tired, find a good spot to rest. (Pause.)

When everyone is rested, we shall return to our classroom and share some of the things that each person discovered on the walk.

Allow a few seconds for everyone to finish her or his fantasy. Students are often very quiet during this time, and it is unwise to rush too soon into the sharing. Generally, when that are through, they open their eyes and send you a smile that says, "Look, I'm back." When most have done so, you can begin the discussion. Now is the time to share the individual discoveries. Your questions guide students in recreating some of their sensory observations.

The guided fantasy involves sensory recall on two levels: first, students use sensory recall to engage in the fantasy during the sidecoaching, and second, they use recall in order to talk about their own special adventure. Many guided fantasies can be replayed as a sidecoached narrative pantomime, and the sensory recall is further reinforced as the players translate their perceptions and feelings into movement. Whatever follow-up uses you make, it quickly becomes obvious that the guided fantasy not only stimulated lots of ideas but also generated strong feelings. This affective dimension of guided imagery play can also make a contribution to both initial and advanced work in drama.

Sensory recall: moods and emotions

Sensory recall not only lays a fundamental role in any work with the imagination, it is also useful when recreating moods and emotions. The ability to establish a mood and generate feelings becomes ever more important as students increase their skills in drama. Story dramatization of literature, original improvised scenes, and work in characterization all involve increasing competency in establishing moods and communicating feelings.

When the class has collectively engaged in a guided fantasy, you can probe that shared experience to discover dominant moods and emotions. The guided fantasy through a woods in later summer did not include any strong conflict or particularly scary situation; however, some students might characterize the mood as one of "loneliness," while others would describe it as "peaceful." For some, the prospect of being alone in the woods to explore would be exciting; others may find it rather frightening and would have preferred to have been there with someone else. Some delight in discovering a multitude of fat bugs, worms, perhaps a snake or turtle; others prefer to find nonliving things. When the guided fantasy offers a wealth of possibilities, each student can utilize her or his own unique treasury of sensory experiences to recall and apply and, thus, remain in control of the kinds of moods and feelings evoked.

■ RECREATING FEELINGS THROUGH SENSORY RECALL

Narrative pantomime, visualizing poetry with strong sensory suggestions, and guided fantasy experiences all afford opportunities to examine moods and express feelings. However, you may want to specifically focus on the relationship between sensory recall, moods, and emotions as a primary objective. The following are short activities that can be used for that purpose.

Request students to think back to a particular occasion, to recall the sights, sounds, and other sensory manifestations. You might say, "Recall the last time you did something special with a friend. See if you can see the scene in your mind's eye. Were there any special sounds, textures, smells associated with the experience? Imagine the scene as vividly as you can. Now, how would you describe the mood of the place or event? Recall your feelings; how would you describe them? How do you imagine your friend felt? If there were others there, how would you describe their feelings?

Another possibility is to suggest a mood (joyous, somber, sad, mysterious, silly, terrifying, etc.) and ask players to recall a time when they were in a situation where the mood created would best be summarized as _____ (name a mood). Suggest that they recall the sights, sounds, tastes, temperature, odors, and so forth associated with that mood. Discuss how each person felt, what emotions were a part of the situation. You might follow the guided recollection by exploring a range of moods and emotions as a group, stimulated by poetry, pictures (works of art or photos), colors, tactile exploration, and music.

To the extent that students can tap into their own past experiences, whatever motivational means is used can work. For example, big-city children listening to a piece of pastoral music "hear and see" different scenes than country children. Consequently, the music suggests different moods and feelings for each.

An example of the variety of responses possible was vividly provided by a class of students exploring a space flooded with red light. Some students moved with great excitement and energy; others interpreted the color as associated with frightening things and events. One student, however, moved through the red environment in slow motion in a drowsy fashion. Later, when discussing the prevalent mood created by the red light, "exciting" was offered by several. They related it to being "downtown," "being part of a crowd gathered to watch firefighters battle a large blaze," and other high-energy situations. Some described the mood as "scary"; they associated the color with sirens, "my house is on fire," even "blood." The student who drifted slowly through the space described the mood as "sleepy"; his explanation was that a nightlight in his bedroom made the whole room glow with a soft, red light. It was what he remembered as he drifted off to sleep each night. Every student identified a mood, but what a range they covered— yet all were equally appropriate responses, as they were honestly evoked by past personal experiences. As a consequence, the feelings expressed were sincere and of substance, drawn from within rather than simply "put on."

Sensory awareness and recall are very important to creative drama at whatever level. However motivated, such experiences are necessary to stimulate and recharge the imagination, to establish moods, and to elicit sincere feelings. From simple activities (such as listening to sounds and exploring objects visually and tactually) to more sophisticated techniques (such as guided imagery and the visualization of literature), drama requires that participants activate the senses. Students who are able to keep their imaginations alive and well during the later years of childhood are well equipped to progress in drama and to move into more formal work in the theatre arts both as performers and as audience. They are also better prepared as creative problem solvers who can put their abilities to synthesize, visualize, and engage in divergent thinking to a variety of academic, personal, and social uses.

PRE- AND POST-PLAYING: IMPORTANT TIMES

All of the preceding activities, used separately or in combination, may stand alone to provide review for experienced players or as introductory work for beginners. This is often accomplished by integrating short, highly focused drama activities into learning in the content areas. However, these or similar activities may also be used to provide orientation and warm-ups (practice) as the exercises are extended into full-length lessons that offer more complex and challenging experiences in creative drama. Indeed, the more extensive and intensive the drama work becomes, the more students need to engage in such preparatory activities. They need practice in using their imaginations, in expressing through movement and pantomime, in discovering how to establish a desired mood and express feelings, and to use their voices and bodies to portray a variety of roles.

It is this writer's observation, based on many years of working with players of all ages, that some of the most exciting and rewarding drama happens during the pre-playing work. This practice time can encourage experimentation, risk-taking, and opportunity to try-out and try-on before making decisions that will affect the main event.

Warm-ups

There are other good reasons for providing ample pre-playing time and a variety of warm-up experiences. When students spend most of their days utilizing rational, linear, cause-and-effect thinking (as required for much of the content area work), they need special opportunities to "shift gears" and to recharge their imaginations. Before engaging in longer or more complex drama work, such as the dramatization of a story or the development of original small group scenes, they need to engage in some concentrated divergent thinking. They need to become comfortable with ambiguity and to explore events and situations, and especially problems for which there can be several answers or solutions, all equally "right" or possible.

This is a time to practice brainstorming ideas without being evaluative or judgmental of each other's contributions. Short exercises in sensory recall, probing possibilities through a variety of what-if questions, and visualizing scenes via guided fantasy all make excellent warm-ups to get the creative juices flowing. Furthermore, the content of these "tuning" activities ought to introduce the topic or theme of the lesson so that the entire experience is one of cohesiveness and unity.

When moving toward more in-depth work in drama, the pre-play time should also include short, highly focused activities designed to let students practice specific skills that will be required in the longer activity. This often includes work with body awareness and control, spatial perception, and exploring vocal possibilities. For example, if the main drama work is to be the dramatization of a story using pantomime, in-place pantomimes such as the ten-count freeze could be employed as warm-ups, or the group might create an environment appropriate to the setting of the story using the "creating an environment" activity. A short sequential pantomime game would be useful as a reminder that the ordering of events is often critical to the telling of a story. An add-on scene can reinforce the importance of a dramatic structure with a beginning, middle, and ending that all fits together with unity.

■ WARMING UP THE BODY

If the story dramatization will require moving over or through a variety of surfaces or special environments, warm-ups could include in-place pantomime in which players practice appropriate movements or, perhaps, a short, sidecoached narrative pantomime where everyone moves through the larger space in ways responsive to the several environments described in the narration. The warm-ups need not include all the possible places or situations suggested in the story to be dramatized, nor are they limited to those possibilities. The purpose of the practice activities is to allow the players to explore ideas and experiment with ways to translate their creative thoughts and related feelings into movement and pantomime. Indeed, there appears to be a good deal of reciprocity between the physical involvement required for pantomime and increased creative ideas. The physical activity feeds the imagination and the imagination guides the movement. The most useful warm-ups generally involve both mind and body working together in a synergetic fashion.

■ ADDING VOICE

Warm-ups may also include short activities that concentrate on warming up the voice. The addition of speech to movement and mime is sometimes seen as more threatening or difficult than movement alone. Consequently, even if the anticipated dramatization of a story does not include improvised dialogue, warm-ups related to the story may include the addition of appropriate imitative sounds or words added to simple, in-place pantomime activity. This extra practice in adding speech to exercises that are basically sensory recall/ movement work can pay off in the long run. It lays a foundation for the important part that speech will play in more advanced work, and clearly establishes that creative drama is not simply movement and pantomime.

The following illustrate ways that simple sounds or bits of speech might be added to some in-place pantomime to be used as a warm-up for a longer dramatization involving a visit from a variety of extraterrestrials invented by the players.

Warm-up 1. In self-space, to a ten-count freeze, everyone uses her or his body to create a being from outer space. Repeat this two or three times to allow students to try on different shapes. Still in self-space, the players can experiment with possible ways to move as their creatures.

Warm-up 2. Still working independently, each player chooses the shape he or she likes best, and to a variety of beats you provide on a drum or tambourine, everyone moves about the larger space as their extraterrestrials. Vary the beat to include very fast movement and slow motion. Students may need to adjust their shapes in order to successfully move with the various tempos.

Warm-up 3. Still moving in the larger space, each player adds an appropriate sound or repetitive phrase that fits her or his creature.

Warm-up 4. Still moving in the larger space, each extraterrestrial adds some special way to greet others as they pass. Emphasize that the greeting is done only with movement, only with speech or sound, or with a combination of movement and sound.

As an extension of the pre-playing, and as part of the planning for the longer drama experience (such as the dramatization of a piece of science fiction from literature or a narrative pantomime or story invented by the group), several players might describe their individual visions of their creatures. Such imaging might have been done before the movement and pantomime work began; however, it is often more successful if the movement precedes the visualization. The awareness of the body shape, the configurations that result as the creature moves, even the type of sounds added to accompany the movement—all of these contribute to the students' visions of their own inventions. Each student has begun the process of creating and assuming a role of someone or something other than self. With mind, body, and voice, the student has physically and cognitively made decisions about such details as size, shape, color, texture, and vocal qualities of her or his role.

Through a series of warm-ups, he or she becomes ready to tackle the more demanding drama work. Everyone benefits from such warm-ups, experienced players and novices alike.

Quieting activities

Before looking at ways to move later elementary students into more demanding work in creative drama, it is useful to explore some ideas for bringing *all* drama experiences to a satisfying conclusion. The longer and more intensive the work, however, the more important it becomes to plan some time at the end of the drama to bring the players down, both physically and emotionally. Just as warm-ups are an important part of planning and preparing for playing, so, also, are "cool-downs" an important part of bringing the lesson to a close. As described in chapter 2, you should strive to have adequate time to debrief, discuss, and assess what has happened. For students to be ready for those important aspects of classroom work in drama, they need to "shift gears" once more, cognitively, physically, and psychologically.

Often, you can create quieting activities by looking at what was done during the warm-ups.

For example, the drama that involved students in creating extra-terrestrial beings could provide a cool-down activity in which very tired creatures, having survived the excitement of meeting such a collection of beings so different from themselves, move in slow motion. As they return to their several special places in the galaxies, they bid farewell to all of the others. Slowly each finds her or his way back home where each falls asleep in her or his own way.

The theme of the lesson has been sustained through to the very end; the playing has come full circle, so that there is a sense of completion before moving on to other activities.

When there are so many other things to be done in a day's time, it can be tempting to either omit the quieting time altogether or to rush it, but the few seconds spent allowing students to make the transition from the realm of make-believe back to the world of reality is important. This is particularly true if the drama is to be followed by quiet work of a totally different nature. No matter what is next on the schedule, leader and players alike need a few moments to reflect quietly on what has happened. Many students find it easier to relax and become quiet while still in role or within the imagined situation, than as themselves. Appropriate quieting activities can assure everyone that self-discipline is as important in drama as in any other creative activity, particularly as students move into more demanding work. The drama lesson that is brought to a satisfying conclusion for teacher and students alike paves the way for enthusiastic anticipation of the next drama time.

CHAPTER 4

Building on Basic Creative Drama Skills

POLISHING AND REFINING BASIC SKILLS

When you give students continuing opportunities to expand and extend drama skills, their growth in this form of creative thinking and expression can be as academically and personally rewarding as their increased abilities as writers, mathematicians, musicians, athletes, and so forth. Anyone who thinks that fourth-, fifth- and sixth-graders would find creative drama boring has not seen these students engaged in drama work that appropriately inspires and challenges their best efforts. Just as Show and Tell with early elementary students gives way to more demanding work in oral presentation (oral reports, speeches of various kinds, panels, symposiums, etc.), the goals, objectives, materials, and activities in drama must keep pace with students' new levels of maturity and more sophisticated capabilities. You should add demands for new drama skills, giving students increased opportunities to develop and portray believable and interesting characters, improvise dialogue, and work cooperatively and creatively in small groups with less dependence on you as motivator and guide.

Advanced work requires a much greater understanding of dramatic structure and increased abilities to select, analyze, and interpret literature that can be successfully used as a basis for drama. The content of the materials you choose to dramatize must meet students' new interests and needs. Generally, if your students respond negatively to drama, it will be because your materials or your expectations are not commensurate with their interests, knowledge, and capabilities.

Before moving into new areas of work, spend some time working to polish and refine drama skills already familiar to students, especially those skills that they will continue to use in more advanced work—movement and pantomime, verbalization, and group work for the dramatization of literature and the invention of original scenes. Sometimes it is necessary to help students understand why it is important to do something again and again in order to get better and better at it. You can compare this need in drama to creative work in art or music. Some students can best relate this to the needs of athletes to practice and practice the basic skills required in their sport in order to excel. You can sometimes substitute new materials or different ways of organizing when practicing and refining previously introduced skills and knowledge.

Making movement and pantomime more communicative

Students are often astute enough to recognize that when certain children demonstrate a particular activity, idea, or feeling through movement or pantomime, others can easily understand the player's intentions. Other times it is nearly impossible to gain meaning from the actions. In the first instance, the action is communicative; meaning is shared. Talking with students, you might compare the use of pantomime with oral communication that is or is not easy to understand. Remind them that a speaker strives to create and share meaning with others by choosing the right words, articulating and pronouncing them with clarity, delivering the words with fluency and appropriate prosody, and arranging them in an order that clearly communicates the intended meaning.

Communicating nonverbally may be particularly challenging as students become better and better language users. Like adults, they come to depend on their own and others' abilities to communicate through language and are often unaware of the important role that facial expression and body movement plays in all of their communication. Therefore, helping them to better communicate through movement and pantomime not only contributes to increased skill in drama, but can also help them as speakers to provide more congruency between their words and nonverbal messages. Additionally, they may become more astute "readers" of the nonverbal components of the communication of others.

Several parallels can be drawn between communicative speech and communicative movement and mime. You should encourage students to *unclutter their pantomime;* economy of movement can help clarify meaning just as concise use of words clarifies speech. Beginning work in pantomime often suffers from a kind of "physical verbosity" or informational overload. Clarity of meaning is lost in all of the frenetic movement.

Point out the value of using *pause* to provide clarity and to highlight important ideas. At first, students may accomplish this through your giving them the "freeze" signal. Later, as students take more charge of the drama work, they may need to be reminded that it is not necessary to move all the time— that stillness, like pause and silence in speech, also communicates. The use of the pause functions as punctuation to separate ideas, changes of motivation or mood, and for emphasis.

Remind players to *use sensory recall* in order to concentrate on what they are trying to show. Tell them to keep a clear picture in the mind's eye, using sensory recall to provide the necessary internal resources that permit students to translate ideas and feelings into movement. Simple in-place pantomime as described in the Sensory Recall and Pantomime section of chapter 2 can be used again and again in order to provide the important practice for increased competencies.

The following are some in-place exercises that stress the use of sensory recall, economy of movement, and the use of pause to emphasize and punctuate the pantomime:

1. Each player, working in self-space, determines the dimensions of a table by "exploring" the surface with her or his hands. Next, each player dusts and polishes the tabletop, trying to maintain a consistent, flat surface. Then everyone puts a place setting of dishes (or some other series of objects) on the table.

Urge players to use pauses to separate segments of actions and to concentrate on the properties of each item as it is handled and put in place.

2. Again working in self-space, each player explores a wall directly in front of her or him. Once this vertical surface is established, everyone becomes a painter and, with brush or roller, applies an even coat of paint from her or his individual bucket or pan. The challenge is to maintain a flat, consistent surface with each stroke of the brush or roller. Tempo may be speeded up or slowed down. Even double-time work that is reminiscent of a Charlie Chaplin silent movie should clearly communicate.

3. Each person is responsible for building a fence or wall from stones or bricks. The goal is to maintain a consistent location and to lift and set the materials in place showing the weight and size of each new piece. This activity makes a fine warm-up before dramatizing a humorous folktale "The Wise People of Gotham," in which peasants build a wall with which to enclose a field where a lovely skylark lives. It is all part of a series of silly behaviors to convince the king's soldiers that the people of Gotham are too stupid to be able to billet his troops. An excellent version of the tale is found in Winifred Ward's *Stories to Dramatize* (1952).

4. Each person decides just where to dig for buried treasure. With hands or tools, everyone digs and digs until an ancient chest is located. It is old and fragile and each player must concentrate on removing it without destroying it. This is fun as a warm-up for the dramatizing of *Treasure Island* or children's own stories about buried treasure.

■ DISCIPLINING BODY PARTS

5. This is a series of pantomime activities in which body parts are used with discipline to communicate actions, ideas, and feelings: players concentrate on using hands and arms to raise a flag or hoist a set of sails; feet and legs work in self-space to produce such actions as kicking a ball, moving through various environments, providing a base for several feats of strength; shoulders and heads lean into a gale force wind or push to move a massive rock. Parts of the face are worked independently or in combination to show a series of feelings: eyes and eyebrows communicate surprise, anger, anticipation, excitement, pleasure, sympathy; noses show delight or displeasure,

haughtiness or an imminent sneeze; mouths demonstrate horror, disappointment, anger, hurt, etc.

Some of the very best exercises are those done with students working in pairs. By definition, pair work requires that the pantomime must be communicative to at least one other person. The following pair situations in which later elementary students are challenged to work with economy of movement, use pause to punctuate and emphasize, while drawing on sensory recall to provide a personal resource for guiding the action.

■ POLISHING PAIR PANTOMIME

Have each student find a partner. Instruct the entire group that none of the pairs share a common language and players must, therefore, try to communicate solely through movement and pantomime. Remind them that facial expression and how they share space are also a part of their nonverbal communication. Within each pair, one person (player 1) will have a problem of some kind (you provide the general category). It must be a problem that can be demonstrated through body movement and facial expression. The other person (player 2) will discover this stranger in a predicament and try to help. The playing will proceed until the problem is appropriately resolved (the helper does succeed in helping) or time is called. If desired, the same situation can be done with roles reversed but with the person with the problem creating her or his own situation within the category.

Problem situations that work well for this type of play are these:

1. Some property of player 1 is lost (a pet, a ticket, a piece of jewelry or clothing, a toy, or piece of sport equipment are all possibilities).
2. Player 1 is stuck in some way or place (foot is caught in a trap or escalator step, a hand or finger is stuck in a small space such as a jar or lock, the person is trapped in thick mud or quicksand, etc.).
3. Player 1 is lost (here the challenge may be to communicate where he or she needs or wants to go).
4. Player 1 is trying to operate some piece of equipment but does not understand how to do it (a pay telephone, a revolving door,

a video game, an elevator, a coin-operated machine, an appliance, a piece of athletic equipment, a piece of machinery).

5. Player 1 is trying to locate a specific location or item (an address, the bus stop or air terminal, a specific kind of store or restaurant, a police officer or taxi cab).

The class may continue to make up hypothetical situations along these lines. You might suggest ideas based on literature or materials studied in science or social studies. Whatever the content, the player with the "problem" quickly discovers that the pantomime must actually communicate to her or his partner, and must, therefore, be done with more precision and attention to clarity of movement than required to successfully respond to a narrative pantomime or other teacher-led drama activity.

Reflected pairs. Another pair activity that requires highly communicative pantomime is Reflected Pairs. Have students work in double pairs; in each foursome, assign one pair a task to do cooperatively. The other pair must mirror the lead pair as accurately as possible. Some tasks that work for this activity are these:

1. Playing checkers, chess, or other board games.
2. One person putting stage make-up on an actor, a clown, etc. (no touching allowed).
3. Two people cooperatively giving an animal (a reluctant dragon, frisky puppy, or circus elephant, perhaps) a bath.
4. Bundling and tying a stack of logs or other materials.
5. A small child getting a first haircut (no touching).
6. Trimming a Christmas tree.
7. Hoisting sails on a clipper ship.
8. Picking fruit, hanging curtains, stocking shelves in a store.
9. Putting up a ladder followed by one person handing materials to the person at the top.
10. One person building something with the other assisting.

You can choose topics to correlate with a piece of literature or an area of study within a content area. You can time these activities and then have the roles reversed to allow the mirroring team to lead the action. Following the playing, give each team an opportunity to talk about what happened, with special attention to what was easy to understand and what, if anything, was confusing. As an entire class, time permitting, students may generate a set of guide-lines for making movement and pantomime clearer. (You need not be concerned with the aesthetics of the movement at this point, although such may be a focus of more advanced work.)

Techniques described earlier also work for additional prac-tice in refining pantomime skills. Add-on scenes and sequen-tial pantomime games inherently require a certain attention to precision and clarity. Those with opportunities for interac-tion within several segments are especially useful. The highly structured nature of the sequence game makes this activity highly replicable; the same game can be played sever-al times but with different players working from the individ-ual cards. This can keep player interest high while providing the necessary practice to get really good at the work.

Gaining greater verbal skills

Communicating with movement and pantomime is chal-lenging and fun, but ultimately you will want students to be able to create an original scene or dramatize a selection from literature with both action and speech. Improvising believ-able dialogue is not easy to do. Many adults, when asked to engage in some role-playing for whatever purpose, can attest to their own feelings of insecurity and self-consciousness. Do not be surprised to see similar behaviors with later elemen-tary students; even those who have become quite competent with movement and pantomime may suddenly clam up or get silly and embarrassed when encouraged to add sounds and dialogue. A useful and comfortable way to get students ver-balizing is to add sounds and fragments of speech to warm-ups, especially as you encourage them to use the voice with power, sensitivity, and expressiveness.

Exploring vocal expression

Choral reading or speaking is an excellent way to involve students in exploring a full range of vocal possibilities. So, too, is storytelling and the reading aloud of prose and poetry. As discussed in the Storytelling section of chapter 2, you should provide later elementary students with ample opportunities both to tell stories and to read aloud. No matter how competently or extensively a student reads silently, those experiences do not directly contribute to reading *aloud* with understanding, fluency, and expression. Many highly skilled adult readers meet disaster when reading aloud. For some, it is a lost art that has resulted from years of neglect; others never had sufficient practice to develop and maintain proficiency. Reading aloud from a variety of genres provides excellent practice in developing the necessary fluency, as well as exploring the full range of the voice. The oral reader or storyteller must work with all of the dynamics of prosody: pitch, rate, volume, and inflection. Through sustained practice, students can gain control over the vocal mechanism so that they can use their voices both communicatively and artistically.

Storytelling or reading aloud is most often solo work. Many students, not just those who are reticent communicators, are shy and uncomfortable when forced to perform before others. Choral work offers a more secure environment for reading or speaking aloud; you can use shy students as chorus even when there are solo parts for the more courageous or gregarious. Poetry affords the ideal genre for choral reading or speaking, particularly when vocal exploration and expression are included as teaching/learning objectives. Not unlike music, poetry should be experienced aurally for people to fully appreciate the rhythm, rhyme, and melodic patterns. Most school libraries offer a wealth of suitable materials, but you will want to keep a few favorite collections nearby.

Most older children delight in the poetry of Shel Silverstein, Jack Prelutsky, Harry Behm, and David McCord, as well as the poetry you may recall with fondness from your own childhood. If students seem noncommittal about working with poetry, introduce them to choral speaking arrangements of "The Crocodile's Toothache" or "The Dirtiest Man in the World' (*Where the Sidewalk Ends,* Silverstein, 1974) or

"Bedtime Stories" by Lillian Moore (*See My Lovely Poison Ivy*, 1975). The images in these are sufficiently "disgusting," humorous, or ghoulish to appeal to the tastes of many nine-to twelve-year-olds. Furthermore, the oral interpretation allows students to explore a wide range of vocal dimensions. Of course, poems about all aspects of the natural world are generally enjoyed as well. Excellent choices are readily available.

Generally, you would score the poetry for reading by dividing the class into small or large choruses and assigning any solo parts. There are several ways to score a selection. If there is a refrain (a stanza repeated throughout the poem), it may effectively be performed by students speaking in chorus. The chorus may be one small group, the entire class, or different small groups assigned to do each repetition. Or you might divide the class into two groups who work antiphonally, alternating verses. Later elementary students often like to be divided by gender, with the boys and girls reciting alternate verses.

■ ARRANGING CHORIC MATERIALS

Some lines are most effective when done by solo voices, particularly as this is contrasted with choral work. Line-a-child is a way to organize for a quick reading, with each line of a longer poem assigned to a different student. Do this by simply moving around the circle or up and down the rows of seats. With this method, each segment is brief, so even reticent students should not feel unduly threatened. However, the reading should flow. Thus, a shy child might be paired with another reader who can lend support. Such arranging can be subtly done (so as not to call attention to anyone). The result is a final product composed of several solo lines and a few duets.

Many poems enjoyed by students in grades 4-6 are full of action as well as imagery. Reticent speakers or those who especially enjoy movement and pantomime might accompany the reading through interpretive or representational movement (depending on the content of the poetry).

Often the words of the poem can guide you in selecting a combination of group and solo reading.

For example, you can score the poem "Spring in the City," reproduced in full in the Sensory Recall and Guided Imagery section of chapter 3, for choral reading by selecting a small chorus to do the first four lines, then with a line-a-child format for all but the final stanza, which would be done with the entire group speaking in chorus. If there are more solo lines than students, have volunteers do two lines. You might score the same poem by dividing the class into several small choral groups, with each assigned one verse for verses two through eight and the full class doing the refrain verses at the beginning and end of the poem.

Students should always have an opportunity to read and discuss any poem before presenting it as a choral reading. If you are to urge expressive interpretation, you must make sure that readers have adequate understanding of the material. Furthermore, any choric work worthy of even minimal time and effort should allow for at least two readings in order to make adjustments and polish the rough spots.

From time to time, some work should be even more refined so that students are aware of their own capacities to improve through practice. Poetry that is especially enjoyed may be committed to memory and done with musical or rhythm instrument accompaniment, bits of props, or done against a backdrop of slides or a filmstrip that visually enhances the images in the poem. Such artistic embellishments offer additional ways to involve every student and provide increased opportunities for success. Like other cooperative work, "getting good" in choric work not only offers a sense of achievement for each student but is also a source of group pride, as everyone shares in the accomplishment of a job well done.

Sequential listening activities

Another format for getting students to read aloud with expression is the sequential listening game. In addition to the emphasis on oral expression, this activity requires active listening and reinforces the turn-taking nature of both interpersonal conversation and dialogue within a dramatic offering. Almost every kind of material can be used as a basis for a sequential listening game: you can divide poetry into lines or stanzas so that every student has an individual card with a small segment to be read aloud at the appropriate time, many works of prose are suitable for dividing among several readers, and blocks of specific information from a content area (such as materials to be introduced or review in history or geography) can be written as a sequence game. Prepare your Master List and individual student cards as you did for the sequential pantomime game described in chapter 3.

■ LISTENING FOR CUES

The following sequential listening game, for fifth- or sixth-graders, introduces a drama/science lesson on energy. What follows is a Master List; as organized here, it provides for 23 student segments.

1. You begin by reading aloud: ALL DAY, EVERY DAY OF OUR LIVES, WE ARE BOTH PRODUCERS AND CONSUMERS OF ENERGY. EVERY TIME WE EAT, OUR BODIES CONVERT FOOD INTO FUEL TO PRODUCE THE ENERGY NECESSARY TO MAINTAIN OUR BODY SYSTEMS AND PRODUCE GROWTH. EVEN WHEN WE ARE RESTING OR ASLEEP, WE ARE PRODUCERS OF ENERGY.

2. After you hear, "Even when we are resting or asleep, we are producers of energy," you read: WE ARE ALSO ENERGY CONSUMERS. MOST OF THE TIME WE TAKE FOR GRANTED THAT WE CAN PLUG IN AN APPLIANCE, FLIP A SWITCH, ADJUST A THERMOSTAT, OR START AN ENGINE AND INSTANTLY HAVE ENERGY TO PROVIDE US WITH ALL THE THINGS WE NEED: LIGHT, FOOD AND DRINK SERVED HOT OR COLD, ENTERTAINMENT, COMFORTABLE ROOMS, AND QUICK, EFFICIENT WAYS OF GETTING US ACROSS TOWN OR AROUND THE WORLD.

3. After you hear, ". . . and quick, efficient ways of getting us across town or around the world," you read: SUCH AN ABUNDANCE OF ENERGY WAS NOT ALWAYS POSSIBLE. MUCH OF WHAT WE TAKE FOR GRANTED WAS UNKNOWN OR IMPOSSIBLE TO PRODUCE EVEN IN THE DAYS OF OUR GREAT-GRANDPARENTS.

4. After your hear, ". . . even in the days of our great-grandparents," you read: ANYONE WHO HAS EVER BEEN CAMPING IN A

WILDERNESS AREA HAS HAD A TASTE OF WHAT LIFE WAS LIKE FOR
EVERYONE, RICH AND POOR, CITY FOLKS AND COUNTRY FOLKS,
BEFORE THE GREAT DISCOVERIES AND INVENTIONS THAT GAVE US
THE TREMENDOUS QUANTITIES OF ELECTRICITY AND OTHER MOD-
ERN SOURCES OF ENERGY.

5. After you hear, ". . . before the great discoveries and inven-
tions that gave us the tremendous quantities of electricity and
other modern sources of energy," you read: MOST FOLKS KNOW
THE STORY OF BEN FRANKLIN AND HIS KITE FLYING. AND MOST
WOULD PROBABLY AGREE THAT HE WAS TAKING A POWERFUL
CHANCE STANDING OUT THERE IN AN ELECTRICAL STORM, WITH
THUNDER ROLLING ALL AROUND AND THE SKY AS BRIGHT AS DAY,
WITH LIGHTNING.

6. BUT THE STORY OF THE DISCOVERY OF ELECTRICITY DIDN'T BEGIN
WITH BEN FRANKLIN AND HIS KITE. NO INDEED. FRANKLIN WOULD
PROBABLY HAVE BEEN INSIDE DURING THAT STORM, INVENTING
BIFOCAL EYEGLASSES OR THE FRANKLIN STOVE, IF HE HAD NOT
KNOWN ABOUT SOME EXPERIMENTS DONE IN BIRMINGHAM, ENG-
LAND, BY HIS FRIEND JAMES WATT.

7. IN 1763, WATT, A MATHEMATICAL INSTRUMENT MAKER FOR THE
UNIVERSITY OF GLASGOW, WAS ASKED TO REPAIR A MODEL OF A
STEAM ENGINE THAT BELONGED TO THE NATURAL PHILOSOPHY
CLASS.

8. NOW, MR. WATT WAS HIGHLY AGGRAVATED TO DISCOVER THAT
THE ENGINE HE WAS ASKED TO REPAIR WAS A GREAT WASTER OF
STEAM, AND HE PROMPTLY SET ABOUT IMPROVING THAT MACHINE.
IT WAS CALLED A NEWCOMEN ENGINE AFTER ITS INVENTOR WHO,
IN 1712, HAD AN IDEA FOR A STEAM-DRIVEN PUMP THAT COULD
BRING UP THE WATER DEEP IN THE TIN MINES OF CORNWALL.

9. BUT NEWCOMEN'S STEAM ENGINE WAS ONLY POSSIBLE BECAUSE
ANOTHER FELLOW WITH A SIMILAR NAME, SIR ISAAC NEWTON, HAD
DECIDED THAT GRAVITY DOES MORE THAN CAUSE APPLES TO FALL
FROM TREES. HE DEVELOPED A MECHANICAL WONDER, WAY BACK
IN THE 17TH CENTURY, THAT CONSISTED OF SOME HUGE WATER-
WORKS.

10. NEWTON DESIGNED FOURTEEN WATERWHEELS THAT USED THE
CURRENT OF THE RIVER SEINE NEAR PARIS TO PROPEL THEM. THE
WHEELS RAISED WATER TO A HIGH TOWER FROM WHICH AN AQUE-

DUCT CARRIED IT NEARLY A HALF A MILE TO THE PALACE OF THE KING.

11. FROM JUST THESE FEW HIGHLIGHTS, WE SEE THAT WE CAN TRACE THE HISTORY OF ENERGY BACKWARDS, STEP BY STEP, FROM MODERN-DAY NUCLEAR POWER TO THE MOST PRIMITIVE SOURCES OF ENERGY KNOWN TO MANKIND.

12. IN FACT, WE MIGHT SAY THAT THE FIRST SOURCES OF ENERGY USED BY HUMAN BEINGS WERE THE PEOPLE THEMSELVES—EVERY MAN, WOMAN, AND CHILD, WHO USED THE BRUTE FORCE OF THEIR MUSCLES TO CARRY OUT THE ENERGY-REQUIRING TASKS OF THEIR TIME.

13. AT FIRST, OUR ANCESTORS WERE NOT ABLE TO HARNESS MOST OF THE SOURCES OF POWER THAT EXISTED ALL AROUND THEM: THE HEAT OF THE SUN; THE WIND; THE FLOWING AND FALLING OF WATER; SUCH NATURAL FUELS AS COAL, OIL, AND GAS; THE PRESSURE OF AIR; THE THUNDERSTORM; THE EARTH'S MAGNETIC FIELD; EVEN VOLCANOES AND HOT SPRINGS.

14. ONE OF THE FIRST USED SOURCES OF ENERGY WAS FIRE. IT WAS USED FOR COOKING AND THE BAKING OF POTTERY DISHES. IT WAS ALSO USED AS ARTIFICIAL HEAT WITH WHICH TO KEEP WARM ON A COLD NIGHT.

15. OUR ANCESTORS ALSO TOOK ADVANTAGE OF THE NATURAL FLOW OF WATER TO CARRY LOGS AND CANOES DOWNSTREAM. LATER, WIND WAS HARNESSED TO FILL SAILS AND CARRY BOATS WITHOUT THE HUMAN LABOR OF PULLING BOATS THROUGH THE WATER WITH OARS OR PADDLES.

16. LATER, FIRE WAS USED TO SEPARATE COPPER AND TIN FROM ORES AND THE METALS GAVE HUMANKIND THE MEANS FOR MAKING BETTER TOOLS. THESE IMPROVED TOOLS WERE USED TO CREATE DEVICES WE CALL MACHINES. PRIMITIVE MACHINES WERE INDEED VERY SIMPLE.

17. TWO SUCH SIMPLE BUT IMPORTANT MACHINES WERE THE SLOPE AND THE SLEDGE. THESE EARLY MACHINES USED HUMAN ENERGY AS THE SOURCE OF POWER. HOWEVER, THE SLOPE AND THE SLEDGE PERMITTED PEOPLE TO MOVE MATERIALS UP AND DOWN HILLS AND ALONG UNEVEN PIECES OF GROUND BY SETTING THEM ON A CARRIER WITH SMOOTH EDGES.

18. PEOPLE ALSO CAME TO RELY ON ANIMALS—BEASTS OF BURDEN—
    TO PROVIDE MORE ENERGY TO DO TASKS THAN HUMAN MUSCLES
    ALONE WOULD PERFORM. WITH THE INVENTION OF THE WHEEL,
    AND SUCH OTHER DEVICES AS PULLEYS AND LEVERS, HUMANS AND
    ANIMALS COULD EXTEND THE AMOUNT OF TIME THEY COULD PUT
    TO A TASK BEFORE RUNNING OUT OF ENERGY.

19. ENGINEERS USE THE TERM "POWER" TO MEAN "SO MUCH WORK
    DONE IN SO MUCH TIME." THIS IS TRUE WHETHER THE POWER
    COMES FROM A NUCLEAR REACTOR OR FROM COAL, OIL, OR WATER
    USED TO GENERATE ELECTRICITY—OR FROM THE MUSCLES OF A
    PERSON OR A MULE.

20. THE HISTORY OF ENERGY, THE ENERGY NEEDED TO PROVIDE THE
    POWER NECESSARY TO CREATE AND MAINTAIN MODERN SOCIETIES,
    HAS CONSTANTLY GROWN AND CHANGED, SOMETIMES VERY
    SLOWLY OVER A LONG PERIOD OF TIME.

21. SOMETIMES IT HAS CHANGED SO RAPIDLY OUR UNDERSTANDING OF
    NEW TYPES OF ENERGY SOURCES CAN HARDLY KEEP UP WITH NEW
    SCIENTIFIC DISCOVERIES AND INVENTIONS. THIS MAY MAKE IT DIF-
    FICULT TO DECIDE JUST WHAT IS THE BEST KIND OF ENERGY
    SOURCE TO USE FOR A SPECIFIC JOB IN A PARTICULAR PART OF THE
    WORLD.

22. TO UNDERSTAND THE HISTORY OF ENERGY IS TO GIVE US KNOWL-
    EDGE OF THE HISTORY OF CIVILIZATION; EACH IS A PART OF THE
    OTHER. BUT EVERY TIME WE TURN ON THE LIGHTS, DRIVE TO THE
    GROCERY STORE, OR FEEL OUR MUSCLES WORKING AS WE PUMP OUR
    BIKES UP A LONG HILL, WE ARE A PART OF THE WHOLE HISTORY OF
    ENERGY—EACH DISCOVERY, EVERY INVENTION.

23. SO, THANKS, BEN FRANKLIN! YOUR KITE WITH A LONG, MOIST
    CORD THAT CARRIED THE ENERGY OF THE THUNDERCLOUD TO
    EARTH HELPED GIVE THE HISTORY OF ENERGY A POWERFUL BOOST.

The first five segments show what would be on the individual student cards and are samples of how to do all of the cards for players. It is not necessary to provide the *entire* preceding segment as the listening cue on the following card; generally, either a final short sentence or a partial sentence will be sufficient. Do be sure that each cue is clearly distinct from any other. Obviously, your Master List need not list any listening cues, since it shows the entire preceding segment.

Allow students some time to read their cards over, several times if necessary, to be sure everyone can correctly read her or his card. The game goes more smoothly if students have already received help with difficult words or the pronunciation of unfamiliar proper nouns. To further assist students in reading with both fluency and expression, it is useful to allow time to read the material aloud more than once, particularly if a first reading were rough.

Reading aloud from prepared materials is an excellent way for students to practice fluent and expressive reading in which they can work with all of the dynamics of vocal expression. It does not, however, promote increased competency with spontaneous speech. Other types of activities are required to engage students in verbal improvisation (that is, the spontaneous invention of dialogue). Adding appropriate imitative sounds to movement as described in the Warm-ups section of chapter 2 is one way to begin. The following are additional ways to expand the addition of sounds and speech to movement so that students can build, in a comfortable progression, true improvisation in which both action and speech are simultaneously invented.

Melodramas with group characters. Later elementary students often delight in the ridiculous and exaggerated. The format of the old-fashioned melodrama can provide a simple, humorous way to encourage students to use their voices in a variety of ways.

Divide the class into small groups with each group playing one character in the story. Assign each character an appropriate but highly exaggerated movement, sound, or fragment of speech to do each time the character is mentioned. You can narrate or have a child who reads with dramatic flair do it. (Several stories of this type are available in a variety of language arts materials for teachers. They are also easy to invent, and students may enjoy making up their own melodramas to perform.) The following example requires the class to be divided into eight groups: a smaller number of players might be divided into four groups with each group responsible for two characters. It works best if each group has a chance to briefly practice working in unison before the story begins.

CAST OF CHARACTERS

LOW-SLUNG SPORTS CAR: makes steering movements and says "Vroom, vroom"
MYSTERIOUS FIGURE: looks right, then left and mutters under his breath
MODEST RANCH HOUSE: rings doorbell and says "ding, dong"
LITTLE SISTER: moves hand as if operating video joystick and says "Gotcha"
BIG BROTHER: puts hands to cheeks and says "Oh no!"
FAMILY MUTT: scratches fleas with right hand and says "Woof, woof"
VIDEO GAME: bats eyes and says "Bleep, bleep"
LATEST SPY THRILLER: looks through magnifying glass and says "Ahaaaa"

It was a dark and stormy night. Slowly the headlights of a LOW-SLUNG SPORTS CAR cut through the rain and turned up the drive of a MODEST RANCH HOUSE on the outskirts of town. A MYSTERIOUS FIGURE wearing a long trench coat and wide-brimmed hat quickly extinguished the headlights of the LOW-SLUNG SPORTS CAR and stepped into the shadows. He swiftly moved toward the front door of the MODEST RANCH HOUSE.

LITTLE SISTER cleverly moved the joystick of her VIDEO GAME without taking her eyes off the screen. BIG BROTHER alternated between munching popcorn and turning the pages of the LATEST SPY THRILLER.

MYSTERIOUS FIGURE patted the pockets of his long trench coat, first slowly and then faster and faster. He looked back over his shoulder at LOW-SLUNG SPORTS CAR and an angry look passed over his face, barely visible between his wide-brimmed hat and turned up collar. FAMILY MUTT opened one eye and growled softly. LITTLE SISTER calmly shot down six more space ships while BIG BROTHER'S eyes grew wide as he turned the final pages of LATEST SPY THRILLER. Just then, there was a terrible roll of thunder, and a jagged burst of lightning split the sky. MYSTERIOUS FIGURE swiftly but silently ducked under the broad eaves of MODEST RANCH HOUSE until he reached the window. His face was ghostlike in the flash of lightning. He clenched his fist and aimed it toward the window. More lightning crackled and suddenly the lights went off inside MODEST RANCH HOUSE plunging LITTLE SISTER and BIG BROTHER into total darkness. The VIDEO GAME blacked out, leaving three alien space-ships about to land. LATEST SPY THRILLER crashed to the floor hitting FAMILY MUTT, who let out a mournful howl.

As the storm raged on, MYSTERIOUS FIGURE pounded on the window of MODEST RANCH HOUSE with first one fist and then the other. FAMILY MUTT cowered in its corner. BIG BROTHER suddenly saw the wide-brimmed hat of MYSTERIOUS FIGURE clearly silhouetted by a burst of lightning. His hand was reaching for the windowlock. With one more angry look over his shoulder at LOW-SLUNG SPORTS CAR, MYSTERIOUS FIGURE forced open the window of MODEST RANCH HOUSE and stepped over the sill. BIG BROTHER let out a shriek, FAMILY MUTT whimpered, and LITTLE SISTER screamed, "Hello, Dad! Locked your keys in LOW-SLUNG SPORTS CAR again, I bet!" MYSTERIOUS FIGURE tossed his dripping wide-brimmed hat toward the hall tree, shook his head, and let out a long, slow sigh.

Students may enjoy exchanging parts and repeating the story.

Melodramas are often full of stereotypes and should be carefully monitored to exclude those which are in any way hurtful or insensitive.

Improvised actions with sounds and words. This activity is least threatening if everyone plays independently in self-space, working at the same time and with the same situation. However, each player is free to improvise his or her own movement and speech. You provide a series of situations, allowing a brief amount of time for each segment. It becomes apparent when most students have done as much with the situation as is of value: the noise and action taper off and the players are ready to move on.

■ COMBINING ACTION AND SOUND

The following are events or situations that later elementary students can easily improvise; several offer options to allow for individual decision making.

1. Coaxing a frightened kitten down from a tree or out from under a dark place where it has gone to hide.
2. Urging on a favorite participant in a race. The racers might be competing in a foot race, car race, a swim or ski meet, etc. Each player decides and makes the appropriate encouragements.

3. Talking to yourself as you look for a misplaced item.

4. Trying to teach a trick to an animal of the trainer's choice.

5. Demonstrating and explaining how to operate a simple piece of equipment to a younger friend or to a newcomer in the classroom.

6. Placing a long distance call through an operator and discovering that there is some kind of problem or delay in getting through to your party.

7. Demonstrating and explaining to a friend how to perform some task or feat that you can do well—perhaps something related to a sport, game, or hobby activity. (If students seem at a loss for ideas, you might suggest such activities as potting a plant, trying to make a strike in bowling, saddling a horse, hitting a long drive in baseball, making a backhand shot in tennis, setting up the pieces for a game of chess, or doing some craft activity.)

8. Giving directions to a newcomer for getting between two places in the school building.

9. As a character in a familiar story, explain something about your adventure to a prospective reader of the tale. (For example, Dorothy gives a three- or four-line summary of the Oz adventure to a library patron who may be interested in reading the book.)

10. Showing and explaining to someone why you are returning a piece of merchandise that is unsatisfactory in some way (it is flawed, the wrong size, doesn't meet your needs in some specific way, etc.).

Students can make up their own lists of situations during a brainstorming session. Remind them that each situation should include potential for both action and sounds or dialogue.

One-liners with a prop. Every classroom where drama is a regular part of the curriculum should include a box or drawer of properties available for a variety of uses. You need not store a great many; instead, aim for variety and uniqueness. Such props are not only useful for working with sensory awareness and recall, but can provide excellent motivation for action, speech, and characterization.

■ CREATING SHORT SEGMENTS

One simple activity to encourage improvised dialogue is to pass a prop around the group with each student giving a line of dialogue as he or she uses the item in some special way.

Either select an object to start around the group or allow students to choose something from the supply box. Urge players to use the prop in some imaginative way rather than simply using it as what it is or seems to be. For example, an ornamental brass vase might be used to hold flowers "There, what do you think of this arrangement for the hall table?"), as a mysterious vase from the Orient that can produce a mysterious genie if rubbed and addressed with magic words, or not be used as a vase at all but as a crucible in a laboratory into which secret compounds are poured and mixed as the mad scientist muses, "Wait until the world discovers my power; then I'll get my rightful respect."

Properties that are highly motivating of spontaneous "one-liners" of dialogue are usually those which generate multiple interpretations. Small but unusual containers; outlandish jewelry; intricate pieces of driftwood, seashells, and other natural phenomena of abstract design; old hand tools, antique artifacts, or household items; a small but selective supply of interesting pieces of fabric are all excellent choices and can be used in a variety of ways in drama.

One-liners from the "magic chest." After students have had repeated opportunities to generate spontaneous lines of dialogue working from actual items, it is fun to substitute a "magic chest."

Pantomime bringing into the classroom a large, heavy chest, and finally pushing it into place in a central location. Do this with appropriate grunts and comments to suggest that what is being carried, or otherwise maneuvered into the room, is an old chest full of "goodness knows what."

Another approach is to matter-of-factly ask a couple of students for help. "Would the two of you mind giving me a hand with that old chest over there (pointing to a space nearby)? I wonder if you might be able to carry it over here (an open space where the drama is to take place) and set it down carefully. It looks frightfully old and rather heavy, I think." It works best to choose more outgoing students, ones who will be willing to go along with the fantasy. Of course, once the "chest" is in place, the helpers are generously thanked and complimented on the care and strength with which they moved the chest.

Continue to reinforce the make-believe (and to provide an adult model who is also willing to engage in fantasy) by finding the key, working it into the old lock, and finally getting the lid open. Comments such as, "Well, would you look at this? What a collection of things! Surely no one has looked in this old chest in years," give additional motivation and background.

Once the chest is established, opened, and found to be full of interesting items, invite everyone to come forth, by turn, to make a personal discovery. Ask each player to do something with what he or she finds and to create a line or two of dialogue to give additional hints about each item. The chest may contain a wild variety of things or, if the activity is integrated with a particular piece of literature or content area topic, the contents of the chest may be clustered around the theme. (For example, if the class has been enjoying Mary Norton's *The Borrowers* [1953], they may assume roles of either the borrowers or the family and discover items mentioned in the story. Or the chest might belong to a family from another culture or time being studied in history or geography, and players may select from the chest a variety of articles associated with a particular incident, era, or group.) Remind the players to do something with each item to complement the dialogue.

Improvised speech in pairs

The several preceding activities involve students either working independently (but parallel) in self-space or working one-at-a-time without interacting with one another. In many of the activities, each person spoke as though someone else were present but that "other" was imagined. It is, however, much more rewarding to be able to actually interact. Real improvised dialogue cannot take place until students begin working in pairs or small groups.

■ PRACTICING DYADIC TURN-TAKING

The following pair activities emphasize turn-taking as each student takes a turn adding one line of dialogue to the conversation. The first few times these activities are done it may be both useful and fun to give each pair some token that can actually be passed to the other player after a line has been given. The first player then listens carefully and without interrupting until the token is passed to her or him.

Good news/bad news. Several topics that involve polarities can be used as the basis for this pair activity: fortunately/unfortunately; yesterday/today; today/tomorrow; little/big; wonderful/terrible; kind/unkind are some examples.

The first player in each pair gives a line of dialogue such as, "The good news is that we are going to see a movie in social studies," to which the partner might respond, "But, the bad news is that right after the movie, we are going to have a test in math."

It is not necessary to try to build blocks of related dialogue around one topic; the object is to simply experience the give and take of conversation. If students have difficulty catching on, provide an example or two to get things going.

Here are some additional examples:

"Fortunately, for the farmers, it is pouring outside." "Unfortunately, for me, I forgot my umbrella."

"Yesterday our team won in football." "Today they lost."

"Today my friend is moving away." "Tomorrow we are getting new neighbors."

"Little dogs are easier to care for." "Big dogs are scarier watchdogs."

"Finding a dime in your pocket is wonderful." "Finding a hole in your pocket is terrible."

"Eating a snack in front of your friend is unkind." "Sharing a snack with a friend is kind."

Pair story-starters. Unlike the preceding, in this activity each pair tries to keep building, one line at a time, a complete story.

■ BUILDING A PLOT

This exercise works best if you serve as timekeeper and allow an assigned time for each segment. The time for each encounter should be quite short, to allow students to play with several beginning lines and to let each student in a dyad begin the story. You can furnish beginning lines or the class might brainstorm several possibilities to use. Some suggestions are these:

1. It was the scariest thing that has ever happened to me.
2. No one at our house had ever seen anything like it before.
3. I wish I had never gone there.
4. Did you hear about the silly thing that happened at school last week?
5. I never used to believe in the supernatural, but since the other night, I'm not so sure.
6. The other day I had the nicest surprise.

Each starter line must be open-ended and provocative but need not give much information. Active listening is paramount to success with this exercise.

Students soon discover that even when they do not have a good idea for adding to the story, they can always respond with a question that asks for clarification or additional information, or by paraphrasing what was just said. These techniques are the "tools of the trade" for the active listener in all person-to-person communication. As students develop greater skills with these techniques, you use this same activity for pair work in situation role-playing (socio-drama) or for working with dramatic structure. For the latter, at some point, you will want all of the pairs to use the last several exchanges to bring the story to a satisfying conclusion.

Person-to-person interviews

The interview format provides excellent opportunities for students to practice spontaneous dialogue. Each pair works independently but with all pairs dealing with the situation you announce. At first, it is easiest to have everyone working from the very same situation. Later, individual pairs may choose to create a variation on the topic or situation suggested. When the entire group is working with the same roles and situation, everyone can contribute to a follow-up discussion.

Although there is no emphasis on characterization, students should be encouraged to use their voices and nonverbal behaviors to *suggest* a role. Some will do much more with this than others, but this only encourages the less experienced or more inhibited to try new things with the voice and body. The emphasis in these activities, however, is the spontaneous creation of dialogue, particularly as it may function in an interview situation.

■ CREATING DYADIC DIALOGUE

Before the playing, you might want to have the entire group contribute to a set of guidelines for interviewing. This gives excellent practice in the heuristic function of language (investigative function basic to discovery and learning), as well as an opportunity to discuss the kinds of question that elicit the most interesting responses (open-ended questions, for example). This would also be a good time to talk about the ethics involved with interviewing and what kinds of questions might be out-of-bounds (in terms of invasion of privacy or good taste).

Storybook interviews. Students working in pairs enjoy inventing spontaneous dialogue as familiar characters from literature, especially stories with which they are *very* familiar.

Folk and fairy tales and highly popular, well-known books such as *Charlotte's Web* (White, 1952) are generally good choices. The activity works so well simply because the players are so familiar and comfortable with the characters and plot.

This activity uses an interview format with one character asking a series of questions of the other. Both characters can be from the same story, or the interviewer may be a newspaper or TV journalist or some other person who might conduct an interview. The following give examples of each of those possibilities:

1. Mother Rabbit asks Peter all about where he has been, why he looks as he does, why he is so tired, etc. (Based on the *Tales of Peter Rabbit* by Beatrix Potter.)

2. Wilbur has many questions to put to Charlotte all about spiders and their webs, such as, "How are you able to do that? Why do you spin a web anyway? Could a clever pig make a web if he had a good teacher? (Based on *Charlotte's Web*.)

3. The Troll from *The Three Billy Goats Gruff* is interviewed by a person who has advertised for a security guard to watch her or his property.

4. The Scarecrow, having received a brain, is being interviewed for a position that requires someone who is smart (students could decide just what the specific position might be). (Based on Frank Baum's *The Wizard of Oz.*)

5. Hansel and Gretel are interviewed by someone from criminal justice who is investigating the death of an eccentric old woman who lived alone in the woods. This might be played as either Hansel or Gretel or in groups of three. (Based on the tale from the Grimm brothers, 1886.)

6. The Velveteen Rabbit and a real rabbit have a conversation after the Velveteen Rabbit has become "real." The real rabbit is curious about its friend's former life as a stuffed toy and/or experiences living with people. (*The Velveteen Rabbit*, Margery Williams, 1975.)

7. A reporter interviews one of the stepsisters after Cinderella has married the Prince and gone off to "live happily ever after."

8. A salesperson or someone with a get-rich-quick scheme calls on Jack and his mother after they have become very rich. The

caller may not only want information about how this change of events has come about but also may offer suggestions for investing or using the newly acquired riches in ways to produce even more. (Based on the folktale of *Jack and the Beanstalk*, retold by Joseph Jacobs, 1892.)

The class may create their own situations incorporating favorite characters from literature or popular characters from film or television. Students might also invent interview situations in which they role-play popular, interesting people from real life. For example, a contemporary sports figure might be interviewed by a legendary sports hero of a bygone era, or a modern political leader by her or his counterpart from long ago. Sample ideas could include Babe Ruth interviewing Hank Aaron; George Washington interviewing Ronald Reagan; Christopher Columbus interviewing an astronaut, Jules Verne interviewing Jacques Cousteau; Beethoven interviewing a popular rock musician.

Person-to-person interviews are often suitable for integration with one or more other subject areas, including the arts. Students studying different periods of art could conduct interviews between artists from two very different schools. A violinist might interview a percussionist or a famous Shakespearean actor might interview a well-known comedian.

Situation role-playing in pairs

Another specific use of the pair format is situation role-playing in which one person assumes the role of someone with a problem and the other serves as either a willing listener or advice-giver. Or, both parties are involved with the same problem but each from a different perspective. Such role-playing for problem solving must be handled with carefully articulated guidelines and sensitivity. The kinds of problems chosen should be of a general nature, and the technique should never be used to focus on one individual's problem, personality, family situation, lifestyle, or values. Never use it to invade a student's right to privacy or to turn the classroom into a clinic. This type of socio-drama must never be confused with psycho-drama or play therapy. There are, however, many situations and problems that may legitimately be used for pair, or small group, role-playing. Indeed, for later elementary students this application of drama skills can provide practice in creating spontaneous dialogue and, at the same time, deal responsibly with the types of problems associated with early adolescense.

■ PLANNING DYADIC ROLE–PLAYING

Guidelines for the role-playing should be created by the group, under the guidance of the teacher, and everyone must be kept aware of them. An excellent book for additional help with this activity is *Role-play in the Elementary School* (Furness, 1972). It devotes an entire chapter to some Do's and Don'ts and provides 52 sample lesson plans that deal with common childhood dilemmas. Among the "don'ts," Furness stresses the importance of remaining nonjudgmental of students' solution and efforts, of never using real names for the role-play casts, and of not simply relying on volunteers for every situation, in order to encourage the shy or introverted to participate as well as the gregarious (p. 36).

Topics that are generally useful for later elementary students include dealing with peer pressure, discovering ways to handle communication situations that are difficult (such as asking permission from a parent to participate in a specific activity or to obtain a special privilege), accepting or declining an invitation from a peer in culturally appropriate ways, making an apology, calling on a sick or shut-in friend (child or adult), reporting an observed or suspected misconduct by a peer to someone in authority, reporting an accident, and dealing with someone who harasses or makes a pest of her or himself. At first, you may wish to remain in control of selecting the topics, but you should also encourage ideas from the group. Students' suggestions must meet the same guidelines as yours for appropriateness, good taste, and be of general rather than individual concern.

The organization is the same as for other pair work. Generally the entire group simultaneously deals with the chosen topic, working within an established time. Within each pair, roles are chosen or assigned. For example, one child tries to pressure another to go along with a prank; the other child is torn between her or his own value system and the temptation to join a friend in some activity. When time permits, roles may be reversed and the scene replayed, or the class can go on to another situation. It is important that every student have the opportunity to play different kinds of roles. No student should be cast in a negative role repeatedly (even if the student volunteers to do so), and no student should ever be stereotyped by gender, race, ethnic background, academic abilities, handicap, or talent. Situation role-playing has much to offer, but it must be used with great understanding of its potential for harm as well as good, of what it is and is not, and of its strengths and limitations for solving human problems.

■ ROLE–PLAYING IN GROUPS

Situation role-playing can also be done with students working in small groups. Each group is assigned (or chooses from a list) a suitable topic to discuss and role-play. Topics suitable for pair work can also be done with small groups, but some topics work even better with a larger cast. Some good situations for small group role-playing are cheating in school; peer pressure to participate in a dangerous escapade, mischievous prank, or some unlawful activity; welcoming a new student, particularly one who is in some way different from others in the group; including or excluding a classmate from an athletic activity; dealing with rational or irrational fears; planning a group activity such as a sale or project of some kind; several people witnessing and reporting the same event such as an accident, theft, or fight; and sharing in someone's grief or special joy.

Group verbalizing activities

In addition to small group situation role-playing, other group activities emphasize verbalizing rather than action and speech together. These are often done with students at desks or table and seldom require as much space or rearrangement of the room as more action-oriented drama requires. The following examples can easily be integrated with other subject area learning (and more examples of this kind of drama activity are included in chapter 6).

Celebrity panel. A panel is composed of several "celebrities" who come together to discuss some problem or topic of interest. These celebrities can be drawn from history, fiction, or contemporary life. The balance of the class serves as an audience that has come to hear a particular topic discussed by this panel of experts. Some examples of panelists and possible topics are:

1. Famous scientists from different periods in history come together to discuss a contemporary scientific invention, such as television or computers; or they may explore a contemporary problem, such as air or water pollution.

2. Several of the great explorers give a television interview in the form of a panel discussion of their most exciting adventures, greatest triumphs, or scariest predicaments related to their renowned travels.

3. Important political figures from American or state history present their views about a contemporary problem, situation, or event. The leader of the panel discussion might be a contemporary leader interested in their wisdom and perspectives or an inquisitive young person interested in their views of modern society.

4. Characters in a book being studied might come together to discuss what happened and to predict how the events in the story will influence each of their futures. Students role-play the several parts but without an emphasis on the physical characteristics of the characters. The focus remains on the dialogue.

5. The panel is composed of several well-known historical and/or contemporary figures who represent a variety of careers, professions, or vocations. Each talks about her or his personal experiences as a ____; the moderator fields questions from the "audience" directed to each panelist. This activity integrates well with a unit on career education.

For this purpose, the entire class would be divided into small groups and each group would select a field of work such as Careers in Government, Careers in the Health Care Field, Careers in

Sports, Careers in Music and Entertainment, or Careers in Social Services. Each person would research a prominent and successful person in a specific job within the group's category. As each group presents, the remaining groups serve as audience with opportunities to ask questions of the "experts" after each briefly talks about her or his career experiences.

For all of the preceding, members of the panel need to research the specific celebrity or expert before presenting the discussion. Members of the audience may also need to research the topic in order to interact with the panelists. Audience members may also role-play as individuals with particular concerns or attitudes about the topic under discussion.

Game shows. Many students are game show fans. Several formats can incorporate some role-playing and improvisation of dialogue, since the emphasis on much of this type of programming is on talk. Two familiar "oldies," perhaps better known to teachers than to students, are *To Tell the Truth* and *What's My Line?* Take-offs on either of these can stimulate lively, spontaneous role-playing that requires the invention of dialogue. Both games are easily integrated with subject area study by choosing "guests" drawn from materials being studied in social studies, literature, science, or the arts.

The class is divided into two groups: those who will ask questions of the panel on "guest celebrity" and the panel or individual guests about whom the questioners are curious. *What's My Line?* has obvious potential to integrate with career education, but the format would not be limited to that use. For example, all of the participants might represent a particular historical period or event and the questions and answers would be related to discovering just what each guest did ("does") that contributed to that period in history or that memorable occasion.

To Tell the Truth is also fun when played by historical or literary figures. Everyone must be sufficiently familiar with the event or story in order to ask appropriate questions and give either truthful or purposely false information. You can serve as the moderator who begins the game with a statement such as, "One of these panelists is the renowned teacher of that remarkable woman, Helen Keller. The others are imposters. In the next ten minutes, let's see if our audience can discover who the real celebrity guest is. At the end of the question period, we shall have a show of hands to see whom the audience has chosen as the person who told the truth and is, indeed, our famous guest. We shall then find out who each of our five panelists is. Raise your hand when you have a question, wait for me to call on you, and then address your question directly to Panelist Number One, Two, Three, Four, or Five. One question at a time, please. We'll begin the questioning now." One person on the panel will be Anne Sullivan Macy, but the other players could choose specific roles by which they will finally identify themselves. (Based on *Helen Keller* by Norman Richards, 1968.)

Fans. Divide the class into groups of five or six. Each group chooses (or is assigned) a sport. Each small group becomes fans who are watching an exciting game of their sport. Call out observations such as, "Your favorite team is about to score." or "Oh, oh, . . . looks like your team is in trouble." The activity is not sidecoached, and you may choose to not make any comments at all if each group of fans seems able to keep some dialogue going about the game. The groups may all work at the same time or separately; if the former, the class will need to work at a time and/or place where quite a bit of noise can be tolerated.

Time travel. Divide the class into small groups. Each small group represents the same group of people but in a different historical setting. For example, each group consists of several school children from different periods in American history talking about things of interest to them. One group might be from the future, one from the era of their parents, another from the turn of the century, another from the Civil War period, one from Colonial times or the early days of state or local history. One group might be a contemporary group. Each group will need some time to research its period. Discuss some important events or characteristics before spontaneously role-playing a discussion that could be typical of a group of students their age during their specific time.

Time Travel discussions can be done by students assuming a variety of roles. For example, each group might represent a family from each time period engaged in a similar event, such as celebrating someone's birthday or making plans for moving to a new home.

Students in a rural setting might imagine that each group represents a group of farmers or ranchers from the past, present, and the future discussing their lives and their work. City students might become past, present, and future groups of local shopkeepers who are discussing matters related to their work and times. Generally, some investigation would be required to give authenticity to the discussions. Within each small group, students assume specific roles, but the focus remains on the verbalizing rather than on action.

■ GIVING SPEECH TO NONHUMAN ROLES

Personification of inanimate objects. Another small group verbal activity much enjoyed by later elementary students involves assuming specific roles within an overall category of some type of inanimate object. The emphasis is on developing spontaneous dialogue with little attempt to assume physical characteristics or engage in physical actions.

Introduce the activity by posing the question, "What if inanimate things such as shoes in your closet or books in the library could talk? Wouldn't it be fun to imagine how they would think and feel, what they would talk about?"

After brainstorming some possibilities, divide the class into groups of five or six, assign each group a category of objects, and present a tension-producing situation. Encourage players to make specific decisions about their individual roles, including such things as age, physical characteristics (even though they do not try to display these to any large degree), personality, and whatever else might be relevant. Urge each student to use those decisions as guidelines for inventing dialogue and speaking as the role. This includes all of the elements of prosody (pitch, tone, rate, volume, inflection) and such nonverbal behaviors as facial expression and body posture even though there will be minimal physical activity.

The following are some sample categories; however, students enjoy adding their own ideas to the list, as this allows them to suggest categories of specific interest to them. For starters, you might suggest cars on a used car lot, leftovers in the refrigerator or on the table after a big holiday meal, shoes in the closet, old clothes in an attic trunk, a collection of household odds and ends stored in a basement or garage, toys in a toy box or on the shelves of a toy shop, phonograph records in a record shop, clothes in the laundry hamper, tools in a tool box, a variety of items inside a student's desk, or books on a shelf.

Once students understand that they will be giving voice, personality, and language to their inanimate things and holding conversations with one another as their objects, divide the class into several small groups. Each comprises a distinct category of "things" that have "come to life" and are engaged in a conversation about a specific situation. The following are sample situations that include a tension-producing element around which at least part of the conversation will focus.

1. *Shoes in the closet.* Each player decides who he or she is, what kind of shoe or other item of footwear, as well as something about its life. Although each player can make an individual decision, the group as a whole will discuss those choices so everyone knows who everyone else is. Situation: the family is out and the shoes are chatting about the events of the day. One child's sneaker suddenly discovers that her or his mate is missing. The family's new puppy is the suspected culprit. The shoes talk about the plight of their missing comrade.

2. *Cars in a used car lot.* Each player chooses a specific type, model, and age to portray. The cars talk among themselves about past exploits and possible futures. Tension is produced when they overhear two humans planning a car theft to obtain a getaway car for a crime they are about to commit.

3. *Leftovers in the refrigerator.* Players within the group decide just what they are. You might suggest that some items may be newcomers while others have been there quite awhile. Situation: as they are chatting they overhear a member of the family announce that the refrigerator is past due for a cleaning, especially inasmuch as today is grocery shopping time.

4. *Old clothes in an attic trunk (or barn or other storage place, depending on locale).* Items may represent a long or short period of family history. Situation: as various items reminisce, a new addition

announces to the group that the family is making plans to move to another home.

5. *Miscellaneous items in a student's desk.* These might include any number of different things so the items would be quiet diverse. Situation: the teacher has announced that tomorrow is to be "desk-cleaning day."

When the situation makes reference to humans, it is not necessary that anyone play that role. When you play this activity for the primary purpose of inventing dialogue, the scene does not need to have a complete dramatic structure that includes a climax or resolution of the conflict. You can simply call time and allow each group to tell something about who they were and what they talked about.

As students gain expertise, they may wish to create improvised scenes with a beginning, a middle, and an ending in which a conflict is introduced, a climax is reached, and there is resolution and a satisfying ending. This is particularly true as students develop more mastery of characterization and a greater understanding of dramatic structure. At any stage, this particular activity works well as a prewriting exercise for anthropomorphic writing.

EXPANDING ENSEMBLE SKILLS

Small group work, whether primarily concerned with movement and pantomime or concentrated on verbalization, gives students practice in inventing and expressing cooperatively. Drama is a group art that requires the participants to work together toward a common goal. It is a true ensemble art in which players not only work together interactively but transactionally, adjusting and adapting to one another in the processes of creating and performing. This is somewhat true at all stages of drama development, but is particularly important as students develop greater understanding and skill. As students gain competency in invention and expression through both action and spontaneous speech, they are ready to develop and engage in improvisation in which they invent the circumstances, create and develop characters, and make their own decisions as to how best to present their ideas. This is more easily accomplished with the class working in small groups rather than as a whole. In preparation for developing scenes and stories completely of their own creation, students benefit from repeated opportunities to dramatize a variety of literary pieces, in total or in part.

Dramatizing literature in small groups

There are a variety of advantages to organizing a class into small groups for the dramatizing of literary materials. One obvious "plus" is that few short stories or scenes from longer works explicitly involve large numbers of characters; a group of five or six can often cover the necessary roles. Another advantage is that a *small* number of students, involved in an improvised scene, can easily discuss, interpret, and plan. They can also develop a sense of cohesiveness within their group that can be carried over into their perceptions of the interrelationships among the characters. They can begin to function as an ensemble in which all of the parts complement one another. The following are some useful ways of using small groups for dramatizing literary materials.

Multiple cast scenes

You can divide a story into scenes with each small group playing each scene. Groups may have to be of different sizes to accommodate the diverse numbers of roles. This type of organization allows everyone to have a part in a story or excerpt that does not have 25 or more parts.

Variation. Different small groups play the same scenes with each group developing it in their way. For example, if the story easily divides into three good scenes, divide the class into six groups. Two groups play each scene. During sharing time, have three groups dramatize the story once and then have a second playing using the other three groups. For this type of organization, it is perfectly acceptable for different groups to handle the same materials in different ways. Commonalities and differences can be discussed during the post-playing discussion. When properly guided, the discussion can help students appreciate how differently each perceive the same or similar things, and that differences can delight, mind-stretch, and reinforce each person's uniqueness.

Creating new endings. Another way to use small groups in the dramatizing of literature is to share a story, then stop the telling before the resolution of the conflict, and invite each small group to create and dramatize its own ending. This may work best when the story is new to the group, so that students do not feel locked-in to the author's ending. You might give one group the actual ending to dramatize and have that group share theirs last.

During the post-play discussion, the entire class can compare and contrast the several endings, including the author's. Appendix F lists several stories of various genres that could be done this way. Of course, you can also use familiar stories as the basis for developing new endings. This can be particularly attractive as an exercise to help students understand that there are often several acceptable ways to resolve an issue, deal with a conflict, or solve a problem. This may provide a range of endings; for example, a humorous ending to a story that has a serious conclusion or a surprise ending to a story that has a predictable one.

Crowd scenes

Small groups can be used to add crowd scenes to a story that otherwise has only limited parts. Many pieces of literature, sometimes explicitly but often by implication, suggest that there are groups of people involved besides the main characters in the story.

The Hans Christian Andersen tale "The Emperor's New Clothes" is great fun to dramatize and provides enough roles for a full-size class, particularly if small groups of students are used to enhance several scenes. Early in the story, two swindlers are among the "hosts of strangers" who come regularly to the palace. Of course, the swindlers are important roles to be cast; however, several students, working in a small group, may choose to be other folks who come to call at the palace—tradespeople delivering goods, workers who repair or maintain the premises, artisans with special wares, folks soliciting monies for the poor, and so forth. Within the group, each becomes a role, and as a group becomes part of a cluster of folks seeking an audience with the Emperor. At another point in the story, "everybody in the town was now talking about this splendid stuff," woven by the swindlers. A small group invents roles and plays a short scene in which there is much conjecturing and gossiping about the weavers and their goods.

Two larger crowds can be developed to play the final scene in which the Emperor and his entourage parade through the city to show off the Emperor's new clothes. One group can comprise the royal attendance who exclaim over the fictitious clothing as the imposters help the Emperor to dress. They become part of his entourage as he processes through the city to show off the new clothes. Another group develops roles to comprise the crowd of subjects who line the street and watch from windows as the royal procession passes by. There are many wonderful roles to play to create this crowd—farm families on their way to market, shopkeepers, school children enjoying a special holiday, even a pickpocket or two . . . and, of course, the small child who remarks that the Emperor is wearing nothing at all. This final scene, utilizing crowds, can provide fine roles for everyone, even in a large class.

Crowd scenes take on new importance as students become more adept at the development of believable characters. At first, each player can portray the several roles, doing some simple activity associated with the role. Improvised speech may be limited and only serve to further identify that a person is a farmer, a shopkeeper, or peddler or some kind. Students not yet ready to add dialogue may simply pantomime some activities of their characters.

Whether explicitly mentioned or simple implied, crowd scenes should be used to enhance rather than change the literature. The several group scenes just described are, in fact, specifically suggested in the story. In other stories, groups may only be implied.

In *Mrs. Beggs and the Wizard* (Mayer, 1973), the illustrations show groups of the boarding house guests at dinner, although the story says, "That evening Mr. Alabasium (the wizard) didn't show up for dinner, so Mrs. Beggs fixed him a tray of food and took it up to his room." A delightful scene could be played by a small group who comprise the boarding house guests at dinner speculating about the elusive Mr. Alabasium who does not join them. Later, the story introduces some specific boarders, so these should be included in the dinner group.

Another small group of players can create the several strange happenings that take place as a result of Mr. Alabasium's wizardry—a giant windstorm that blows the laundry about the yard, a rainstorm that thunders into the parlor, and, finally, a group of "strange things" that result from Mrs. Begg's own brand of wizardry and sneak into Mr. Alabasium's room and tie him up, tickle his toes, tweak his nose and perform other delightful business. In fact, this scene can easily be extended and embellished to allow the "strange things" additional opportunities to get revenge.

The classic fairy tales invariably provide several opportunities to translate a suggestion of a crowd (guests at a royal ball, peasants, soldiers, townspeople, and so forth) into small crowds to plan and play. Indeed, this type of embellishment has traditionally been done by Walt Disney and his successors when turning a short folk or fairy tale into a feature-length film. Birds, forest animals, and perhaps most memorably, seven little men, play major roles in telling familiar stories. Additionally, they offer examples of superb ensemble playing, with each complementary role playing off the others.

Creative storybuilding from group ideas

In the preceding, players use both explicitly and implicitly suggested scenes and develop them with small groups to "flesh out" the telling of a piece of literature. However, within each group, students would bring their own creative ideas to the scene as they invent and portray roles which may only be implied. These creative energies have even greater applications as students begin to invent scenes and improvised plays primarily drawn from their own imaginations. Small group storybuilding and dramatizing offers some of the most rewarding creative drama work. It also affords an ideal environment for engaging in cooperative creativity as students experientially learn to negotiate, compromise, synthesize from a variety of peer suggestions and ultimately bring all of their ideas together as they participate, ensemble, in the dramatization of their own original ideas.

Your role remains one of guide and facilitator but in a secondary role, helping only as the players require. Probably your most important contribution is in providing the initial motivation to get each group involved and inventing.

■ BUILDING ORIGINAL STORIES

The following are suggestions for stimulating small group creative storybuilding to be played as an improvised scene or story. For all of these, divide the class into small groups of five or six. Remind students that their stories can have more roles, and each person can play more than one part.

The five Ws cards

Give each group a card with a who, what, where, when and why. Instruct the players that they are not limited to the information on the cards but must incorporate the information presented in their final product. Some typical cards might read this way:

Card 1
Who:　　Dock workers.
Where:　At dockside of an international port.
When:　 Late in the day; almost dusk.
Why:　　Unloading a cargo of exotic (use "zoo animals" for younger children) animals just arrived from Africa.
What:　　One of the crates breaks open.

Card 2
Who:　　A team of spelunkers.
Where:　Inside a large, uncharted cave.
When:　 Now.

Why: Making an initial exploration of a cave believed to be
          of recent discovery.
What: They arrive at a ledge and far below see something
          submerged in an underground river.

Card 3
Who: Hot air balloonists and their families.
Where: An open field.
When: Early morning.
Why: Getting ready for an around-the-world flight.
What: A strong gust of wind tears the balloon from the moorings
          just as it is discovered that a small child is missing.

Note that in each case, the "what" provides the necessary
tension or problem around which the scene may be built.

Sensory experiences. Give each group a card with some sensory
suggestions that must be incorporated into the scene. The cards
may concentrate on only one sense (e.g. sounds only or tactile
experiences) or may be multisensory. In the examples that follow,
the information concentrates on one sense at a time—the sense of
hearing:

Card 1.
Incorporate into your story the following sounds. They may be
varied, repeated, and used singly or in combination. Sounds
are (1) an explosive blast, (2) a chomping, grinding sound, and
(3) a melodic flutelike sound.

Card 2.
(Same lead-in). Sounds: (1) a small, ticking sound, (2) a large
buzzing hum, and (3) a low rumble.

Card 3.
(Same lead-in). Sounds: (1) a whirring sound, (2) a sound like a
million bells of different sizes, and (3) a blaring roar.

Multisensory cards might be like this:

Card 1.
Sound: rushing air. Sight: shape—circles; color—blue. Texture: smooth as glass. Odor: fresh and minty. Taste: sweet.

Card 2.
Sound: ringing sounds. Sight: shape—triangles; color—orange. Texture: gritty. Odor: musty. Taste: salty.

Card 3.
Sound: buzzing. Sight: shape—rectangles; color—green. Texture: very soft. Odor: dusty. Taste: spicy.

Props for storybuilding. Each group selects the same number of props from a supply. They can use the prop in different ways at different times in the same scene. Suggestions for types of properties that work well as motivation in drama appear earlier in the "One-liners with a prop" section of this chapter.

Pictures for storybuilding. Each group is given, or selects, a picture. Students can work with photographs, prints of famous paintings (for example, impressionistic, abstract, or as representational as Norman Rockwell paintings), or their own art work. Groups must use ideas *generated* (inspired) by the picture(s) but should not simply recreate the picture as a "frozen scene."

Variation. Each group selects a picture of a person or group and a scene of some special environment. The "who" and "where" would then be based on or stimulated by the pictures.

Mini-stories. Give each group a card that gives a brief suggestion for a plot. The following examples also include a different genre approach for each very short story.

Card 1. Create a real-life adventure story about some children who decide to go into some kind of business in order to buy an expensive gift for a favorite teacher who is leaving to teach in a developing country.

Card 2. Create a science fiction story about a family that lives near a space launch site. The events should be related to the planned launching of a radically new space ship for a never-before tried voyage.

Card 3. Create a mini-story that is a piece of historical fiction about a family who decides to join a wagon train going west on the Oregon Trail.

Card 4. Create a fantasy story in which some children meet and make friends with an enchanted silver pony. The story may include magic and/or other supernatural actions or events.

Card 5. Create a legend to explain how the earth received both day and night. You may also decide what kind of primitive peoples might have invented your legend to explain these natural events.

■ ADDING CONFLICTS

Each card begins with the instructions that the group should specify its own who, what, where, when, and why. In addition, the card includes a specific conflict or problem to be resolved. The following are examples of conflicts or problems that should be appealing to later elementary students:

1. The birthday party has been planned for a long time; lots of guests have been invited. On the morning of "the day" a terrific electrical story knocks out the electricity and everything is in an uproar.

2. A very secret and important document must be taken out of a foreign country. Create a plan knowing that others are intent on keeping you from carrying it out.

3. A group of people are on a special outing. Through a series of circumstances, one or more are separated from the main group.

4. Within a group of friends, one or more persons decide to play a practical joke on someone else in the group. The joke has unexpected consequences.

5. A group is about to take a trip to a special place and end up in a totally strange and foreign environment for which no one was prepared.

Further adventures. Each group chooses a favorite book, movie, or television show from which they are to plan a further adventure. These are not to be new endings for the existing story but new, short episodes that involve at least some of the characters and circumstances in the literature or film. Later elementary students often choose to work with films or television shows. Therefore, the further adventure may be a new episode of a continuing series (such as *Knight Rider* or the specials about the Peanuts gang) or a new adventure using characters from a single popular film such as *E.T.* or *The Neverending Story.* Choices are made based on what is currently popular with the group.

Personal experiences. Each small group shares personal experiences around a central topic such as "the funniest thing that ever happened to me," "my sincerest wish," "family traditions," or "my greatest fear was realized." When everyone who wishes to share has done so (anyone who wishes may simple "pass"), the group chooses one person's experience to polish into a mini-story to dramatize. The student whose experience is chosen may serve as director for the scene.

Variation. The final product may be a composite of ideas from each person's sharing. This activity is not intended to be a sociodrama exercise, and players should feel free to add elements of fiction to their offerings. One important purpose of this activity, which can also serve as an excellent prewriting exercise, is to encourage students to find ideas for stories within themselves and drawn from their own experiences.

Character collections. Each person in each group pulls a slip from a box. Each slip contains a common noun character. Each group then is challenged to create a mini-story in which their randomly selected characters might interact with one another in ways that contribute to a storyline.

Prepare character slips by putting a brief amount of information on each one. Examples are a TV actor, a small-town shopkeeper, a big-city journalist, a business tycoon, an inventor, a high-society person, a visiting ruler, a geologist who looks for oil deposits, a private investigator, a ship's captain, a curator of a museum, a cattle rancher, a rock musician, a mining engineer, a salesperson. Note that all of the characters might be either male or female, young or old, pleasant or not, successful or "down on their luck," and so forth.

At first, the group may do little with rounding out or exploring more in-depth dimensions of each character. Students will simply use their characters in obvious ways in their story and dramatized scene, but they are to be sure to include every character drawn by the group in some way. The extent to which the characters are developed will be related to the experience and skill of the group. This will be equally true of plot development. Less experienced players may not add a conflict or bring the scene to a very satisfying conclusion; more experienced players may present a complete story with all or most of the elements of the dramatic structure.

Small groups, working with short, improvised storybuilding and dramatization need not spend a great deal of time with either the planning or performing of their scenes. However, if they are to build expertise, they will need repeated opportunities to engage in this kind of creative drama work. You may want to use different formats and types of motivational stimuli to keep interest levels high. Occasionally, everyone should be encouraged to spend some extra time refining and polishing work for sharing with others. These original scenes make excellent products to be shared with peers serving as audience. During the post-playing debriefing and discussing, strengths and weaknesses can be discussed and suggestions made for making good work even better.

During the debriefing is a good time to introduce new ideas for making everyone's drama work even better—more in-depth work in character development, greater understanding of dramatic structure, and the importance of conflict to drama, for example. As facilitator, you lead the discussion and provide the role model who encourages everyone to participate in constructive commentary. When you suggest that the players seem ready to go on to more advanced work next time, students feel validated that their efforts at "getting good in drama" (making real progress) have been worth their very best efforts.

CHAPTER 5

Achieving Advanced Creative Drama Skills

Drama is doing; it is also *being*. Experiences in creative drama make a special kind of contribution to each child's exploration and understanding of what it means to be human. This need to know "who we are" is first evident in the dramatic play of preschoolers as they imitate the behaviors of others and try on roles. When they try on roles, however, it is the self engaging in an action, or set of behaviors, that they have observed in someone or something else. Indeed, imitating the actions of mommy or daddy is not necessarily more insightful for the child than trying out the actions of the dog or some television creature.

DEVELOPING CHARACTERS

By the later elementary grades, as students move into formal operational thought, they move away from their egocentricity and are concerned with and about others. Evidence of this is demonstrated by their increased interest in what others think and do, especially as it affects them. Peer influence emerges. Students become more anxious about and vulnerable to the expectations and pressures from peers than from parents and other adults. As a result, by early adolescence, students begin to question, even challenge, many beliefs and values hitherto held. They discover that not everyone looks at the world in exactly the same way, that what is right or important or of value to one person may not hold true for another. In addition, they are better able to accommodate such variables in human nature as "intentions" and "means to an end."

137

They discover that each person is a composite of many facets of personality and that this is also true of themselves. They are ready to go beyond the simple imitation of roles to the exploration of what it would be like to be someone else; to discover what "makes others tick." In the process, they are also discovering additional facets of self as they probe characters and invent roles.

The experiential nature of drama can provide a safe environment for such exploration. As students try on different attributes of character, they not only get insights into others, but they may also be able to assess and evaluate how they themselves are like or different from those characteristics. Are these qualities they wish to have? Does a character hold a point of view or values they have not previously known or considered? In what ways do these different perspectives illuminate their view of what it means to be a human being? Are there ideas, feelings, and behaviors associated with a character being explored through the drama that they might want to assume or adopt in their own lives? Students probe these and other issues as they begin to try real characterization, developing roles internally rather than just externally. Students need help in making this transition. Fortunately, a whole world of literature is available to provide a remarkable, almost endless variety of characters to explore and try on.

Developing characters from literature

A Critical Handbook of Children's Literature (Lukens, 1982, p. 29) describes character as "the aggregate of mental, emotional, and social qualities that distinguish a person." We know these qualities of character in self and others through our observations of actions, speech, and appearance. We also know about ourselves and others through interpersonal interaction.

■ USING LITERATURE FOR CHARACTER WORK

In literature we observe characters for ourselves and also share observations that those characters make. In stories written in first person narrative, we are also privy to the thoughts and feelings of the central figure as they happen. And many stories are written from the perspective of an onmiscient narrator who reveals not only the innermost thoughts and feelings of the central character(s), but of others as well.

Literature explores the human condition through the revelation of the thoughts and feelings of the characters. Students in grades 4-6 prefer some degree of omniscience (Lukens, p. 127), which fits with their increased abilities to be cause-and-effect thinkers themselves. Knowing the unspoken thoughts and feelings of a person helps others understand her or his actions; therefore, the cause that precipitates an effect may be easier to see and understand.

Literature offers drama exactly what it needs to first engage students in the development of characters with believability and some degree of depth. To begin using literature this way, teach students about the ways characters are presented in literature. That knowledge is an excellent springboard into deeper understanding of characters as students analyze a story for playing.

Types of characters

The following are generally accepted categories of types of characters as determined by the degree of information readers have and how the characters are used in telling the story.

■ DEFINING TYPES OF CHARACTERS

Stock character. A type of character that appears again and again, especially in folk and fairy tales. These are flat, one-dimensional characters, either good or bad, and thus very predictable. Examples of stock characters in classic children's literature are witches (good or bad), the beautiful princess, the wicked stepmother, the handsome and heroic prince, the greedy ruler, the honest and hard-working miller's son. Contemporary literature also has its share of stock characters, also one-dimensional and predictable. Examples are the rich brat, the mean older boy, the whiny little girl, the helpful policeman, the stern neighbor.

Stereotype. A character who seems to possess only a few characteristics (and those supposedly result from being a member of a particular group or class of people). Many times such stereotypic portrayals are blatantly bigoted misrepresentations of a class or group of people. Look very carefully at literature that includes stereotypes and do not use stories that present qualities of race, gender, age, ethnic heritage, or religious orientation in discriminatory and prejudicial ways. Stereotypes generally play a background role, allowing readers to see limited facets of their personalities

Flat character. A character about whom readers know very little. They are important to help tell the tale and carry the action. Because we know little about them, we respond to them in a superficial way. Flat characters populate the folktales, fables, myths, and legends—stories that deal swiftly and to-the-point with good and evil with good triumphing at the very end of the story.

Round character. A character about whom much is known and with whom readers can, therefore, closely relate. We often know both the strengths and weaknesses of these multidimensional characters. Round characters, be they animal with-human-characteristics, science fiction creatures, or humans, are believable. As we come to know them, we can predict their behaviors and accept it when they surprise us with an unpredicted response.

The central figure, called the protagonist, is most apt to be the most rounded character, the one we most relate to and care about. Two such heroines in contemporary children's literature are Kit in *The Witch of Blackbird Pond* (Speare, 1958) and Harriet in *Harriet the Spy* (Fitzhugh, 1964). Both are multidimensional, have strengths and weaknesses, and are, therefore, both heroic and vulnerable. Students can relate to and believe in them.

Static character. A character who does not change over the course of the action. A static character may be good, like Charlotte in *Charlotte's Web* (White, 1952), or evil, like Captain Hook in *Peter Pan* (Barrie, 1928), but they stay the same throughout. Round characters may or may not change; flat characters and stock characters do not. That would be antithetical to their flatness.

Dynamic character. A character who changes in one or more substantive ways in the course of the story. Wilbur in *Charlotte's Web* grows, matures, and changes over the course of the action; even Templeton the rat, who seems a rather stock character, turns out to be less flat than one anticipates. (Templeton, on occasion, shows some feelings for another in a very unratlike manner.)

The preceding extended definitions offer enough information about types of characters to meet the needs of later elementary students. Fortunately, there is a good deal of familiar literature from which to draw highly correlative examples. Indeed, the definitions per se are neither particularly necessary nor useful, except as they are used in conjunction with examples and applications. This does, however, provide a background for the development of characters in drama. The following are some preplaying activities to help students put their enlarged understanding of characters to use in getting ready to dramatize literature with heightened awareness for portrayal.

■ DISCOVERING DIMENSIONS OF CHARACTER THROUGH DYADIC INTERVIEWS

In pairs, two characters from a familiar story interview one another. When working with round characters from literature, students should use all of the information, both explicitly and implicitly provided, in the story. When working with flat characters, students use what little is known to predict information that goes beyond what is told. In the process, the flat character begins to take on some further, though limited dimensions.

After the pair interviews, put the names of the characters on the board, listing as many descriptive phrases under each as the class can provide as a result of the interviews. Then, as a group, information that was clearly provided in the story is keyed with a "T" (*told* in story,) and what was *implied* is keyed with an "I." Information *created* by a player in order to answer a question that could not be answered with either textual or clearly inferred data would be keyed "C." The results become a basis for discussion during which the players can provide rationales for their decisions.

■ ROUNDING A FLAT CHARACTER

Folk and fairy tales provide a wealth of flat characters that might be rounded out through a full class discussion or with students working in small groups. Precisely how you organize the activity depends on the experience and maturity of the group and the amount of time available.

For less experienced and/or younger students, choose one character highly familiar to the entire class and work as the large group. Students find it both fun and insightful to work as a class with the wolf from the story of "The Three Little Pigs." All of the characters in the story are typical flat characters found again and again in folktales, although each pig is "slightly rounded" (as befits pigs). However, the wolf is also a stock character and a stereotype of how wolves are regularly presented in a variety of literary offerings— mean-minded, devious, and violent.

Use the following series of questions to lead students through a process of rounding out a flat character (in this case, the wolf).

■ EXPLORING A DIFFERENT POINT OF VIEW

1. We recognize the wolf has a problem. What do you think its main problem is? Is it hunger? Are there reasons why the wolf may be especially hungry (a spell of bad weather; it has been too sick to look for food; humans have built homes or a shopping center where it usually foraged)? Maybe it is old and toothless, or very young and inexperienced. Perhaps its peers have been making fun of it for being a poor hunter, unable to compete. Maybe it has a real or imagined grievance against pigs for something very unkind they have done to it or one of its kin.

   Brainstorm a list of motives. Encourage students to give a rationale for their choices. It is not enough to simply decide that the wolf is hungry or even *very hungry*.

2. Describe the wolf, its attractive characteristics as well as its unattractive ones.

3. What is it like as a personality? Does it have a sense of humor? Is it ever philosophical about its situation or does it simply feel angry, misunderstood, frustrated, annoyed most of the time?

4. What is its lifestyle? How does it live? Where? Is it from here or has it come from someplace else? Does it have any friends? If so, where are they in its moment of need? If not, why not?

5. What are its talents or lack of talents? Are these related to its current plight? If so, in what way?

6. What is its name? We simply call it "wolf," but what does its family or friends call it?

7. Based on certain decisions we have made about the wolf, how would it move (perhaps it limps because it was once caught in a trap set by a pig seeking wolf skins for a winter coat)? How does it talk? Is it a cultured wolf, etc.? (Its speech would reflect other decisions already made about personality, current mood, etc.)

8. Any other questions generated by the class discussion.

After the class has agreed on an extended description, everyone should have a chance to play the wolf. You might sidecoach a narrative scene in which students meet the wolf as it prepares to go seeking pigs for dinner.

After the playing, compare how students might have played the wolf before the discussion and how they chose to play it after. Compare and contrast different players' interpretations of the wolf.

In rounding out a flat character, it is important to know what motivated her or him. This is always an important element to explore when developing more believable and rounded characters.

Understanding motivation

To help students better understand motivation, you might do the following:

■ ANALYZING MOTIVATION

What turns you on? This can be done as an in-place pantomime. With everyone working in self-space, briefly describe a series of short actions to play; each action includes some information to motivate the action beyond just the action itself. Here are some examples:

1. You played too long at a friend's house and missed dinner. You are tip-toeing downstairs to raid the refrigerator.
2. Your mother told you to hurry home from school so you can help her with some chores. You're walking with a friend who wants to window shop and you don't want to tell her or him that you have to get home to help your mom.
3. You are weeding the garden (or some other chore familiar to the class). Your dad is working nearby. You are anxious to meet your friends (as promised) to play ball.
4. You are following your big brother down the street to see where he is going but you don't want him to know you are following.
5. You didn't read the assigned out-of-class book and now the teacher is leading a discussion of the material.
6. You are sitting at the kitchen table reading and writing a report that is due tomorrow—the same day you are participating in the championship skateboard contest right after school.

Talk about how the feelings related to each motivation caused students to use their bodies. What were some of their facial expressions? Identify the motivation in each instance. Discuss which were internally and which externally motivated. Next, discuss examples from literature where a character might have felt similarly motivated even though the situation was very different. For example, Cinderella must leave the ball at midnight, but she could not tell the Prince why she had to go; Tom Sawyer was supposed to be whitewashing the fence for his Aunt Polly, but he wanted to be playing.

Follow the discussion with additional in-place pantomime using characters from literature.

■ IDENTIFYING UNIQUE ATTRIBUTES

Writing a news release about a character. Divide the class into small groups. Working from the same or different stories, have each group use the information provided (or strongly implied) in the story to write a short public relations article or news release about a character in the story. If all of the groups are working from the same story, have them choose different characters to showcase.

Each group must probe the literature for as much information as they can find. Inferences must be credible, and each group should be able to support the accuracy of what they create. When the groups are finished, one person from each group assumes the role of a newscaster or public relations promoter who reads the piece with appropriate expression. For example, one group might create a news article describing the remarkable feats of Mafatu (*Call it Courage,* Sperry, 1940), with special attention to the personal attributes that allowed him to survive his ordeal in an heroic manner. You would encourage students to look below the surface to discover as much as they can about Mafatu.

Keeping a diary. Have each student choose a favorite character from a story. Next, all students must do a careful reading of the material, even if they think they already know it well. The purpose is to discover as much as possible about the chosen character. Have students generate five or six journal or diary entries written *as* the character—entries might deal with events in the story or something else that would be a part of the character's life and world. Later, have students share these writings in small groups, with special attention to why each person wrote as he or she did (explaining in terms of dimensions of character).

You can use this activity to explore point-of-view, by having students choose different characters from the same story and write about the same events, with each student writing from the perspective of a different character.

All of the preceding can be done either concurrently with story dramatization or in preparation for doing drama based on literature with increased attention to characterization.

Actively preparing for dramatization

Two additional activities for students are actively involved in the preparation for dramatizing.

Sculpting a character. Divide the class into pairs. In each pair, one person is the sculptor and the other is to be made into a character from a story to be dramatized. Before the work is begun, the "raw material" tells the artist as much about him or herself as possible: this would include information revealed in the story through the character's speech and actions, what others say, how others relate to the character, and inner thoughts and feelings of the character as revealed by an omniscient author or a first person narrative character. (The telling can be done with a series of "I" statements.) Then the artist begins to shape the "raw material" so that the statue formed accurately portrays important qualities of the character. When the artists have finished, you give a signal that brings the characters to life and they move in appropriate ways.

To extend further, each character gives one line of dialogue using voice and language in suitable ways. Later, players reverse roles so that everyone plays both artist and statue.

Imaging a role. Every student chooses a character from literature. (Discourage students from selecting a piece that has been made into a film, because they often feel locked into the portrayal in the movie or television version.) You lead students in visualizing their roles through a series of sidecoached suggestions. Everyone sits with eyes closed to encourage concentration on the mind pictures being formed. Ask them to focus on everything they know about their character. The narration might go as follows:

■ ASSUMING A ROLE INTERNALLY

You are about to become your chosen character. Concentrate on everything you know or feel about her or him. You are going to become this character. What are you wearing? Is this what you usually wear? If not, why? Are you standing, sitting, or moving about?

Look at your posture. What are you doing with your hands, arms, feet, and legs? Are you full of energy or tired? How can someone tell by looking at you?

Look at your face. What expression do you see there? Why do you look as you do? How are you feeling inside? Is this a special feeling or a usual one?

Look at the scene around you. Where are you in the scene? Is it unusual for you to be here? How do you feel about this place? Why are you here? What are you doing? How do you feel about what you are doing?

Think about your thoughts. What is on your mind more than anything else?

Another character from the story has come into the scene. Who is it? How do you feel now? How do you look? What are you doing now?

Allow enough time between suggestions and questions for the players to think and visualize. Afterwards, encourage students to share through both discussion and showing.

Variation. When students are preparing to dramatize a story and roles have been chosen (including additional roles created to enhance the story through crowd scenes that provide roles for everyone). The same kinds of questions are used to get each player to visualize the character to be portrayed. After the visualizing, the group would move immediately into the dramatization. Remind each player to hold the vision of her or his character as the play begins.

■ GIVING PHYSICAL FORM TO A ROLE

Body work for characterization. Discuss a character from a story that the class is reading or working with in drama. Talk about what is told in the story that gives clues about the physical appearance of the character. List those on the board.

With everyone in self-space, have the players assume the body stance and a facial expression each person considers characteristic of the role. Done to the ten-count freeze, everyone quickly glances around and observes how others have formed the character. This may be followed by discussion.

Next, the group may concentrate on separate body parts; for example, shoulders, feet and legs, arms and hands, head, jaw, eyes, nose and mouth. It is especially fun to work from personified animal characters who walk upright with a more or less human stance. The Cowardly Lion in *The Wizard of Oz* is an example with whom students can relate; he is in all ways leonine in appearance, gait, and voice, yet is played upright. Familiar, easier-to-play animals can be followed by more difficult ones such as serpents, birds, and butterflies. The characters from C. S. Lewis's *Narnia Chronicles* offer a wonderful variety of human and animal characters to play, but with everyone walking upright (as befits personified animals). The story of St. George and the Dragon is much more effective with the dragon played upright rather than crawling about on all fours.

Whatever the content of the activity, after working with individual body parts, everyone again creates the entire character using the full body and facial expression. While still in their character shapes, players can add a sound or fragment of speech creating a voice appropriate to the role. Conclude the activity by comparing the initial shapes with those created after working through the separate body parts.

■ ADDING SPEECH TO CHARACTERIZATION

Character one-liners. Discovering the voice for a character is generally easier once everyone has had an opportunity to create the physical appearance. For this activity, divide the class into small groups. The size of each group corresponds to the number of characters in the story assigned to it. Familiar folktales or fables work well as a basis for this activity because they have flat characters, fewer roles, and the story depends on the action.

Put the characters for each story on individual cards, and have each person in the group draw a character card from an envelope. (The group will need a copy of the story for quick reference.)

Next, each player works independently to create the physical appearance of her or his role. While maintaining the physical appearance, each player gives one line of dialogue, either improvised or taken from the story, using an appropriate voice.

Within each group, have players experiment and discuss and adjust until you call time. Now, introduce each group to the rest of the class: "May I present the cast of *Hansel and Gretel* (name the story) . . ." Each player assumes the physical appearance of her or his character and gives one line of dialogue using the type of speech and vocal qualities invented for the role.

Crowd scenes. When you add crowd scenes to enhance the playing of a story from literature, encourage each player in each crowd scene to create a unique character, one with its own physical attributes and personality. Not only does this enrich the playing of the story, it provides quality roles for everyone. Remind the players that even in a crowd, everyone is unique, with an individual appearance, ideas, feelings, experiences, and interests.

Though there may not be an occasion within the playing of the story to showcase each of these personalities on an individual basis, each player makes specific decisions that will serve as guidelines as to how to move and speak and be within the story. Techniques for helping students create these added roles are explained in detail in the next section, where we explore character work for scenes and stories built from original ideas.

Developing characters for original stories

Later elementary students especially enjoy creating their own stories and scenes for dramatization. Here all of their dramatic skills and wealth of literacy background can be brought together in very creative ways. Drawing from their familiarity with characters, settings, themes, and plots invented by others, they tackle more complex improvisation. When inventing characters for their own stories and plays, students often base them on characters from literature (or television). It is not unusual to meet familiar characters in student creative writing and you should expect this to also happen in drama. These literary and film characters provide excellent models, especially when students have been exposed to a breadth of quality materials. (You will also meet derivatives from television, movies, and comic books of not-such-high-quality served up in revised forms.)

There are some strategies you can use to divert students from simply recycling familiar characters as they invent their own scenes to play. One of the most useful activities employs a series of questions put to the entire group as they contemplate a given situation. (You can use similar questions when students are creating additional characters for crowd scenes when dramatizing literature.)

Building characters in original crowd scenes

For this activity, the class works as a whole. Present a situation that involves an indefinite number of people. Have each student imagine that he or she is one of the people involved. The following is a narrative example of how this is done.

■ DEFINING UNIQUE ROLES

"Everyone get comfortable and close your eyes. I am going to describe a place and a situation. Each of you is involved in this scene, and each of you may be involved in a way very different from anyone else.

"The place is just outside a large stadium. It is a pleasant afternoon and some popular entertainers have come to give a concert to raise money for a charity drive. The proceeds from the concert are to be used to help people in another country who have suffered from a terrible disaster.

"There is a great deal of excitement as people outside the gates await the opening. In your mind's eye, see the stadium. Look around at what you can see and what you cannot see for the crowd is enormous. Notice all the sounds around you—the odors, the colors. As a character you are about to invent, you are a part of this crowd.

"Invent your character by concentrating on the questions and supplying your own answers. As you make each decision, in answer to a question, you will be building your role. When you can, begin to imagine what you look and sound like and see and hear yourself in your imagination. Ready?

"Are you here alone or are you with someone else? If you are with someone, is it one person or are you a part of a group?

"How did you get here? Are you from this city or someplace else?

"When is your next birthday? How old will you be on your birthday?

"What are you wearing? Are you carrying something? What is it? What do you have in your pocket(s)?

"How do you feel about being here?

"When you are not here, what would you be apt to be doing at this time of day and week?

"Have you ever done anything like this before? Seldom? Often?

"What is your name?"

(The questions may be varied considerably to reflect the given situation.)

"See yourself there in the crowd, this character that you have just become. Notice yourself in relation to others around you and think about whether they may be noticing you. Now, with your character clearly in mind, open your eyes, and we will find out about some of the people who make up this huge crowd."

Take the time to hear each person briefly talk about her or his character. As players describe, they are firming up their ideas and making their characters more concrete and believable.

You may want to have students develop their characters even more, using some of the techniques previously described to work with physical appearance and voice. The group need not play out the scene each time this activity is used. (It is also a first-rate motivational prewriting activity and can sometimes led directly to writing rather than drama.) However, some situations should be further developed into a scene to be played, allowing the cast to provide direction for the action. What evolves may not be a complete dramatic structure with a beginning, middle, climax, and ending; however, the potential is there.

Situations to be used for this activity should have a strong appeal to later elementary students, although you shall encourage students to draw on vicarious knowledge as well as on real and personal experience. Some places and situations that work with many such groups are these:

1. Bus and train stations, air terminals, or dockside just as an arrival/departure is scheduled.

2. Sports events of all kinds, particularly when a very important contest is to take place—a championship or world competition, for example.

3. Celebrations of all kinds. This is fun to do with any of the regional or national patriotic occasions or ethnic festivals, especially familiar ones.

4. The arrival of a famous person or some other event in which a celebrity is to be honored.

5. A natural disaster of some kind that strikes at a time and place that involves a great many people—a hurricane, tornado, or an unusual snow or ice storm.

6. A school event such as a school carnival, dedication of a new gym or library

7. A shopping center during rush hour, perhaps just before closing on a holiday.

8. An auction, especially when something very special is to be sold.

9. A county or state fair, perhaps during a popular competition.

10. A traffic jam downtown in a big city that brings everything to a halt.

Class characters. The preceding technique can also be used by the whole class working together to develop a series of "class characters." This technique works well when you want to break down stereotypical portrayals of stock characters. The emphasis on creating a highly individual character should be antithetical to stereotyping. Additional questions to engage even greater individualism can include these:

1. What is the most unusual thing about you? What sets you apart from everyone else in a very special way?

2. What is your greatest strength? Your greatest weakness?

■ REDUCING STEREOTYPIC PORTRAYAL

Each small group will develop a character sketch of various characters that are often played in stereotypical ways: elderly people, down-and-outers, rock musicians, athletes, police, business executives, teachers, factory workers, farmers. Groups might choose to work with such supernatural characters as witches, creatures from outer space, dragons, or personified animals—bears, tigers, apes or gorillas.

Each group takes one "generic character" from a list. Each player within the group, using the internal questioning technique, creates a specific character. After everyone has had time to answer all or most of the questions, students share within their own groups. When time permits, full group sharing is fun to do, especially when there is an opportunity to use several of the characters to create a composite story developed by the whole class.

Writing character "autobiographies"

Put common nouns (for a person or something that could be personified in a play: man, woman, boy, girl, horse, car, monkey, wind, tree, etc.) on individual paper slips. Have each student draw one from the box. Students then assume their roles and each writes a short "autobiography" about the character that is picked. Encourage those with other than human characters to be sure and give them human qualities but ones that would fit. For example, "wind" might always be rushing around, playing tricks on other folks, capricious and constantly changing her or his mind, full of gossip and sometimes known to tell tall tales. Her or his real name is "Westerly" but friends call her or him "Whoosh."

Later, have students share their short descriptions.

Variation: An excellent variation on this activity is to divide the class into small groups after everyone has written a description. Then pass all of the characters from one group to another, so that no group works with its own inventions. Then each group uses the clusters of characters to create a short scene to play.

If the characters include a variety of human and personified nonhuman characters, the story must be a fantasy. If all of the characters are human, the group can decide on the genre depending on the details of each character. At first, groups with unusually diverse roles may panic and not see how they can put such an assortment together in one scene. They may need some special hints or encouragement to get started, but once they see how this can make their story even more unusual and fun, they are generally excited to work in every character in some interesting way.

Character development, particularly from original ideas, naturally leads into the creation of original stories to dramatize. By grades 4-6, students should be looking at literature in a somewhat analytical way. Drama, through the creation of original scenes to play, offers a unique, experiential way of analyzing dramatic structure at a level later elementary students can handle. Pulling everything together to invent even a simple, limited-action story requires some understanding of how a story is built. By contrast, students inventing their own stories can use literature as their models for guidance. Combined with opportunities to develop simple stories in creative writing, literature and drama can engage students analytically and interpretively with dramatic structure in ways commensurate with their cognitive abilities. Through drama, students can experientially analyze and understand concepts that they might not otherwise be able to handle until sometime in secondary school.

EXPLORING DRAMATIC STRUCTURE

Elements of dramatic structure may first be explored by looking at a favorite story, one everyone knows and understands. This has already been introduced through several activities built on the concept of the five Ws: who (characters), what (plot), where and when (setting), and why (some tension-producing element that sets everything in motion). These are the concerns of the journalist who probes and records the essential elements in order to report with accuracy and objectivity. Obviously, the creative writer will want to embellish and elaborate on the basic elements in order to subjectively explore and comment on the human condition.

■ USING LITERATURE FOR ANALYSIS

By grades 4-6, students are ready (at least experientially) to look at a piece of literature not only in terms of the five Ws but also to examine each of those parts in detail. They can begin to use the language of literary interpretation, at least some of the more basic terminology: characters, plot, setting, theme, mood, conflict, climax, rising action, falling actions, and ending. Fifth- and sixth-graders who begin to use and understand these terms should be well prepared to do more sophisticated analysis later on. You may want to begin by focusing on plot and characters with some attention to point-of-view and the introduction of the conflict. Terms such as beginning, middle, climax, and ending are useful when first looking at a story in terms of structure.

Discovering elements of a story

Each time you share a story aloud, you can introduce the class to how pieces of information relate to the dramatic structure.

■ COMPARING TYPES OF PLOTS

Before telling a story, suggest that everyone listen so that later they will be able to answer some questions about how the story is put together. You may put questions on the board (not too many, for you want students to be able to understand and enjoy the story as a unit). The following are sample questions that might be asked, a few at a time:

1. What is the setting of the story (time, place, environment)?
2. Whose story is it? (Titles do not always tell us even when the title is a name of a character; e.g. *Charlotte's Web* is actually the story of Wilbur.)
3. What happened at the very beginning of the story that told us something about what the story was to be about?
4. What was the most exciting thing that happened in the story? What led up to that most exciting or important action?

5. Did the story end the way you thought it would? If not, explain.

These questions can be used with a story with a progressive plot.

Folk and fairy tales are sometimes episodic and have several lesser events in a series of problems to be resolved rather than one large problem that leads to the climax. When reading episodic stories, you may ask students to identify each of the short, individual incidents that are unified around the common theme of the story. Several contemporary stories, many of which are about the adventures of children or personified animals, are also episodic in structure. *The Adventures of Tom Sawyer* begins this way; other longer works with episodic plot development include *The Wind in the Willows* (Grahame, 1908), *Pippi Longstocking* (Lindgren, 1950), *Harriet the Spy* (Fitzhugh, 1964), and long sections of *Alice in Wonderland* (Carroll, 1865). Each of the episodes may well make a scene to dramatize, since each incident often includes a beginning, a middle, a climax, and an ending—to form a complete entity within the story.

■ IDENTIFYING THEME

Students may listen to stories in order to identify the common theme that holds the entire story together. The autobiographical stories of Laura Ingalls Wilder are basically episodic in structure, with all of the incidents held together around the common theme of the struggles of life on the frontier. In *A Wrinkle in Time* (L'Engle, 1962), all of the exciting struggles within a progressive plot are tied together around Meg's attempts to free Charles Wallace from the antagonist IT. In both examples, one a personal narrative of pioneer life and the other a rather abstract piece of science fiction written by an omniscient author, the unifying theme deals with the struggles of a young girl. Comparing and contrasting how this similar theme is handled can give students insight into experiencing both style and point-of-view as well as comparing genres.

As students begin to invent their own stories for drama, they can apply their developing insights into literary structure to make their own stories more successful. Drawing on well-known models, they can create stories with a beginning that sets the scene and introduces characters and conflict, a middle that moves the story along, and a climax that provides a turning-around place and leads to a satisfying ending.

Building a setting

Sometimes in their early improvised original stories, students are so anxious to get to the action that they do not establish where and when the story takes place. Literature may handle this by simply announcing, "Once upon a time . . ." This works fine in the story told through words, especially if the setting is simply a backdrop for the action. However, when the story is to be told through drama, and the players must move within a particular time and place, and especially if the setting is integral to the plot, then the setting must be clearly identified and established.

The "Creating a Place" activity, borrowed from Viola Spolin's *Improvisation for the Theatre* (1963), is useful. Once the group has made decisions about the time and place where the story is to happen, the players use pantomime to put the necessary furnishings into the scene. They create both a setting and a set that everyone can visualize.

Although this is time-consuming and need not be done each time an invented scene is to be played, it is a useful technique on occasion. It clearly establishes the importance of setting, that all stories take place within some time and place. Stories can even be built from the established setting. Once they have a setting, students can brainstorm about who lives there and what happens that creates a problem to be solved.

Manipulating elements in a story

Divide the class into groups. Give each group the same short story—a fable, legend, folk or fairy tale. Use familiar stories or ones the class has recently read. Have each group change some basic element in the story in some significant way: time (from period to contemporary or in the future), place (city to rural, perhaps), point of view (protagonist/antagonist roles might be reversed), or mood (serious to humor, for example).

Give the players several minutes to plan the playing of the scene with the prescribed change. After each group shares, have the class discuss the impact of each change on the story.

Working with simple, familiar stories is just as productive as working with more complex materials. This activity works best if you assign a specific type of change; it is a challenging activity and works best with experienced players. It is an excellent way for students to experience the important role that each element contributes to the overall product.

■ INVENTING COMPLETE STRUCTURES

Small group round-robins. Another way to reinforce dramatic structure is to use small groups with each charged to create and play each successive section of a story.

Group 1 is responsible for creating the beginning scene in which setting is established, characters introduced, theme revealed, and the mood established.

Group 2 picks up where the first group leaves off. This group adds a conflict.

Group 3 develops the plot up to the resolution of the conflict.

Group 4 resolves the conflict.

Group 5 creates a satisfying way to end the story.

At first the steps may simply be planned and shared. Experienced players might do each improvised scene as an add-on, but that takes a great deal of practice. Keep scenes short so that the groups can do several.

In successive rounds, have the groups shift parts so that group 2 begins and group 1 provides the ending. The class may decide to play one story with pantomime or with action and speech together.

Working with mood

Mood is closely associated with the feelings of the characters in the story, but it is projected by other elements as well—where the story takes place, the kind of conflict, and the style in which the story is told all contribute to a dominant mood.

In the following activities, students have opportunities to both experience and manipulate mood in order to develop a better understanding of what it is and how mood is conveyed.

Five Ws with mood. Divide the class into small groups. Give each group the same instructions about who, what, when, where, and why. But assign each group a different dominant mood. For example: "who" are workers and visitors, "where" is an amusement park, "when" is opening day. Each group is assigned a different mood such as "excitement," "suspense," "hilarity," "eerie," "foreboding." Each group decides what is happening, using the given information and the assigned mood. Scenes are created and shared. Afterwards, the class discusses how the different moods influenced what happened and how the scene was played.

Change of mood. This is done with in-place pantomime with everyone playing independently of others. To a count of ten, each student uses her or his body to project a specific mood as you call it. Next, instruct them to "change to . . ." Provide a count of ten for each mood change. Follow-up discussion might focus on how different moods were portrayed by different players, what body parts were most often used to indicate a mood, and what moods were easiest to show. Discussion may also include reasons why someone's mood might change with the analysis focusing on the introduction of problems (conflict) and the resolution of problems.

USING CONFLICT AND CLIMAX FOR SATISFYING CONCLUSIONS

At the heart of drama is conflict. Indeed, "no conflict; no drama" is an easy reminder to students inventing their own stories. If the story is to have a dramatic structure that can be played, there needs to be a problem of some kind. Another way to reinforce the importance of conflict is to look at several examples of favorite stories. Children's literature, particularly that which endures, abounds with excellent examples of the several types of conflict: person-against-person, person-against nature, person-against-self, and person-against-society.

■ DEFINING TYPES OF CONFLICT

Some stories include examples of most or all of these categories of struggle. For example, in Armstrong's *Call it Courage*, Mafatu struggles against his own fear of the sea and against the forces of nature that set him adrift on the water only to be washed ashore on an island which is used by cannibals for their sacrifices. In addition, part of his personal turmoil is induced by his humiliation in the eyes of his people who see him as a coward. For the son of a Polynesian chief to fear the sea is unnatural and a cause for rejection by his own people. Although the overriding struggle is with the self, each of the other types play a significant role in the telling of the story and in its final resolution.

Folk and fairy tales abound with examples of good people against evil ones; myths and legends often center around the struggles of a person or group of people (or deities) with the forces of nature. In many excellent stories enjoyed by later elementary students, the chief antagonist is society (perhaps as embodied in one or more specific characters). Robert O'Brien's *Mrs. Frisby and the Rats of NIMH* (1971) and Richard Adams's *Watership Down* (1974) are both personified animal tales in which the basic struggles are against the forces of human society. By contrast, Peter Rabbit's enemy is clearly Farmer McGregor. Older boys and girls, with less egocentric views of the world, enjoy the full range of conflicts and begin to personally relate to all of them.

By pointing out examples of different kinds of conflict in literature, you provide models for students to use in inventing their own stories for dramatization. This may suggest other types of stories than simply the "good guys" vs. "bad guys" plot. The following activities focus on types of conflicts.

Adding conflict to beginnings

As a whole, the class creates the beginning of a story. They choose a setting and add a central character. For example: This story will be about a ten-year-old girl who has come to spend the summer on her uncle's cattle ranch.

Next, the class is divided into four groups. Each is to have one type of conflict:

Group 1: the girl against some person or persons

Group 2: the girl against herself

Group 3: the girl against nature

Group 4: the girl against society

Students may need additional help in getting started. If so, you can lead the entire group in brainstorming several possible examples under each category. This may be particularly useful for group 4 (person against society); students generally need to identify specific members of society as the antagonist, although adults perceive those persons as representing certain values or attitudes (ethical, political, religious, etc.) held by a portion of society.

After each group has added the conflict and finished their planning, each group shares their scene. During debriefing and discussion, the stories can be compared and contrasted. The different conflicts will provide different climaxes and endings so that the entire structure of each scene can be compared with the others.

Manipulating conflict

In an activity similar to the one just described, students work with a piece of literature. As a whole group, the class takes a favorite story and changes the type of conflict or changes the antagonist in some significant way. Considering the change, students talk through the problem to climax and resolution. Then they compare the new story to the original.

The story matrix board. For this activity, the class creates a board on which students enter ideas under several elements of a story. The number of elements and degree of sophistication will depend on the age and experience of the class. For most later elementary students, the following is sufficiently challenging yet useful. (Later, the story matrix board could be expanded to include theme.) The headings might be as follows:

CHARACTERS	SETTINGS	CONFLICTS	MOODS

The group may decide that there should be a minimum of three characters within each box under the character column. More could be added later (if a group so desires). In each box, under each of the other headings, will be one choice or set of choices. For example, under "Settings," each box should contain a specific time and place (2001, a U.S. space station); a struggle of some kind should be in each box under "Conflicts" (an invasion of grasshoppers); and one dominant mood should be in each box under "Moods." Urge students to use conflicts that include the different kinds of struggles.

Divide the class into small groups. Each group selects one box from each element so that they work from one set of characters, a setting, a conflict, and a mood. For this information, the group creates a story to be dramatized.

Stress that students are not *limited* to the characters from their box, but they must use those furnished. Likewise, they must use the chosen setting, at least initially, as well as the conflict and mood.

Add things to the story matrix board from time to time. It makes an excellent tool for creative writing as well as for drama. Having the proper terminology in place adds a sense of professionalism to all of their creative efforts.

■ DEFINING CLIMAX

Without setting out to memorize a list of terms or definitions, students working with dramatic structure (using both literature and scenes of their own invention) need to know appropriate terminology and delight in being able to use it, especially as they move toward formal work in theatre arts.

As they gain skills, students should also extend and expand their working drama vocabulary. Young students discuss the climax as "the most exciting part of the story"; older students refer to the "climax," but without an understanding that this is more than just the "most exciting part" (sometimes the most exciting part is not at the climax); mature students understand that the climax is the moment when the audience (reader or viewer) knows how things will work out.

Looking at literature and identifying the climax in stories helps students in drama see how to build toward the climax when planning a scene. This is true for drama that is episodic as well as for drama that has a clearly progressive action plot, for there is always one final struggle that turns things around and leads to the ending. The following activity allows the players in creative drama to manipulate the climax in order to provide different outcomes.

Manipulating climax

Just as students can manipulate the conflict in order to change the plot, they can substitute different climaxes and change the final outcome of the story in highly significant ways. The moment of climax determines whether the story has a happy or tragic ending; a serious story may become comedic by a different resolution of the conflict. The class may substitute different climaxes in familiar tales to exper-ience the impact on the outcome and ending. You might facilitate this by posing questions: What would be the out-come of the story of "The Three Little Pigs" if the wolf, having entered the third pig's house through the chimney, had survived its fall into the pot of boiling water? (Perhaps it repents and is invited to stay for a sumptuous dinner. Per-haps it turns the table on the pigs, tosses them into the pot, and eats a hearty meal after which it stays on as a noble wolf who live out its life as a respectable homeowner of one brick house.)

Creating multiple endings

Working from literature or original story ideas, have the entire class discuss and work with the same story right up to the climax. Then, with students working in small groups, have each group decide how the conflict is resolved and create an appropriate end-ing. (This is particularly fun to do using a film version of a piece of literature and stopping the film just before resolution. At that point, the groups each decide on a climax and ending.)

You can use this activity to reinforce what makes a good ending: one that is satisfying and makes sense. This is also a time to intro-duce sixth-graders to the term *denouement* with the simple defini-tion that it is the part of the story that begins at the climax and at the point where they feel certain they know what will happen to the protagonist.

The best endings, from the perspective of children, wrap up the details in happy and satisfying ways during the falling action that follows the climax. Creating simple yet satisfying endings is not easy and often requires a good deal of work. Bringing a story to a good conclusion is even more difficult in drama than in a printed story for how can you "show" that "they all lived happily ever after?"

If the class has worked with a film version of a familiar story, after students have invented their own endings, it is good to look at the ending of the film to see how another satisfying ending was "shown." Compare the filmed ending with the words used to end the printed literature.

All of this analysis and work with dramatic structure is not only important to advanced work in creative drama but paves the way for formal work in theatre arts. By secondary school, students who have this kind of background are generally well prepared to deal with more in-depth analysis of literature and to tackle the performance of scripted plays.

DOING FORMAL DRAMA

Concurrently with more challenging work in creative drama, later elementary students can bring a wealth of understanding and skill to related art forms, some of a more formal nature. One of the most satisfying forms is the oral interpretation of literature. Unlike a formal play in which scripts must be memorized and speech and actions coordinated, in oral interpretation (including a variety of forms of readers theatre), the literature is generally shared from the manuscript. The reader becomes the means by which an author's work(s) is shared. Obviously, in order to do this well, the reader must do as much as possible to analyze and understand the author's words and the milieu from which they came. All of the elements, character, plot, setting, theme, point of view, style and tone need to be considered. Selecting suitable works means exploring a variety of pieces and looking at them in terms of dramatic appeal.

Literature in performance has different requirements than literature to be silently read for one's own enlightenment or enjoyment. Vocal skills, practiced and developed in creative drama, can make the words come alive for an audience. Whether for others in the classroom or for guests, the selection and performance must be done with the audience in mind. Therefore, audience analysis is an important part of selecting and performing the literature.

Readers theatre

Readers theatre is a rather generic term that covers a variety of ways to present literature (of all kinds) so that "the literature becomes a living experience . . . both for the readers and for their audience" (Coger & White, *Readers Theatre Handbook,* 3rd. ed., 1982, p. 7). For those who remember this art form as some readers seated on tall stools reading aloud from manuscripts resting on music stands, Coger and White offer the following description to cover the wide variety of techniques currently used in readers theatre.

> In nature it is theatrical; in content, human. Readers Theatre draws on a wide range of styles: presentation with stools and stands and no movement, presentation without stools and stands and much purposeful action and interaction of the involved characters, with and without settings, with and without costuming, with and without special lighting, with and without a stage, with and without a theatrical curtain, with and without memorization, with and without multiple casting (one reader taking more than one role), with or without onstage or offstage focus . . . , with or without make-up, with or without music, dance, sound, and mechanical and vocal effects. (p. 4)

Readers theatre is such a flexible art that performers of all ages and abilities can participate. In this regard, it is a theatre art highly correlated with creative drama, for it can provide for everyone who wants to participate to have some role in the production. Although intended for sharing with an audience, like drama, readers theatre is also very process-oriented. It is to be a "living experience" for readers as well as audience and certainly, when used within the classroom, is a means for students to become intimate with good literature as well as skillful in their interpretation and performance of it.

Choosing materials for readers theatre

Generally, the size of the cast would not be large enough to include everyone in a regular classroom. More often, materials for readers theatre utilize five or six readers to a piece. However, you can divide the class into several casts sharing materials around a central theme. Therefore, when selecting materials it is not necessary to look for something with 25 or more parts. For conventional readers theatre, a range of materials are suitable and available: plays, dramatic and narrative poetry, epic poems, and nondramatic literature.

For *chamber theatre* (where characters may memorize lines and use contentional stage blocking), characters often speak in the third person and the past tense. Therefore, narrative fiction is a preferred genre. With the class working in small groups to present around a central theme, materials may be chosen to accommodate various reading levels and group preferences.

■ SELECTING AND ORGANIZING

Later elementary students may enjoy putting together a whole program of readings around the theme "Sometimes Growing Up Is Hard to Do." Excerpts from Mark Twain, Judy Blume, and a breadth of traditional and contemporary poets might be used together in an insightful and delightful program.

Whatever is chosen must be strong enough to hold the interest of both readers and audience primarily through vivid vocal expression.

Most often readers theatre is done with few embellishments. Strong sensory language, highly articulate dialogue, and passages that create action in the mind's eye are all desirable when choosing materials for reading aloud, regardless of the exact format used.

■ USING PREPARED SCRIPTS

For beginning experiences with readers theatre, you may wish to purchase prepared scripts especially designed for students in grades 4-6. These are not only professionally done but provide excellent models for later programs to be designed by you and your class. Readers Theatre Script Service (P.O. Box 178333, San Diego, California 97117) offers packets for all grades from early elementary through secondary. Each packet contains step-by-step instructions as well as fully edited scripts. Among titles currently available are these: "The Pied Piper of Hamlin" by Robert Browning; two of *Aesop's Fables,* "The City Mouse and the Country Mouse" and "The Tortoise and the Hare," available in bilingual Spanish/French/German with English versions; "The Ballad of the Oysterman" by Oliver Wendell Holmes, done in simple, staged, chamber, and story theatre formats; and "The Little Girl and the Wolf" and "The Unicorn in the Garden" by James Thurber. Materials are available for all grade levels, so students with special reading or interest needs can be accommodated.

Creative Drama and readers theatre

Delightful theatre arts experiences can be provided by employing creative drama and readers theatre in a single program.

Divide the class into four groups. Have two groups prepare materials to be read aloud as simple readers theatre (using manuscripts and without actions). The other two groups become small casts who pantomime the literature as it is read.

Four groups are suggested to permit the reading and pantomiming groups to be of about equal size and yet include everyone in a regular classroom in the production. A central theme may tie the entire program together. The pairs of groups provide audience for one another. This type of program is often something that the class would want to refine and polish to present to guests, child or adult, for a special occasion. If that is the case, the groups will want to keep the special audience in mind as they select and prepare.

Puppetry and readers theatre

Readers theatre and drama skills can be further combined by using a readers theatre cast to tell a story done as puppet theatre by another cast. Students who are communication-apprehensive or those with severe reading problems can tell the story with puppets while others narrate using a readers theatre format. Rather than the single narrator, the use of multiple readers can provide a variety of voices for the several characters as well as a separate narrator to carry the storyline. Chorus work, spoken and sung, and sound effects can be added to increase the effectiveness of the entire production.

Shadow puppet plays and readers theatre

Readers theatre may also accompany a shadow puppet play performance. The reading cast may be "offstage" while other players use their hands, arms, and other body parts to create characters through shadow play behind a backlighted curtain, screen, or bedsheet. Shadow puppetry is a wonderful way to portray lots of action without players actually engaging in pseudo-combat. Stories about famous battles; dueling knights; invasions by land, sea, or sky; science fiction; and all the hero tales of mythology make excellent materials for both readers theatre and shadow puppetry. The two art forms can combine to give everyone an important role, while allowing each student to contribute in a unique way.

This kind of program is also fun to share with another class or as part of a special school program. Enhanced with sound effects and a musical prologue and epilogue, a simple story theatre program can become a full-scale theatre event.

Reading a play aloud

Readers theatre includes the reading aloud of plays written in playscript format. This can make an excellent introduction to working with a playscript. Indeed, materials provided by the Readers Theatre Script Service are prepared in playscript form, although they are based on various genres of literature. Readers theatre can also be done with materials originally written as plays.

Few later elementary students have read a play and, at first, may find it awkward and hard to follow the storyline, yet plays and radio scripts are some of the easiest materials to adapt for reader theatre. But not all scripts work equally well. Plays that depend on a lot of physical action in order to reveal character motivation and attributes of personality, or where the climax is basically action-oriented, need to be adapted to work primarily through words and vocal expression. When combined with puppets or pantomime to help carry the action, however, even very physical plays can work for a children's readers theatre program.

The scripted play

Students who are experienced in improvisation and the dramatization of literature through creative drama will eventually want to do a scripted play, especially if they have had opportunities to do some readers theatre of various kinds. It is this writer's opinion, based on many years of working with students and theatre arts education, that there is time enough in secondary school for students to move into formal theatre work. However, some teachers and students may choose to work with a scripted performance in grades 4-6.

To direct a play is a special experience and requires some different skills than leading students in creative drama or even guiding them in a readers theatre performance. Unless you have personal experience and/or training, it is challenging to select suitable materials, adapt them for young players, prepare a Prompt Book with all of the details related to production, cast the play, rehearse it, provide technical assistance, and finally bring it to an audience. This might be a shared project with another teacher or with the media or music specialist. If you choose to tackle such a project, you will need all the help you can find.

It may be useful to first work with playscripts performed as readers theatre or as a puppet play. In both these formats, the players need not memorize the lines or they may memorize only limited amounts of the material (those places where two characters interact face-to-face, for example).

Scripted plays for puppet performance

A problem that all inexperienced players have with doing a scripted play is following the script, remembering the lines, and staying in character at the same time (both physically and vocally). Two advantages of the puppet play in which the puppeteers work from a formal script are that there is no need to memorize the lines and that the puppet maintains a physical constancy of the character. The movement and voice of the puppet must be consistent throughout, and this is challenge enough for young puppeteers. However, the puppet is not apt to be suddenly overcome with the self-consciousness that results in breaking character and spoiling a scene.

Directing a puppet play is also a good medium for the teacher who is inexperienced in directing a complete production. Directors, by definition, are considerably more autocratic than facilitators of creative drama. When directions must be enforced in order to have successful final product, you are *directing* puppet characters and their "handlers." This may allow for the requisite amount of authoritativeness without undue hurt feelings among the puppeteers. Furthermore, the separate parts of the play may be rehearsed, adjusted, polished, and *then* put together for the final product.

The script must be rehearsed with the manipulation of the puppets in order to pace both the timing of the actions and the speaking of the lines. When you are satisfied with the timing, you may want to record the script on tape so that the puppeteers can concentrate on the manipulation of the puppets. Students not handling puppets can serve as technical crew to manage the tape recorder, add lighting effects if desired, and help with the "front of the house" responsibilities such as seating guests, handing out programs, and serving as model members of the audience.

The emphasis in rehearsal must be on creating and maintaining consistent voices and movements for each of the puppet characters. You must listen and watch and help each puppeteer develop and maintain consistent characters. The same student need not provide both the voice and the movement for each character, but they must be carefully coordinated to work—voice and movements must be more than in sync; they must make a compatible, unified whole. As part of rehearsal, the puppeteer might mime the character as the voice speaks. Mime provides the kind of uncluttered, disciplined movement required to manipulate a believable puppet character.

Additional puppet activities

Upper elementary students often enjoy putting on a polished puppet play for younger students. Familiar folk and fairy tales are dependable choices, enjoyed by players and audience. The following are activities to do in addition to plays.

1. Choric work with puppets. Class or teacher scores a narrative poem such as Robert Browning's "The Pied Piper of Hamelin." Children choose roles, make appropriate bag or rod puppets, and speak assigned lines. Poems may use line-a-child or antiphonal arrangements, duos, small choruses, and so on. Choric work with puppets can be exciting when done as a shadow puppet activity.

2. Situational role-playing with puppets. The use of puppets can reduce anxieties when older children are engaged in role-playing as a way to explore different points-of-view in conflict situations. Example: One puppet whose garden has been trampled confronts the puppet ballplayer who did the deed chasing a home run. Or, puppets may engage in buying and selling, persuasive dyads, and other activities that work well with children playing in pairs.

3. Job interviews. Upper elementary children use puppets to practice interviewing skills of all kinds including the special skills required for the job interview. This combines well with a unit on career education.

4. Small group problem-solving. Each child creates a puppet with a name, voice, and unique personality. The class divides into groups of five or six and each is assigned a problem to solve. Each puppet contributes to the discussion in ways appropriate to his or her personal attributes. Sample topics are: developing ideas for a school money-raising project, new ideas to encourage everyone to read lots of books over summer vacation, deciding what to do to honor a favorite school employee who is retiring, creating a list of good citizenship rules.

5. Showcasing different cultures or countries using small group puppet work. Each group selects a different culture. Puppets, appropriately costumed, share information and folklore. This activity can be combined with a social studies unit.

Viewing scripted plays

Reading a play script, noting dialogue and stage directions, makes excellent preparation for seeing plays of all kinds. Commercial television networks sometimes make available to schools scripts of upcoming programming for children. These can provide a basis for a stimulating discussion of the content as well as script analysis. The class can present sections as readers theatre. Whether the script is provided or not, networks regularly distribute viewer's guides that include discussion questions and interesting commentary on the content and background of the program, the author, and actors involved in the production. Such program notes can motivate insightful discussion both before and after the program airs.

Prior to seeing a live performance, you can prepare students to view it with deeper understanding by teaching them about the play, the playwright, the period in which the play was first staged, etc. This is also a good time to talk about how a formal production is staged, extending students' knowledge of theatre terms so that they can talk about the play as seasoned theatregoers.

THEATRE TERMS FOR CHILD VIEWERS

The following is a limited glossary of terms; however, even this is more than later elementary students need at one time. You may wish to introduce several of the most useful terms (for a particular play and/or student audience) and provide the class with a short vocabulary list. Adjust the exact language of each definition to suit the age and sophistication of the viewers.

acting area: the area enclosed by scenery used by the actors during a performance.

actors: performers in a theatre production.

antagonist: the chief opponent of the protagonist (the main leading character). Not all plays have a single protagonist with a complementary antagonist, however. (See sections on "Conflict.")

arena theatre: also called "theatre in the round" because the audience may be seated on most or all sides of the acting area. Many productions for young people are done this way, including participatory theatre where the audience joins in some of the action as guided by the actors.

auditions: trial hearings of actors, musicians, and others who wish to be considered for participation in a stage production. (Often called *try-outs*.)

blocking: the director's overall conceptualization for each scene in terms of where everything is placed and where actors are to be at any given time.

business: the physical actions and movement used by the actors to characterize their roles. It is what projects the action of the play to the audience. It includes posture, facial expression, and gesture, as well as entrances, exits, how hand props are used, standing, sitting, etc. The director plans the *required business* in advance; *supplementary business* is that which is not demanded by the script but is added by the actors and/or director to enhance the effect and clarify meaning.

director: the chief job and responsibility of the director is to coach and direct the performances of the actors.

downstage: any position on the stage near the footlights (toward the audience).

drop: a large sheet of canvas, fastened to a batten at the top and bottom and hung from the gridiron. This often represents the sky or skyline.

entrance: the point in a script where a performer begins. Entrances are designated on the playscript and in the director's Prompt Book as "Enter." Further stage directions will tell how and where.

exit: the point in a script that designates when a performer leaves the scene. Further stage directions will tell how and where.

fly: to lift scenery up above the level of the stage floor by lines from the overhead gridiron.

footlights: one or more rows of lights set in recess outside the curtain to produce general illumination from below.

front of the house: in a proscenium theatre, the auditorium where the audience sits.

gelatin: the most commonly used material to produce color. Made of ordinary gelatin and dyed, thin sheets of "gels" cover the various light sources to produce required colors.

gridiron: the framework of steel or wooden beams above the stage which supports the rigging so that scenery can be raised or lowered.

illumination: describes the lighting of the acting area, both generally and in specific locations. (Often used synonymously with *lighting*.

left stage: any position on stage to the left of the actor while facing the audience.

masking: a piece of scenery used to cut off the view of anything that should not be visible to the audience.

offstage: any position on the stage outside the acting area.

pit: the section directly in front of the stage in a proscenium theatre that conceals the musicians. (Sometimes called the *orchestra pit*.)

prompter: one who has a complete copy of the director's Prompt Book and can assist an actor in recalling a line.

properties: any article except scenery and costumes used as a part of a dramatic production. Hand props are those portable items that are actually used by the players.

proscenium: the wall that divides the stage from the auditorium. The opening through which the audience views the play is called the *proscenium arch* or *proscenium opening*.

right stage: any position on stage to the actor's right when facing the audience.

set: all of the units and pieces of scenery that represents a single locale.

stage crew: all of the people involved with the behind-the-scenes work in putting on a play. (Often simply called the *crew*.)

stage hand: a person who works backstage in a theatre.

technical crew: the people responsible for handling the technical requirements of a production. This includes the people who handle the lights, the sound effects, the amplifications, etc.

strike: to take apart and remove a set of scenery after it has been used, at the end of an act and at the close of the play.

upstage: any position on the stage away from the footlights (away from the audience).

Children often find great satisfaction in being able to talk knowledgeably about anything "adult." This would include both seeing a play and, later on, taking part in the production of a formal performance. The use of proper theatre terms can be as important as the use of technical language in sports and games or working with the computer. All of these experiences are associated with becoming grown-up, worldly, and making the transition from elementary to secondary school.

Later elementary students can begin to put their theatre vocabulary to work as they invent original stories and dramatize them through improvisation, as they analyze a piece of literature to do as readers theatre, or as they develop a puppet play from a script to perform for a group of younger students. It allows them to discuss and take part in theatre arts at a level commensurate with their increased experience and maturity—and to do so in a natural progression that fits their changing needs, interests, and aptitudes.

CHAPTER 6

Integrating Drama with Content Areas

Whether drama is used to help students experientially understand dramatic structure and characterization in literature, or literature is used as the basis for creative drama, the integration of these two areas of language arts lets them mutually enhance one another. By grades 4-6, there are few instances in which creative drama does not serve to introduce, reinforce, or enrich learning in one or more of the content areas. Drama is always about something; there is always a content—drawn from history, literature, the world of scientific exploration, or a combination of ways people explore and reflect on both the human and nonhuman dimensions of the world. Almost all of the activities in the preceding chapters combine both drama and one or more other areas of study in ways that foster integrated, holistic exploration and discovery. This chapter offers additional suggestions for integrating drama and other content learning (with occasional references to activities previously described, since those also employ integration).

CREATIVE DRAMA AND THE OTHER LANGUAGE ARTS

It would be redundant to reiterate the many interrelationships between creative drama and the study and enjoyment of literature. Not only are the several genres of literature the most often-used basis for story dramatization, they provide the stimuli for other types of creative drama work as well. Poetry and short pieces of prose can often be used to introduce the drama lesson or as the basis for various warm-up activities invoking sensory recall. Conversely, such drama devices as guided imagery and narrative pantomime serve to subjectively involve the listener in the richness and excitement of language invented by the poet or storyteller. Through drama, students are drawn into the world of literature with increased intimacy and pleasure. Reading can be encouraged as students discover the excitement of books. However, the integration of drama and literature is only one way in which drama and the other language arts can be mutually reinforcing.

Drama and prewriting

Whether the writing assignment requires students to think imaginatively to invent a piece of creative writing or to concisely and precisely articulate information, data, and evidence in expository writing, the key requirement is always motivation. In order to write well, the writer must have both something to say and an urge to write about it. Creative drama can provide both the content for the writing and the initiative and excitement to want to put ideas and feelings on paper. Several of the exercises in the preceding chapters provide excellent prewriting inspiration for both creative and expository writing. For example, the creation of a special place can provide the setting for a story. The furnishings offer clues about who lives there and when. The addition of a conflict provides all of the necessary ingredients for an original story.

■ WRITING ORIGINAL ENDINGS

Another prewriting device is the use of drama to begin the story but with options for everyone to create individual endings. Using contextual cues provided in the drama, students are motivated to predict and devise satisfying conclusions. The opening can be done as a narrative pantomime, as story theatre with the teacher as narrator, or as an improvised scene. Everyone plays a part, and every writer has an immediate experience on which to build. No one should lack "something to write about."

Guided imagery and poetry. Guided imagery does more than simply ask the participants to create pictures in the mind as suggested by the leader. The visualization, is, of course, an important part; however, most experiences in guided imagery are multisensory—suggesting that the student recall shapes, sizes, colors, sounds, tastes, odors, textures, and temperatures.

Students cannot create in the mind's eye experiences totally outside their own realms of experience, but they can be guided to look at the familiar in new ways and to synthesize experiences into new combinations—for example, to see in the mind's eye the familiar route to school, but noticing such detail as the shapes and colors of buildings, cracks in the sidewalk, colonies of ants, perhaps bits and pieces of candy wrappers swirled about by gusts of wind. These images are the stuff of which a poem can be made. Later elementary students may capture their imaged recollections with haiku or cinquain poems—short, sensuous, and vivid as seen through a child's eyes.

Pantomime and poetry. Creative movement and pantomime can motivate action poetry. In-place pantomime in which a student explores different body movements while discovering how to discipline the arms, hands, legs, shoulders, torso, and head to imitate actions or create a character provides a wealth of different ways to experience movement. If students' poems and stories are full of creatures who simply "walk, walk, walk, and sometimes, run," the actual doing in drama in which *they* slide, glide, slither, slink, tarry, tip-toe, bounce, balance, and blast-off should conjure up an extensive list of exciting ways to describe locomotion.

Interpretive movement and metaphor. Interpretive movement provides another avenue for exploring ways to express action, perhaps more metaphorically. Mirroring to music or letting the melody and/or rhythm guide the players as they move through a larger space should suggest using their bodies as other dynamic forces—a breeze, a hurricane, a sandstorm, a tidal wave, for instance. Used prior to writing, this experience lets students bring the metaphor to life and then use the personal experience in the writing.

Drama and Expository Writing

Activities in drama may instill a degree of curiosity about all kinds of things and provide motivation for library research and introductory work in writing papers. Again, the personal involvement required for the drama can generate heightened interest in topics explored. The research may lead into other areas of curriculum. The dramatization of historical fiction may produce several written reports on a specific era.

■ MOTIVATING RESEARCH THROUGH DRAMA

One group of students became interested in World War II after dramatizing several scenes from *The Lion, The Witch, and The Wardrobe* (Lewis, 1950). They were fascinated by the idea that many English children were sent to the countryside without their parents in order to escape the bombing of London. They later did some drama with *Carrie's War* (Bawden, 1973) dealing with the same topic. This spawned an interest in other situations in which children have been sent to live away from their parents in order to be safe. Ultimately several students researched and wrote about child evacuees in different times and places. This interest in a rather mature subject was a direct outgrowth of the drama experiences.

■ GENERATING PRACTICAL WRITING

Other kinds of expository writing that might be generated by drama include these: letters to characters or as characters in a story, writing invitations, thank-you notes, and letters of sympathy to or as literary figures.

Many favorite stories to dramatize involve food and eating. A class cookbook is fun to do after students have dramatized the Mad Hatter's tea party or Marcia Brown's *Stone Soup* (1947). The latter is a picture book enjoyed by children of all ages because of the excellent artwork and its appeal as drama. One class of fourth-graders, after playing this story and while still motivated by the subject, created their own "Guide to Eating Out . . . Just for Kids." The latter became a popular volume in the school library.

An older class would enjoy putting together an ethnic cookbook of favorite dishes representing their own heritages after doing drama related to various places and cultures. A drama about getting lost resulted in one class producing a book of maps showing how to get to various important (and popular with children) places in the neighborhood and community. It was dedicated to "All the New Kids in Our School."

Many prewriting ideas can be used as motivation for giving oral reports and short speeches. Formal speech work is seldom stressed in the elementary grades, but this is a good time to encourage students to give informal talks before their peers. The self-confidence that comes from participating in drama can pave the way for other speech work.

Drama and the oral curriculum

Drama is part of the oral curriculum: those areas of language arts that deal with listening and speaking, including the nonverbal components of speech. Several of the activities described in earlier chapters engage students both in drama and in developing listening and speaking skills for other purposes beyond the drama.

Drama and listening

Listening in order to follow directions is required in order to do any sidecoached activity, ten-count pantomime, and variations on listening games. Listening for comprehension is reinforced through storytelling, creating new conclusions for open-ended stories, and sequential listening games. Listening for information is practiced each time the class does round-robin storybuilding. These activities also require players to listen in order to predict.

■ MEETING LISTENING NEEDS

Another important need is to be able to listen empathically. This is a skill (and an attitude) that is difficult to teach except by doing. To do it, we must listen beyond the words to the feelings of another and to try to put ourselves in another's place. Work in role-playing and characterization can provide this kind of experience as students move from egocentricity to being able to see another's point-of-view. Before playing the following, talk about how to listen to another in order to see how it is with her or him. You might say, "This means that we try not to prejudge what another is saying or leap to our own conclusion. It means listening for feelings as well as words and giving supportive feedback that says you are listening and care."

Empathic listening activity. Divide the class into dyads (pairs). In each dyad, one person needs someone to listen with a "kind ear," not necessarily to give advice but just to listen. Possible topics for each dyadic conversation are: "My best friend is moving way across country." "My pet died." "My brother (sister) gets to do things that I am not allowed to do." "Somebody took my favorite _____ and broke (or lost) it." Avoid any situation that may seem related to a particular child's own circumstances. Like any work in situation role-playing, it should not be used to pry or as psycho-drama. After five minutes of play, call "time" and have the class discuss what kinds of comments (feedback) helped and which did not. Then, reverse roles and let the listener describe a "problem."

This type of listening is not easy for anyone, children included. Do not worry if students are not able to do more than make sympathetic responses or offer unsolicited advice. Being an empathic listener is a tough task.

Barbara S. Wood (*Children and Communication,* 2nd ed., 1981) discusses several communication situations that are particularly difficult for some children. She includes in her book an instrument that teachers can use in helping students identify those topics and relationships that are hard for them to handle interpersonally. Whether you use the instrument or not, you might have the class identify a list of possible "tough communication tasks," real or imagined. You might then choose a few from the list to be role-played in pairs. (The same format can be used as in the empathic listening exercise.)

Drama and speaking

One type of interpersonal communication that many people find difficult is persuasion. As novice cause-and-effect thinkers, students often do not think ahead to the consequences of their actions and do not understand when someone else (often an adult in authority) turns down a request because it may have negative results. They are also not very astute in backing argument with evidence; they tend to rely on "what they want." The following activity works well after a discussion of different ways to present an appeal, the value of supporting requests with evidence or rationale, etc.

Persuasive dyads. Students work in pairs. In each, one player has a special request or wishes to persuade the other to do or not to do something. Urge the persuader to present the argument in the best possible manner (based on the prior discussion). Ask the other to listen and respond to the extent that the persuader is truly persuasive. Some possible topics for this age group are these: a child trying to convince a parent to allow her or him to stay up late on a school night to see a special TV show; a little brother or sister asking to borrow an older sibling's favorite record, sweater, or bike; a child asking a peer for help with some project. Students may also enjoy some humorous situations in which they can practice persuasive techniques: a mouse who does not want to be a cat's dinner, a turkey pleading its case to a farmer just before Thanksgiving, a speeder and a police officer, an antique chair and an overweight "sitter."

Students are not as astute as adults in "reading" other people's nonverbal communication. Work in pantomime, particularly sequential pantomime games and pantomime guessing games are useful in focusing attention on body actions, gestures, and facial expressions. The following activity requires players to use their pantomime skills in communicating and to also read another's nonverbal behaviors.

■ OBSERVING NONVERBAL CUES

"I might have said that!" Divide the class into groups of five or six. Have each student draw a card with a character and a situation, for example: a dentist pulling a tooth, a baseball pitcher trying to strike out a batter, a child looking for a lost pet, a mother trying to coax a child to try a new food.

Working in the small groups, each person takes a turn pantomiming her or his character. When a person thinks he or she knows the character, *rather than guessing the role or situation,* that player offers a line of dialogue that the character might say. If the line is correct, everyone in the group quickly adds another appropriate line; if not, play continues until every player has offered a line. The characters might all be clustered around a theme or drawn from several pieces of literature familiar to the group. Themes to use include holidays, the circus, sporting events, celebrities, and related occupations such as the different categories of community helpers.

Doing the news. A class of later elementary students may first practice and then actually assume responsibility for providing the rest of the school with daily news and special announcements. To prepare for requesting to assume that responsibility, the class may role-play a newscast. Every student should be involved in both the practice role-playing and in handling some aspect of providing news, weather, and announcements for the building. Encourage communication-apprehensive students to participate; if they are unable to do so, assign them to writing scripts or other less threatening jobs.

Speaking and listening activities are often taught through integration with other content areas such as social studies and literature rather than as separate skills. Therefore, additional oracy activities are included in some of the following sections. One special area of study that integrates well with drama and deals directly with speaking and listening is foreign language study.

Drama and foreign language study

The kind of introductory work in a foreign language that is most often done in the later elementary grades integrates well with drama. Simulated conversations in which students practice foreign words and phrases as introduced in exploratory study can utilize a variety of drama skills: role-playing, pantomime, and the expressive use of the voice to complement the language and make it more communicative.

■ EXPLORING FOREIGN CULTURES

Students are often self-conscious about trying to pronounce words in another language with appropriate accents, inflections, and gestures. It is different, however, when they are speaking in the *role* of a member of a group who are native speakers of the language. The emphasis then is on the total communication, both verbal and nonverbal. This activity works well with students in pairs or small groups. It helps the self-conscious child become more risk-taking.

Moving to foreign verbs. Adding pantomime to pronunciation of verbs is useful when practicing foreign verbs just as it is with English work. The speech and movement complement one another, and the movement reinforces the meaning of the word. Later, students may add modifiers to the verbs as they practice common adverbs and adjectives. They will speak the phrase and move accordingly as they practice it several times.

■ ROLE-PLAYING FAMILIAR SITUATIONS

Introductory foreign language study in the elementary school may include learning about the customs and everyday lives of native speakers. Have students use selected vocabularies as they role-play ordering a meal; asking and giving directions to such places as shops, transportation depots, the post office; inquiring about the time or weather. To allow all students to practice at one time, divide the class into pairs or groups, with each choosing its own situation to play as long as it involves vocabulary words previously introduced.

Celebrations and festivals. Students can also employ a limited vocabulary as they recreate some historical event from a country where the language is spoken. This may focus on the celebration of a national holiday or an important festival. With a multiarts approach, the class may turn a simulated celebration of Bastille Day, *Cinco de Mayo,* or *Diaz y Siete de Septiembre,* into a special event. Parts of the celebration will be done with creative drama and enhanced with the addition of native songs, dances, and rituals. It is exciting to add such real-life embellishments as ethnic foods and beverages, songs, and artifacts. Decorating the room with appropriate flags, banners, etc., creates a stimulating setting.

This activity may become a multidisciplinary experience that combines foreign language study, history, geography, and cultural anthropology, as all are explored through drama. One of the most exciting and rewarding integrations of drama and a content area is with the breadth of subjects that comprise the social sciences.

DRAMA AND SOCIAL STUDIES

The chronological nature of history is a perfect match for several types of creative drama activities, particularly sequential pantomime and listening games and add-on scenes. History deals with actions, so almost any event can be translated into a sequential pantomime activity. A few possible topics for later elementary classes are these: the Great Explorations, the events that led to the Revolutionary War, the defense of the Alamo, the trek west to California or the adventures along the Oregon Trail, the Lewis and Clark Expedition, the exploration of the poles, the use of the "underground railroad" during the Civil War, the history of flight and space exploration, and the laying of the transcontinental railroad.

Drama and history

The following sequential pantomime could be used for the celebration of Columbus Day or as part of the story of the Great Explorations. The game is played as explained in chapter 3.

■ PARTICIPATING IN HISTORY THROUGH DRAMA

Columbus discovers a new world. This sequence game is designed for a maximum class size of 30 students, though fewer can play if you give some students a second card. Several of the segments are designed for small groups of players; the number in parentheses is a suggested number who can play that particular part.

1. (3) You begin. You are a sailor on the Santa Maria. You are scrubbing the deck with a big mop. The sea is very rough, and it is hard to do your job. Empty your mop pail over the side of the rolling ship. Return to your seat.

2. (1) After you see sailors mopping the deck of the ship, you are the cook. You are stirring a big pot of fish soup. Wait for others to join you, then give each of them a bowl of the soup. Return to your seat.

3. (3) You are a sailor. When you see the cook stirring a big pot of fish soup, join the cook. He will give you a bowl of soup. It is not very good. Show that you do not like it very much. Return to your seat.

4. (1) You are Christopher Columbus. When you see sailors eating their fish soup, go to the deck and look for land through your spy glass. Show that you do not see land and walk slowly back to your seat.

5. (1) After you see Columbus look for land through his spy glass and return to his seat, you are a sailor looking over the side of the ship. You see something in the water. You are very excited. Motion to other to come to see what you have found. Wait for others to join you and show them what you have found. Go back to your seat with them.

6. (5) When you see someone looking over the side of the ship and motioning to other sailors to come and see, be a sailor and go and see what was found. Crowd around the sailor who found something. Show how happy and excited you feel. Go back to your seat with the others.

7. (5) After several sailors have looked at something over the side of the ship, run out on deck and begin working the lines on the sails. Others will help you. Pull hard on the ropes. Go back to your seat with the others.

8. (1) You are a sailor. After you have seen other sailors pulling hard on the ropes that work the sails. go on deck and look through your spy glass. You see land. Show the others what you have discovered. Wait for others to join you. When they have, show them the land, then go back to your seat with them.

9. (4) You are a sailor. When you see someone point to land, run on deck. Show how excited and happy you are. Look toward the land and show others where it is. Return to your seat.

10. (1) After the sailors who were looking and pointing toward land have returned to their seats, be Christopher Columbus. Step out of your landing boat. Kneel down on the shore. Stay

until you are joined by your sailors. After someone shows a sign to the class, go back to your seat.

11. (4) You are a sailor. When you see Columbus step out of a landing boat and kneel down on the shore, join him and kneel down also. Stay until someone shows a sign to the class. Then go back to your seat.

12. (1) When you see Columbus and the sailors kneel down on the shore; while they are still kneeling, show the entire class your sign. Then return to your seat. Sign says:

OCTOBER 12, 1492

COLUMBUS REACHES THE NEW WORLD

AND

YOU WERE THERE!

(Teaching with Creative Dramatics, pp. 78-80)

History is, among other things, a record of famous persons, their deeds and times. Sequential listening games that highlight the lives of famous Americans, state and local founders, heroes of important battles, and men and women whose acts of courage or creativity have influenced the course of history are all excellent subjects for sequence activities, especially listening games. The following is a good example. Here, complete cards are shown for the first three segments only. From card 4 on, only the part to be read aloud is given. All cards for the students, however, must include both cue and action. (See chapter 3.)

EARLY LIFE OF GEORGE WASHINGTON

1. YOU BEGIN BY READING ALOUD: "George Washington was born in Virginia on February 22, 1732. His parents were Augustine and Mary Ball Washington."

2. After you hear, GEORGE WASHINGTON WAS BORN IN VIRGINIA ON FEBRUARY 22, 1732. HIS PARENTS WERE AUGUSTINE AND MARY BALL WASHINGTON, you read aloud: "When George Washington was born there was no country called the United States of America. Virginia was one of 13 colonies which belonged to England and was ruled by the King of England."

3. After you hear, WHEN GEORGE WASHINGTON WAS BORN THERE WAS NO COUNTRY CALLED THE UNITED STATES OF AMERICA. VIRGINIA WAS ONE OF 13 COLONIES WHICH BELONGED TO ENGLAND AND WAS RULED BY THE KING OF ENGLAND, you read aloud: "George Washington's great-grandfather had come to Virginia from England, and he had built a plantation near the seacoast. Away from the seacoast, the land was wilderness where Indian tribes lived."

4. "When George was a little boy, his family moved to another plantation on the Rappahonnock River. The plantation was called 'Ferry Farm.'"

5. "George Washington had three younger brothers and a sister. He also had two older half-brothers."

6. "Life on the plantation was very busy. Besides the main house where the Washington family lived, there were barns and shops of all kinds."

7. "Many people lived and worked on the plantation—blacksmiths, carpenters, shoemakers, people who spun yarn and wove cloth, candlemakers, and all of the men, women, and children who worked in the fields."

8. "Young George liked to explore the plantation, fish and swim in the river, pitch horseshoes, and watch the barges on the river."

9. "Every summer a big ship arrived from England bringing furniture, tools, clothes, and many other things. The ship took back to England the tobacco which was raised on Ferry Farm."

10. "George Washington loved to watch the ship unloading and loading. He listened to the captain giving orders, and thought he would like to be a captain on a big ship when he grew up."

11. "Young George did not go to school like children today. His teachers came to the plantation to teach him to read, write, spell, and do arithmetic."

12. "There are many stories about George Washington when he was a little boy. The best known one is about George and the cherry tree."

13. "Another favorite story is about young George and his mother's favorite colt. The colt was very frisky and hard to ride. One day George decided he would ride the colt and make it behave."

14. "The colt began to buck and jump, but George did not fall off. Finally the colt gave a big leap and fell down dead. It had broken a vein. George knew he had done a foolish thing, but he went to the house and told his mother."

15. "Even though his mother was sad about the colt, she was glad George had been brave and told her the truth."

16. "When George was about ten, his two half-brothers came back from England where they had gone to study. George listened to his brother Lawrence tell of his adventures when he had fought for England in the war with Spain."

17. "George especially liked the stories about Lawrence's brave commander, Admiral Vernon."

18. "George liked to play that he was a captain in the army. He and his friends played soldiers with cornstalks for muskets. They drilled up and down in a vacant field."

19. "When George was 11, his father died. His father left most of his property to his oldest son, Lawrence."

20. "Lawrence soon married, and he rebuilt the house on the largest family plantation on the Potomac River It had been called 'Hunting Creek,' but Lawrence renamed it 'Mount Vernon' after his commander in England."

21. "After his father died, George knew he would not be going to England to school like his older brothers. He went to a new school in Virginia and studied hard."

22. "When George was 14, he began to plan for his future. He wanted to go to sea and become a naval officer. He was all set to sail for England."

(*Teaching with Creative Dramatics*, pp. 53-55)

Later elementary students may enjoy creating their own sequence game after they are familiar with the format. As a writing activity, it provides practice in organizing in sequential order.

Historical add-ons. A famous or significant historical event may start with only a few people involved. Others join in as the situation escalates, takes on greater importance, or the

problem grows. Add-on pantomimes (with or without improvised speech) work well to recreate a piece of history through
experiential learning. Discoveries of all kinds are one category that fits this format well: the discovery of gold in Alaska
or California, silver in Colorado, oil in Texas and Oklahoma,
rich farm lands in the Midwest, open ranges in the prairie
lands were all events that began with the arrival of just a few
explorers or adventurers and attracted more and more folks
to that place.

■ DISCOVERING LOCAL HISTORY

Settling a community makes an excellent basis for an add-on.
This may begin by "building a place" to establish the setting. One or
two persons or families come and settle. Soon others join them;
churches are built; a school is opened; a newspaper begun; shops
and tradespeople arrive to join the growing population; a doctor
and dentist open practices. Students can use their developing skills
in building characters to research and recreate well-known early
settlers. They may also create all of the folks who are not recorded
specifically but who also came and made important contributions to
the growth and development of the community.

Giving these roles unique personalities, various motivations and
points-of-view, talents and needs makes these roles satisfying to
portray. This activity may or may not involve a conflict beyond the
struggles of people engaged in carving out a community from
unsettled lands.

To do this well requires students to become familiar with their
own community's past. It would be fun to do after visiting a local
history museum, looking at early architecture, exploring an old
cemetery as a group, or interviewing older residents and obtaining
some oral history.

Dramatizing historical fiction. In addition to history as it is
presented in textbooks, many excellent pieces of historical
fiction are well researched, based in a specific time and place,
and deal with real events but use fictional characters to tell

the story. Examples of historical fiction with strong appeal to students in grades 4-6 include these: *Can't You Make Them Behave, King George?* (Fritz, 1977) and *Johnny Tremain* (Forbes, 1944), two books about the Revolutionary War; *Cyrus Holt and the Civil War* (Hall, 1964) and *A Gathering of Days: A New England Girl's Journal* (Blos, 1979) set before the Civil War but concerned with slavery; *The Tilted Sombrero* (Lampman, 1966) about the Mexican War of Independence; *Squaw Man's Son* (1978) and *Once Upon the Little Big Horn* (1971) also by Evelyn Lampman that focus on real events involving Native Americans; and the several "Little House" books by Laura Ingalls Wilder. The latter are autobiographical but read as fictional stories. All of these offer exciting scenes to play and interesting characters to develop. Important historical events can also come alive through people who *might* have shared in the experiences.

■ VISITING OTHER LANDS THROUGH DRAMA

Drama and geography

Whether an event took place in this country or is some far corner of the world, it always involves a setting and specific groups of people. The story dramatizations of literature (both fiction and nonfiction) that are set in various locales and reveal the lives and customs of other peoples help students experience geography rather than simply read about it. A breadth of excellent fare that appeals to later elementary students is available. Several titles in the appendices to this book can be used in conjunction with the story of lands and peoples around the world. Some additional titles for specific regions of study include the following. *Shadow of a Bull* (Wojciechowski, 1964) is set in the Andalusian region of Spain and deals insightfully with bull fighting and a child's cowardice and ultimate courage. *The Wheel on the School* (DeJong, 1954) is set in Holland; it beautifully pictures the unusual topography of that country. *The Forever Christmas Tree* (Uchida, 1963) is set in Japan and shows the traditional reverence of the Japanese for the elderly. *The Spider, the Cave, and the Pottery Bowl* (Clymer, 1971) shares many aspects of a Native American child's heritage. *Makasa* (Nagenda, 1973) the story of an African child's life as an educated member of his tribe, is set in Uganda.

Other activities that use drama to reinforce learning in geography include these: a sidecoached narrative pantomime to explore various terrains and natural topographical features such as moving as nomadic peoples over a desert, touring Mammoth Cave, exploring a glacier; using pantomime to create a special environment; using small groups to showcase different lifestyles around the world as different peoples engage in similar activities such as farming, traveling, or going to school; and organizing character panels in which each participant assumes the role of a travel agent who describes the attributes of a particular country or part of the world to encourage tourists to visit.

Experiencing population density. Begin this activity as described in chapter 3, with students exploring what can be done in self-space, in shared space, and in space combined with other pairs. Next, have the groups combine so that there are eight players in each group, using the combined space of eight individuals. Each then discusses some activity they can pantomime in the larger space. This generally requires some discussion and planning. Groups often develop some kind of organized game to pantomime.

Finally, instruct some groups to leave their space and move into the space of another group. The "invaded" groups should be careful not to expand their space to accommodate the newcomers. Now the enlarged groups should invent something they can do. It will probably take even more discussion and planning to come up with an activity that satisfies everyone (or most): majority rules. Allow sufficient time for the discussion and some beginning participation in the activity before calling "time."

To conclude the activity, have students sit down where they were when time was called. This should create islands of empty space but also groups crowded into small amounts of space.

Have students talk about how they felt when they were working in self-space, shared space, and in the large combined space. Discuss the kinds of activities they pantomimed in each. Take particular note of the planning for the activities in the combined space. Typical observations and comments might be these: "More people sharing space generally requires more planning. Did everyone have an equal chance to be heard? If not, how did those people feel? Did you plan activities that included some 'rules' for participation? Why do you suppose that happened?"

Finally, ask the groups that had to give up their space and move in with others how they felt. Compare their experiences and feelings with situations in which people must give up where they are (Native American tribes, for example, who were moved off their lands and onto reservations; evacuation of Japanese-Americans during World War II; others as related to their knowledge and/or information provided in class). Discuss how the original "owners" felt when others moved into their space and wanted to join their activities. Talk about what happens in neighborhoods when more and more people move in bringing with them their belongings, interests, needs, etc., but no additional space. Discuss ways to help both those who were already there and the newcomers to recognize each other's feelings, needs, and frustrations. Have the class suggest ways to deal with the human problems involved.

■ COMBINING MULTI-SUBJECTS THROUGH DRAMA

Drama/speech/geography/history/political science. This culminating activity is planned and carried out over several class periods. It incorporates several areas of social studies as well as drama and speech. It is incorporated into the story of colonial America, the events that led up to the Revolutionary War, the issues and personalities involved. The final product is a recreation of the Continental Congress.

Each student chooses a role, researches to discover as much as possible about the person's point-of-view, background, etc. You will want to be sure that the leading characters are covered and that different perspectives will be provided. The class, as a whole, carefully studies the issues, factions, etc. When students are ready to convene, call the Congress together and serve as leader and guide for the discussions.

DRAMA AND SCIENCE EDUCATION

The experiential nature of both drama and science make for easy and rewarding integration. Simulation through drama may also help some students understand and retain scientific information, concepts, and procedures. Students' need to be aware of and to use their bodies in drama can be combined with learning about how their bodies function; integrating drama and health education may utilize a variety of drama skills.

Drama and health education

The following is a pantomime/creative movement activity that can help children better understand a complex biological system.

■ REINFORCING HEALTHFUL PRACTICES

Exploring the cardiovascular system. Assign students different roles. Several work together to create the heart as the left ventricle opens to receive arterial blood and then contracts to drive it into the aorta; others form the right ventricle that receives venous blood from the right atrium and then drives it into the pulmonary artery. Several others make both large and small "bridges" that represent arteries and blood vessels. The rest of the players become the blood cells and move (as you sidecoach them) through the system.

The activity may be accompanied by a beat on the tambourine, indicating a slowing or speeding of the heart action. Later, have students demonstrate how their bodies function if there is some breakdown (a clogged artery or a bleeding vessel as a result of a wound) in the system. As a follow-up, students might write a short story about the journey, or letters to their "person" urging certain behaviors such as proper diet, exercise, etc., to make their journeys safe and dependable.

■ PANTOMIMING HEALTH-PRODUCING ACTIVITIES

Drama can be used to practice good eating habits, daily exercise, and dental hygiene. Students can create their own small group scenes to show either good or bad health habits. Following the several presentations, the class can compare and discuss those activities that contribute to good health and those that do not. You can prepare activity cards for each group that suggests what they demonstrate or have the groups show a positive or negative activity of lifestyle in their scene.

Safety procedures

Later elementary children generally have more freedom to go further from home, work with various tools, and otherwise begin to engage in activities that have different elements of danger than those to which younger boys and girls are exposed. Proper safety procedures can often be practiced using pantomime. In addition to discussing the more ordinary situations in which these students need to be able to work and play safely, you may want to do some situation role-playing related to such hazards as drug and alcohol abuse. Whether discussed as part of the science program or generated by literature or news events, the use of socio-drama is an effective way to explore the dangers and learn ways to protect oneself from involvement.

Drama and the world around

Other areas of science can also be integrated with drama or taught by using drama skills. Special areas of study may include ecology, astronomy, and an introductory look at scientific methodology (doing things like setting up an experiment, doing careful observations, keeping accurate records, etc.). The sequential nature of much scientific investigation and application also fits with sequence activities in drama. The pantomime game in chapter 3, for example, deals with landing on the moon; the sequential listening game in chapter 4 gives an overview of the history of energy.

The following activity uses pantomime and creative movement to simulate the behaviors of gas molecules in a confined space under different conditions. It is based on an idea from Barb Diol, a classroom teacher.

Magic molecules. Prepare cards, mark half of them "molecules" and the other half "side cells." Have masking tape available. As a warm-up, have students imagine themselves shrinking until they each fit inside a pop bottle full of fizzy pop. While in the bottle, each person is to "catch" a bubble and explore its shape and notice how it feels. Next, with eyes closed, each person imagines shrinking into a bubble. Again the sides of this new container are explored. Players move slowly as they explore and show how they would interact with another bubble. This can be done to a ten-count freeze. They are reminded to move slowly and carefully without damaging other bubbles.

As the next step, everyone becomes part of a bubble using the "molecule" and "side cell" cards you provide. The cards are randomly distributed with half the students as molecules and half as side cells. The cards are taped to each player to identify her or his role. The "side cells" make a big circle by clasping hands; the "molecules" are to be inside this big circle. The molecules, to a slow ten-count, move about very slowly. Remind them to interact with the side cells as they move because the amount of air pressure depends on this interaction. Students should try to move at the same speed and in a methodical manner.

Next, the molecules are to respond to a change in the bubble. It is heating up; the pop is setting in a warm place. To a count of ten, the side cells should move out until only their fingers touch. The molecules are to rebound more frequently off the side cells demonstrating increased pressure.

Finally, suggest that students reduce the pressure inside the bubble. Tell them to cool the bubble by putting the bottle of pop in the refrigerator. To a count of ten, the side cells move toward the center until their shoulders touch. To a slow ten-count, the molecules should slow down their rebounding. After each change in the bubble, students may discuss what they have observed about the behavior of molecules in environments with more or less pressure; how the bubble responded to heat, cold, etc. to reinforce the concepts involved, the players may exchange cards and replay the activity.

You can also combine verbalizing activities with science. The following activity might be used with either a history or science lesson for the study of great inventions and their creators is both history and science.

■ USING ROLE-PLAYING IN SCIENCE

Inventor's round table. Each member of the panel researches and role-plays her or his famous inventor. The balance of the class, as a group, brainstorms an extensive list of questions they may wish to put to the panel. When everyone is ready to play, the panel functions as a symposium with you as chair. Each inventor has five minutes to talk about her or his invention. (Be sure the panel is as multicultural as possible with both women and minority scientists represented.) Following the short presentations, the chair (you) takes questions from the "audience."

This activity can be done with great leaders, humanitarians, literary figures, artists and composers, adventurers, etc. or a panel of renowned scientists such as Marie Curie, Jonas Salk, and George Washington Carver.

DRAMA AND GROWING UP

Almost by definition, participation in creative drama provides assistance to the emerging adolescent. The subjective involvement with literature explores a range of values as characters express, through words and actions, their points-of-view. Students are encouraged to try on different ways to think, feel, and be. The events, particularly the conflicts presented and resolved, afford experiences in handling the challenges of life. The judicious use of situational role-playing allows students to explore optional views and responses to the problems of growing up in their culture. Exposure to drama as both participants and audience provides a kind of catharsis as feelings are explored and expressed.

■ GAINING COORDINATION AND GRACE

In addition, the "doing" nature of drama requires students to be aware of their own bodies and to use them as important parts of their communication behaviors. One of the special ways that drama can contribute to growing up is through the use of movement and pantomime to help students gain and maintain coordination and grace.

Drama and physical education

Drama activities, particularly those that emphasize rhythmic movement and body awareness and discipline, are often integrated with physical education. Although students in grades 4-6 enjoy the competitive nature of games and sports, they should also be striving to develop coordination and grace. This is true for all students, not just those with natural athletic abilities or a talent for dance. It may, in fact, be particularly important for those who seem to have "two left feet." Sometimes it is easier for students to show coordination and graceful movement when they are in roles rather than when being themselves, particularly if they see themselves as awkward.

Using in-place pantomime to develop and practice roles that require coordination, grace, or athletic prowess makes a good warm-up before moving interactively with others. The following is a sample exercise that stresses body discipline through the invention of various roles.

Getting into shape(s). To a count of ten, have students assume the following roles, giving special attention to the shape of the body and the physical stance: a world class diver poised at the end of the high diving board; a downhill skier waiting for the "gun" in the Winter Olympics; a batter getting ready to hit a home run in the World Series; a champion figure skater bringing a brilliant performance to a dramatic finish; a tennis player serving an "ace" to win the Wimbledon Lawn Tennis Matches; a famous gymnast finishing a prize-winning routine.

Other drama activities to emphasize coordination and grace include these: playing imaginary sports to music while varying the speed from double-time to slow motion on cue; creating machines with the bodies and running them at various speeds; doing a scene and repeating it with the jerky movements of a silent film; creating fantasy characters with the body and maintaining the shape while moving to a beat.

Multiarts expression

Combining the fine arts is another way to accommodate different students' needs, preferences, and abilities. Creative drama, like all theatre, is an excellent place to pull all of the arts together to enhance one another. This also provides optional ways for self-expression. The communication-apprehensive student, for example, may find it easier to express through movement and pantomime, dance, art, or music than to improvise dialogue or read aloud in a readers theatre presentation. The learning disabled student who is not able to read at or near grade level often does very well in one or more of the arts.

It is very important for early adolescent children to feel that they belong. Drama, especially in combination with the other arts, offers every student a variety of ways to contribute and participate. This is equally true for all special children as well—from the educable mentally impaired to the talented and gifted, and including those with physical and/or emotional handicaps.

CREATIVE DRAMA WITH SPECIAL STUDENTS

By the time special children are in grades 4-6, most have come to accept their differences and to function, in most ways, as normally as possible. In addition, however, they have a strong need to be a part of the group, to relate and interact with their peers, and to feel accepted by them. Where special children have received the kind of extra help they deserve, they often require (or expect) little special treatment. However, their peers in the regular classroom may require extra help in order to recognize that differently-abled students are in most all ways like them, whatever their differences. These attitudes are critical in the classroom with mainstreamed children.

■ SENSITIZING OTHERS TO SPECIAL PEOPLE

Creative drama, including the dramatization of literature that deals with handicaps and special people, can provide all students with deeper understanding, sensitivity, and appreciation for the multiplicity of the human condition. Work with characterization that strives to reduce stereotyping promotes greater understanding. So, too, do opportunities to see and hear handicapped artists perform.

Perhaps only a few students will have an opportunity to see the wonderful work of the National Theatre of the Deaf, but most are familiar with the talents of Stevie Wonder and Ray Charles. You can also point out, at appropriate times, that there are many famous people in all areas of life who have made remarkable contributions to humanity through their intellectual and/or artistic contributions. Others have modelled great courage, patience, and spirit. Use some of these examples as a basis for scenes to play. The following are biographies of people with whom later elementary students can relate. All have possibilities for drama, particularly with the older students in grades 4-6.

Axline, Virginia. *Dibs in Search of Self.* Boston: Houghton-Mifflin, 1965. The trials and ultimate triumph of an emotionally impaired child.

Bigland, Eileen. *Helen Keller.* New York: S.G. Phillips, 1967. An excellent telling of the life of a most unusual child who grew up to become an internationally admired woman.

Haskins, James. *The Story of Stevie Wonder.* New York: Dell (paperback), 1976. The story of a contemporary blind black singer enjoyed and admired by children and adults

■ MAKING EVERY STUDENT A PLAYER

When physically or emotionally handicapped children are mainstreamed into the regular classroom, include them in all of the drama activities. Often they find their own ways to adapt or adjust to an exercise; however, you should anticipate and make it easier for special students to take part. They can often make special contributions derived from their own experiences.

Hearing-impaired students, especially those with speech and language difficulties, are often talented nonverbal communicators. It is not unusual to find that they have advanced skills in pantomime and are excited to participate.

Visually impaired students, in contrast, are often very verbal and enjoy the verbalizing activities including the invention of spontaneous speech. A visually impaired student can serve as narrator for a story theatre production as others perform the actions. However, you should encourage partially sighted students to participate in movement and pantomime. Working in pairs provides each student with a buddy and instills confidence. Even the mirror game is possible when the partners put palms together or lightly touch fingertips and move in time to the music.

Orthopedically handicapped students can often substitute one kind of movement for another. Arms, hands, and fingers can interpret music, give physical qualities to a character and explore an invented environment when legs cannot. Creative drama in grades 4-6 provide such a variety of ways to participate, especially in more advanced work, that there are always ways to include everyone.

Creative drama is never more *creative* than when you find ways to integrate in a multitude of ways—by incorporating holistic learning, by integrating drama and subject materials, and by providing opportunities for all students to contribute to the experience in their own unique ways. When you emphasize the importance of each person's participation, the drama is enhanced and each student feels valued.

CHAPTER 7

Creative Drama and Mass Entertainment

Breathes there a child, particularly one about to enter that best of times/worst of times known as "adolescence" who can possibly imagine a world without television, movies, AM/FM radio, and cassette players? Yet, it was not so very long ago that many American children did not see or hear much in the way of mass entertainment beyond the occasional movie, radio programs and records that seemed to appeal more to parents than to youth, and whatever live performance they were fortunate enough to see at school. Today's children, however, live "knee deep" in the products of the electronics revolution—with everything from personal computers to wide-screen movies presented in stereophonic sound.

■ LOOKING AT THE ROLE OF TV

From amongst this astonishing array of media products, one stands out not only as the captor of children's time and attention, but perhaps of their childhood as well. The age of television heralded a new era of mass entertainment for everyone, particularly for children and youth. Almost overnight, in the historical scheme of things, nearly every child in the country—rich, poor, urban, suburban, or rural—became a major consumer of not just plays and entertainment designed for children, but theatre of all sorts produced for people of all ages, backgrounds, and tastes. Media ecologist Neil Postman, in *The Disappearance of Childhood* (1982), declares that, "So far as symbolic form is concerned, 'Laverne and Shirley' is as simple to grasp as 'Sesame Street'; a McDonald's commercial as simple to grasp as a Xerox commercial.

Which is why, in truth, there is no such thing on TV as children's programming. Everything is for everybody" (p. 79). And Postman predicts that this may spell the disappearance of childhood, at least as we have come to view it. As you listen to and watch children, it is not too difficult to see his point.

As a teacher, you may sometimes feel that the one greatest competition for the minds, time, and allegiance of your students is the "tube." There is certainly data to support that concern. According to *Encyclopedia Britannica* (1980), 40 percent of the world's television sets are in the United States. And these TV sets are used: "at any given moment in prime time, approximately 38 million sets are turned on" (Charren and Sandler, *Changing Channels,* 1983, p. 22). The figures continue to climb as more homes have cable, own videocassette recorders, and subscribe to additional programming.

A study conducted by Comstock et al. *(Television and Human Behavior,* 1978) reported that the heaviest viewers are children eight through twelve who average 2½ hours per day (8-year-olds) to 4 (12-year-olds). In a study by Lyle and Hoffman (1972), "Television in Day-to-Day Life: Patterns of Use," results indicated that 25 percent of the sixth-graders in the study watched television for 8½ hours on Sunday and 5½ hours on school days. The amount of television viewing varies widely; however, some children are certainly heavy viewers even by adult standards. Whether specific children are light, moderate, or heavy viewers, television consumption in the United States is a fact of life—one that can be turned into either a "prince" or a "frog" depending on how we decide to use, or ignore, its influence.

CHILDREN, CREATIVE DRAMA, AND TELEVISION

That television is the single greatest source of exposure to the theatre arts is as true for children as for adults. It would, therefore, seem to follow that theatre arts education must recognize and consider not only the influence of television on children in the broader sense but also as it specifically impacts on a child's understanding of theatre. Whether you approach the integration of drama and television from a perspective of "if you can't beat 'em, join 'em" or because you see possibilities for using television as a source for enriching drama, there can be some excellent consequences.

■ USING TV TO ENRICH DRAMA CONTENT

Many fine programs on television (both commercial and public) can be used as a basis for a drama lesson. The superbly done wildlife shows, for example, can provide the location and inspiration for a narrative pantomime adventure through a special environment. Integrated with a science lesson, the information and inspiration of such programming can provide a basis for group scenes about ecological concerns and issues. Combined with a variety of books from the library dealing with the same or similar topic, the inclusion of the TV show as part of the background for dramatization reinforces the notion that television and books can complement each other. It is antithetical to our purposes to communicate that it is a television versus books world.

Teachers who keep abreast of TV offerings can integrate television viewing into a lesson by planning ahead and suggesting specific shows to watch, but you lose your advantage if you recommend programs that are pedantic or dull. This means that you do your homework; you become an astute viewer and actually spend time watching programming that is either aimed at the child audience or that draws a large viewership of children.

■ DEMYSTIFYING THE MEDIA THROUGH DRAMA

You can learn much about children by listening to them and noting what they draw from TV, particularly during creative drama work. For example, TV characters can be used as a basis for character analysis—identifying stereotypes, flat and rounded, dynamic or static characters. You can discuss how the actor prepares and compare this to how students develop their own roles in creative drama. Saturday "kidvid" can be used as the basis for analyzing dramatic structure. What shows have episodic plots, progressive action, or a combination of both? What are the most usual types of conflict? Students can compare those programs that are totally predictable in terms of outcomes with those that offer surprises, and discuss which is more satisfying.

The more students understand about television production and programming, the easier it is for them to put it in proper perspective. Later elementary students are cognitively ready to understand some basic elements of television production. Drama, combined with literature, music, art, science, or social studies, can provide the catalyst to encourage students to create their own television shows.

■ PLANNING A TV PROGRAM

Have students form small groups and have each group create an idea for a television show that the group feels would appeal to viewers like themselves. They should discuss whether it would be a special or a series, cartoon or live, etc. Give them 15 minutes to come up with an idea and 5 more minutes to plan how to "sell" their idea to a prospective producer or sponsor.

Each group then gives a presentation with the rest of the class serving as the potential producer or sponsor. When all groups have shared, discuss the merits of each proposal.

As a class, choose one idea, and in the small groups, write a *treatment* for the show or first segment of a series. (A treatment is a short summary of the basic story and action in the show. It is written as if one were actually viewing the production.) The different treatments can be shared and compared.

The treatment activity can be followed by having each group (or the entire class) produce a *storyboard.* (A storyboard is a series of pictures showing consecutive segments that follows the action in the treatment. It might be compared to each blocking segment in a play director's Prompt Book.) If students wish, they can paste the segments of the storyboard in sequential order on a long roll of paper. Each end is then fastened to a roller so that as the story unfolds, the preceding segment is rolled up.

Presenting the story one frame at a time (through an opening cut in a cardboard box) simulates the separate frames that create a movie or television show. Music and sound effects can be added.

Students can serve as voice-over storytellers; or if they are experienced with improvised dialogue, they can actually speak for the characters in each picture. This activity utilizes drama skills and offers an experiential comparison between the making of a television show and doing live performance.

■ LEARNING TV TALK

Students enjoy creating the kind of storyboard show just described, but they may also want to incorporate knowledge about television cameras and how they are used to provide different kinds of shots to enhance the telling. For example, the first frame shows the setting for the story, the "establishing shot"; subsequent pictures will show faces close-up, midrange, or panoramic scenes, etc. Students love to learn the technical language of the television experts and use it in making their TV shows. They can assume various roles, and use the correct titles for each job.

For assistance with technical terms and job descriptions, you can find all you need, and more, in the excellent glossaries provided in *Getting the Most Out of TV* (Singer et al. 1981). Later, students may actually work with a videotape machine or super-8mm camera to turn a story dramatization into their own television special.

■ DISTINGUISHING BETWEEN REALITY AND FANTASY

Drama activities can be used to help children further distinguish between reality and fantasy on television programs. For example, when students create their own sound effects to accompany their play would be a good time to talk about how sound effects are produced to make television programming more believable and exciting. Working with imaginary cameras doing different lengths and angles of shots provides opportunities to discuss how these techniques are used to make things look smaller or bigger than they really are and how the camera can make faraway things look very close. If students have made their own TV show using pictures on a roller, this could be compared to animated films and contrasted with their own drama when they do it "live."

Students may enjoy the challenge of creating an animated cartoon segment, and there are some excellent films that show how animations are done. *Gene Deitch: The Picture Book*

Animated (1977) shows the animator making several films based on popular picture books. Seeing the artists at work vividly impresses the reader with how the drawings are done to fool the eye.

■ EXPLORING HOW TV CREATES ILLUSIONS

The following activity suggests another way of exploring how television appears to turn fantasy into reality.

Eye games. Begin by discussing how television cameras are used to emphasize, clarify, and distort reality. Talk about close-ups, long shots, use of tilt (up or down), zooming in and out, and wide-angle lenses, for example. Encourage students to offer examples from their own viewing.

Ask for volunteers to dramatize a scene showing a rescue of some kind—a cat from a tree or a helicopter attempting to rescue people adrift in a disabled boat. Give the players a few minutes to plan the scene while the rest of the class continues to discuss ways to use the cameras. In addition to describing different types and lengths of shots, discuss how cameras can shoot in slow motion or speed up action for clarification or effect. Have students play the scene.

Afterward, the class can discuss how a camera crew might shoot the scene to make it look the most exciting and dramatic, or how they might shoot it to give the most clear and accurate portrayal. Explore what aspects might be played up or down depending on the desired effect, how they would begin the scene and end the shooting.

Drama can provide other ways of reinforcing the role that special effects and theatre techniques play in making make-believe look real in movies and television. For special drama events, it is always fun to add some trimming: properties, bits of costuming, face painting or makeup. (See the Special Drama Event section of chapter 8.)

This would be an excellent time to explore how actors in movies and on television are made to look like different characters, including fantasy and nonhuman ones. It helps children to further separate reality from fantasy when they understand that under the makeup, wigs, and costumes are ordinary people. If students have been backstage at a live performance, they have seen players up close in makeup and costumes. However, the camera can do even more to change the appearance: for example, an actor of ordinary stature can become a giant if the camera is tilted up from a low position. The camera can also be used to manipulate the size of properties and create various unusual effects with sets and scenery. Leading children into an understanding of how things are done will not destroy their enjoyment of movies and television; it can, however, help to demystify the media.

■ PUTTING TV VIOLENCE IN ITS PLACE

Many of the folk and fairy tales used in drama contain fight scenes and other violent acts. Adventure stories, so popular with later elementary students, may include battle scenes or terrifying situations for the protagonist. When students are discussing how to show these events and actions in their own drama without actually hurting one another is a time to discuss how actors and stunt performers create violent scenes. This might include talking about how natural disasters are created and filmed, fights are simulated, and cars crashed in a multitude of ways. This is also a time to talk about what television does not generally show—the consequences of violence and tragedy.

■ SENSITIZING THROUGH GUIDED IMAGERY

The following activity is suggested for children who are sufficiently mature to handle the experience and later discuss it with sensitivity.

Visualizing the consequences of violence. Begin by posing such questions as "Is the real world more or less violent than the world according to television?" Next, discuss a variety of violent acts regularly depicted on television. Pick one type of TV violence (e.g. car crashes). Have the students close their eyes and use their visualizing skills. Sidecoach as follows:

In your mind's eye, see a car driving along a country road at a high rate of speed. At a curve, the driver loses control and the car sails through the air. It crashes into a tree and comes to a sudden stop with wheels still turning. See the people in the car bounce around inside or fly out of the car on impact. See the terror on the faces. See how their bodies hit and bounce. Maybe they are bleeding. Next, see the victims bandaged, in casts, and so forth. Imagine how the injuries really feel and how the people cannot resume a normal life until the injuries heal.

Afterwards, compare the real-life consequences with television and movie scenes in which victims walk away without a scratch, often looking quite neat and clean. Talk about students' memory of such programming when they were younger, compared with their perceptions and attitudes now. End with a discussion of stunts vs. real-life violence.

The following are additional activities appropriate to use with students who are interested in knowing and doing more with television.

Talking back to TV. Using the one-liner technique, have all students think of one line of dialogue they would like to say to any television personality, real or fictional. The line may be a question, a comment, a compliment, or a criticism.

Each student begins her or his statement by addressing the TV character or personality to whom the remarks are directed. For example, "Mr. Cosby, I like the way you take time to listen to your kids on your show," or "Ms. Newscaster (use name), how do you decide what events should be reported on the six o'clock news?"

Move around the group, allowing each child one offering. Afterward, discuss the one-way nature of television communication and how that differs from face-to-face communication when people have a chance to interact with one another and their ideas.

■ EXAMINING CHOICES

Our Emmy Awards . . . a class act. Select the categories the class wishes to honor. Possible categories are these: Best Saturday Cartoon, Best Comedy Series, Best Actor or Actress in a Show Kids Like, Best Musical Show, Best Prime Time Show with Appeal to Children, Best TV Commercial, Best Special for Children. Limit the categories to six or eight.

A week prior to the Awards, each student nominates a show or performer in each category via a secret ballot. The class elects a committee to take the nominations and make final selections. Using the information received, the committee must come to consensus for each selection and should be prepared to give a rationale for each choice.

Slips are then prepared that contain the names of all nominees, plus a sufficient number of other television personalities so that everyone in the class (except members of the committee) draws a "role slip." Each person should be prepared to give a few words of acceptance should he or she be a winner.

On the day of the Awards, the committee present their choices. Members of the committee may also role-play a celebrity as they present and give a short summary of the outstanding features of each choice. Celebrities and shows honored are represented by those in the audience who drew corresponding role slips.

As the announcements are made, the winners come forward, say a few words, and accept their awards. After the show, the class discusses the choices made. As a special art project, the class might hold a contest to design and name its own awards contest.

■ APPLYING TECHNICAL SKILLS

Videotaping a class play. Students enjoy actually learning how to use video cameras to film a *short* piece of drama. If it is not feasible for students to use school equipment (or it is not available for students), you or the media specialist could do the filming. The finished product would then be viewed and critiqued by the class.

Variation. Use a movie camera to film small group improvisations based on a genre of literature (for example, fables, legends, or scenes based on poems by a favorite writer).

Variation. Students can film a polished puppet play using super-8mm cameras. Record any musical background and the dialogue and narration on a tape recorder. A 35mm camera can also be used. Instead of processing the film as separate slides, have it processed as a filmstrip. This requires a filmstrip projector that accommodates 35mm film.

Imagining a world without TV. Ask the class to imagine a world without TV, radio, movies, etc. Talk about the role of the media in their lives. Brainstorm as many ideas as possible that reflect ways that each person's life is influenced by media, especially television.

In small groups, dramatize something people do as a direct result of exposure to media. (Remind the players that it is "no fair" to simply show people sitting and watching television!) Afterward, discuss how students might live their lives differently if it were not for mass media.

Drama and tv advertising

No discussion of later elementary students and media, especially television, would be complete without a look at TV advertising. On the one hand, later elementary students think very much like adults. They can hypothesize, predict, and relate cause and effect. These abilities to think in a more mature way ought to make them less vulnerable to shabby or distorted advertising. On the other hand, they are at the beginning age and stage of intense peer pressure and the concomitant need to be accepted, to "belong."

Drama skills can be used to help students understand that the purpose of advertising, whether in electronic or printed media, is to make a person feel a need and to then satisfy the perceived need by buying the seller's product. Studies by Ward, Reale, and Levinson (1972) and Ward and Wackman (1972) confirm that by age eleven most children have become cynical about the purpose and credibility of commercials. By that age, children suspect the motives and feel they are often lied to by advertisers (Liebert et al., *The Early Window*, 1982, pp. 96-99). Creating their own commercials can help students recognize the constructive side of advertising and deal with the ethical issues involved.

The following activities include suggested grade levels.

■ USING DRAMA TO EXPLORE ADVERTISING

New products with a prop. (grade 6) Divide the class into small groups. Give each group an item from the properties box. The item should not be a commercial product of any kind. The groups have five minutes to turn their props into new products, give them names, and decide their uses.

On the board, list different kinds of appeals: to a sense of well-being (safety, physical or mental health), economic (saves you money or helps you to make money), pleasure (entertains or makes life more fun), popularity (makes a person more attractive, well liked, or admired).

Have each group create and share a television commercial for their product that incorporates at least one type of appeal. The follow-up discussion should explore whether the appeals seemed ethical, honest and valid.

"But first, this message." (grade 4 or 5) Divide the class into small groups. Give each group a card that describes a machine to make, using bodies and sounds. Samples might be a machine to plant and weed a garden, a "homework machine," a machine that cleans your room, a machine that clears the table, etc.

The groups have 15 minutes to cooperatively create their machines. In addition, they should give the machine a name that will "sell" and list six reasons why children their age should urge their parents to purchase the machine (or why they should save their money to buy it for themselves). (Experienced players may develop and dramatize commercials for their products complete with catchy slogans, jingles, premium offers, and/or endorsements by famous people.)

After all have presented, the class will discuss whether each product seemed fairly and honestly presented and the different strategies used to persuade.

Cleaning up a commercial. As a class, watch and analyze several commercials on television, especially ones aimed at young consumers. Identify the appeals in each and rate them in terms of integrity and clarity. Choose one or two that the class feels do not measure up to their standards of ethical advertising. Have students, in small groups, create their own commercials for the same products. Share and discuss what they changed and why.

Television as a resource

Several excellent publications offer ideas for utilizing children's high levels of involvement with television and turning this to positive use in the class. (See appendixes.) Many of the suggestions can be combined with drama work; nearly all incorporate television viewing and/or production with the several content areas.

In addition to printed resources, many television stations are equipped to send personnel to the schools to talk with elementary students and teachers. This kind of public relations is an important component of the public service commitment required of television stations and is, therefore, provided free of charge to the schools. Some stations may also conduct tours of their facilities, where students can see a television show being made. In many places, there is also a community access station where the classes could actually air a program of their own creation and production.

It seems shortsighted to lament or ignore the important role that television plays in the lives of children as a source of information and entertainment. Television affords the single most direct encounter with the theatre arts available to most people, and as educators we are wise to seek constructive ways to capitalize on the love relationship that exists between many of our students and television.

CHILDREN AND OTHER MASS ENTERTAINMENT

Although television is without question the number one entertainment medium of children, many children are also avid consumers of a variety of other media. In addition to the many movies they see on television, including those not rated for child audiences, many boys and girls regularly attend movies at theatres.

Movies vs. television. Sometimes there is a movie that nearly everyone has seen that is also shown on television. Have students watch both versions and compare how a movie produced for the large screen translates to the television format. What works well and what does not? After the class has dramatized a story, they might talk about how it might be done as a movie made for large screen and compare with how it might be done for television.

Later elementary students often own their own radios, record players, and audio cassette players. The proliferation of relatively inexpensive audio players has created a market for tapes for listeners of all ages. With students in grades 4-6, contemporary music by their favorite performers is the most popular fare. The popularity of the music videos on television contributes to students' desires to own recordings of the music.

Making music videos. Using records or tapes, the class can make their own music videos—using drama, dance, and multimedia effects (such as slides) for background. As part of the activity, discuss the range of music videos presented on television. What is good? What is objectionable and why? Discuss how this media presents minorities and women, how violence is handled, etc.

THE VALUE OF LIVE PERFORMANCE

Television, movies, radio, records, and tapes overwhelmingly provide the mass of entertainment and exposure to theatre arts for most children. We cannot reiterate too often, however, that all children should have regular opportunities to see live performance. It is equally important that teachers and parents demand that what is offered for the child audience is of high quality. Never accept the notion that something done for children can be "less." It ought to be the very best.

Possible sources of quality programs for children and youth are college theatre departments who may offer shows both on campus and toured to the schools, community theatre groups who may be willing to do theatre for children if assured of school support, and professional touring companies. State and local arts councils often are able to provide at least partial support to bring quality theatre to child audiences. A troupe might even be sponsored by local philanthropic organizations who support projects for children. It may be necessary for you to take the initiative in exploring possibilities so that all children can see quality live performance.

Schools committed to theatre arts education will want to supplement classroom experiences in creative drama with supplement classroom experiences in creative drama with exposure to plays, musicals, puppet theatre, and perhaps ballet and opera when possible. Never assume that children will not or cannot understand or enjoy any specific theatrical form: *The Nutcracker* ballet and the opera of *Hansel and Gretel* can hold a child audience spellbound. Nothing takes the place of seeing the performers bring a story to life, hearing the music, and seeing the dancers with your very own eyes and spirits.

Generous amounts of creative drama can help children better understand and enjoy live performance of all kinds. Dramatization of literature and original plays that include different kinds of conflict provide insights into the nature of conflict and conflict resolution. All of the activities suggested in chapter 5 provide background and skills in identifying dramatic structure, characterization, and some of the technical elements of theatre.

Doing drama and seeing live performance of drama is a reciprocal process; each experience enhances the other. Recall that a policy paper on "Theatre in Elementary Education" produced by the American Theatre Association affirms that creative drama and "seeing plays of the highest possible educational value and artistic quality" are both "essential to basic education."

For students engaged in classroom drama, one of the most rewarding experiences is to attend a live performance as a group. It can be an excellent way to explore the elements of drama. It can also provide a basis for teaching students how to critique a performance and that criticism means discovering all of the good things (as well as discussing anything they did not like or understand). Relate this to the debriefing sessions that follow students' own creative drama sessions.

Often a class that has enjoyed a play together will want to do something special, related to the play or its topic, in drama. Stimulated by the "smell of the greasepaint," they will approach their own work with excitement and vigor. Even for children addicted to television, a live performance is special and exciting. There is really nothing else quite like it.

COMPARING TELEVISION, FILM, AND LIVE THEATRE

Although many theatrical offerings are done both as film and live theatre, there are conventions unique to each form.

The movie screen is particularly suitable for the extravaganza or spectacle. Great vistas and large casts afford "bigger than life" possibilities. By contrast, television is an intimate medium, viewed in small and often private settings. It also has the capacity to deal with events as they are happening so there is often immediacy as well. Both media can provide exciting and unusual effects by the manipulation of the camera and diverse technical equipment. The zoom lens and dissolve techniques, for example, make ordinary events look extraordinary. Computer graphics and other special effects (both video and audio) create illusions difficult to transfer in a live performance.

Live theatre depends largely on the actors, the story, the stagecraft, and the presence of an audience willing and able to suspend disbelief in order to create the illusion. The role of audience is, therefore, critical to live theatre in ways quite different from viewing television or film.

Audience etiquette for formal theatre

1. Arrive on time; avoid climbing over others; be courteous.
2. Do not take food or drink into a formal theatre show.
3. A real emergency is the only reason to leave during a performance; wait until intermission before leaving and return with respect for others who have remained seated.
4. Save conversation and comments until intermission or after the show. Even "stage whispers" are disruptive.
5. Be responsive in appropriate ways. Applause, laughter, and so on are appreciated, but whistles and shrieks are not.
6. If part of a group, stick together. Note where adult leaders are located and take any special cues from them.
7. Wait for final curtain or house lights to indicate end of performance; then exit in a quiet and orderly manner.

CHAPTER 8

Writing Workable Plans

Writing unit and lesson (or teaching) plans in drama is very much like writing plans in any of the content areas. Some lessons concentrate on the development of competencies in drama and others use an integrated approach in which drama skills already gained are used as a teaching methodology or strategy in one of the content areas. Perhaps the most useful approach is the lesson that combines and integrates ongoing work in drama with ongoing work in some other area of study. To use drama as a teaching/learning methodology, it is best to use drama knowledge, skills, and attitudes with which students have already acquired a degree of mastery. By contrast, drama lessons and integrated drama-/content area plans focus on building competencies in both drama and content area while using the drama to enhance and enrich the subject matter learning.

However and whenever you teach drama, you will want to be able to clearly state your goals and objectives for the drama work. From the beginning of the school year on, you will have identified and articulated both long-range and short-range goals in drama and should be able to translate those goals into student objectives that provide the information necessary for individual student assessment. One of the major challenges in identifying and stating goals and objectives is determining readily where students are in their mastery of drama. In drama, unlike most of the content areas, student records may not clearly show what work has been previously done and how either the group or individuals schools where drama is regularly and generously included in curriculum, student records should indicate both previous experiences and levels of competency—in other words, what kinds of drama experiences have been done, how often, and how well have the students progressed. Nationwide, however, this kind of background information is the exception rather than the rule. Lacking such information, both discussion with students and actual participation in drama will help you appraise where the group is and where they need to go. Even when most of the students have had a good deal of drama work, you should begin with some review and build some common drama experiences with the class as a newly constituted group.

UNIT PLANS FOR DRAMA EDUCATION

The very idea of a unit suggests that the activities will be conducted over an extended period of time and that they will coalesce around a central idea or concept. For example, a useful drama unit in grades 4-6 may be designed to give students information, skill development and application, and appropriate attitudes for using drama techniques to explore and enhance how people function and work in groups as responsible members of society. Separate lessons within the unit may integrate drama with literature, socialization skills, current events, history, and career education. In the unit, you would include everything you *might* cover in the teaching (recognizing that you will probably not do all of the activities suggested in the plan). When you actually begin to develop teaching plans from the unit, choose the activities that seem best suited to more narrowly focused purposes, objectives, and occasions.

■ PLANNING LONG-RANGE GOALS

The following is a format for writing a unit plan for drama:

1. The unit plan should contain an *overview* and *rationale*. This will include a brief statement of the *nature and scope* of the unit. It will clearly describe where, when, and how to

begin and what is to be covered; also, what the final outcome should be. The length of time devoted to the unit will be stated.

For example, the unit may concentrate on a variety of ways that groups are used for drama work and may be integrated with other applications of groups such as groups for problem-solving and accomplishing tasks.

The *scope* of the unit should describe beginning and exiting skills. It may start with several drama activities in which players work independently in self-space to accomplish tasks that are best done individually. This might be followed by various kinds of pair work. Finally, the major lessons of the unit would explore various applications of group work both in drama per se and in drama integrated with other content areas.

A unit of this scope would probably be planned for approximately six weeks. The *overview* should identify how much time each day, or each week, will be devoted to this work. The *rationale* is a briefly stated justification for the unit and highlights the value and importance of dealing with the content, skills, and attitudes for your stated population.

2. The plan should clearly state the most important *goals*. If the unit primarily deals with concepts, such as the concept of groups, most of the goals will deal with concept development. Other goals will cover skills to be practiced toward a desired level of competency, and attitudes appropriate to the content of the unit.

3. The next step is a statement of *major objectives,* written in observable terms that relate to the stated teaching goals. Only the major goals and objectives should be stated, however. You miss the point and lose the value of this kind of planning if you include vast numbers of goals and objectives in either a unit or teaching plan. You can become so embroiled with the mechanics of the plan that you lose sight of what you really wish to accomplish and become inundated with trivia.

Be sure that you have identified at least one student objective for each goal. If such a minimum is not possible, question the validity or importance of that goal in this particular unit.

4. *Activities* are listed next. These are the heart of the unit. This term is used to cover anything you or the students will do. For example, this includes teacher introductions to the unit such as a special film, stories, field trip, a guest who shares some expertise or experience, and so forth.

This section will also include all of the drama and related activities for other subject or content areas to be integrated into the unit. It is good to overplan, to include more ideas than may actually be taught. This section of a unit plan is a kind of "wish list" that contains everything you might like to do if time and student interest allows.

Some activities may be designated as necessary for everyone to do; others may be integrated into content learning centers and might be selected by only some of the students. For example, the plan may include extra ideas for individual library research or writing or speech activities. Useful unit plans, particularly for the later grades should include copious options and alternative ways of meeting goals and objectives.

5. *Ideas and methods for assessment and evaluation* should be included in the unit plan. These are derived from the goals and objectives stated at the beginning. In drama, assessment and evaluation is often of an informal nature. It may also include self- and peer-evaluation. The fact that you seldom (if ever) use pencil-and-paper tests does not make assessment and feedback less valid or necessary. You should plan how to handle this in a general way when you develop the unit plan.

6. In this section, list all of the *printed materials* that will be used in teaching the unit—the children's books, stories, poems, plus all of the professional materials that you will consult. It is advantageous to make these references complete so that the unit can be used again and again (or

put on hold, if necessary, and used later than originally conceived).

7. Finally, the unit plan should include titles, sources, etc., for any *other materials* that may be used: films, records, cassette tapes, filmstrips, resource persons, properties, projectors, and other miscellaneous materials.

Once a unit plan is developed covering a specific set of learnings that you want to include in the curriculum, you can use the plan again and again, with appropriate updating, revisions, and adaptations to accommodate different groups of students and your own changing interests and expertise. The initial time and effort can be considerable, but over a period of time, such thorough and flexible plans can be priceless.

Unit plans for other content areas can include goals and objectives related to creative drama, just as unit plans in drama often include goals and objectives in the content areas. This is so often true in grades 4-6 that it is difficult to know whether a unit should be labeled drama/(content area) or the other way around. The use of drama as a teaching/learning methodology has so much potential that you must keep alert to the possibilities for using drama activities when developing units in all of the content areas. Similarly, you may often include in a drama unit activities that are not drama per se. Art, music, and literature activities not directly involving drama can be included in a drama unit to provide additional motivation and optional ways to express ideas and feelings, and to accommodate individual learning styles and interests of pupils.

Unit plans are most rewarding when they are planned for great flexibility. There should always be room to insert something new, to be able to expand or extend on an activity that is really working, and to be able to take advantage of something new that comes along after the unit is in progress. A special program offered in the media center that relates in some way, a new book, the sudden opportunity to see a play as a group or have a guest come to class are things you would not want to miss simply because they were not included in the original plan. It is especially useful to keep alert to special television programming that may relate in some unique way to the unit. You may even generate a "viewing guide" that directs the students' involvement with the program in ways that complement the goals and objectives already identified.

Flow chart planning

Some teachers prefer to use *flow chart planning* to design curriculum rather than unit plans. You begin this type of planning by choosing a theme or topic around which work in the content areas and the arts may cluster and from which all or significant segments of the curriculum "flows."

■ PLANNING FROM A THEME

Imagine that the curriculum topic for a fifth-grade class is "Our Community/Our World." You would identify all of the skills and attitudes that should be covered by the students during a given block of time (perhaps one marking period) in all of the curriculum areas (or several specific ones). You then teach those skills and attitudes using information, concepts, and interests related to looking at the local community as a microcosm of the world. For example, work in geography would be done by looking at the various ethnic groups represented in the local community. Census reports, community organizations, even the telephone directory can provide the important demographic information. Once major groups have been identified, you might divide into small groups and have members of each group research everything they can find about the history of the group in the community, as well as studying the geography, history, and culture of the part of the world to which members of the group relate as the source of their "roots." The contributions of outstanding members of each of the target groups (both locally and historically) in the areas of literature, science, and the arts can provide interesting ways to integrate into those content areas as well. Creative drama, with its attention to role-playing and the incorporation of literature makes a natural alliance with flow chart planning. Indeed, all of the arts very naturally and conveniently fit into this approach.

Rather than individual unit plans for each of the content areas and arts, flow chart curriculum development requires an overall plan for the time period, a kind of master plan *with lots of options*. This requires an ability on your part to synthesize and integrate a variety of areas into one cohesive plan while making certain that everything that needs to be covered is included. Many optional ways to meet goals and objectives are generally provided, with activities for whole class, small group, and individual work. Assessment and record keeping can be especially demanding, since few students would be working lockstep. This kind of long-range planning is exciting, demanding, and very rewarding; however, it assures the arts a central role in the curriculum.

LESSON (OR TEACHING) PLANS

Lesson plans become *teaching plans* when they are adapted or created for a specific population of students. Obviously lesson plans, or ideas for such plans, included in this or any other resource book for teachers will require adaptation to convert them into useful plans for a particular classroom. The following format for drama lesson plans offers one set of guidelines that works well for a variety of populations, teaching purposes, and drama activities. This particular format consists of ten steps, all of which would be centered around a specific theme or topic.

Format for a drama lesson

Step 1. Identify the *theme* and/or *topic* for the lesson. If the theme is rather broad, pick a more narrowly focused topic. At this point, it is also useful to note anything special related to the particular population for whom the lesson is planned, and information about when, where, and for how long the lesson is scheduled.

Step 2. State your *teaching goals* (sometimes called *purposes*) for the lesson. As with a unit plan, list only the most important goals on the lesson plan.

Step 3. State the most important *student objectives* designed to meet the teaching goals. Describe these in observable terms and include relevant conditions and criteria when necessary. For example, when introducing new ideas, skills and so forth, anticipate what percentage of students ought to be able to successfully meet student objectives and at what level of competency, in order for you to feel that goals were adequately met. There would be no point in going on to more advanced work until such minimum expectations were met by most of the students.

Step 4. State *materials* to be used and *bibliographic information* here (or at the end of the plan). Include all that should be on hand in order to teach the lesson: films, books, music, audio-visual equipment, properties, and so forth, as well as specific drama materials developed for the lesson, such as the materials to do a sequential game, cards for small group scenes, or copies of poetry for choric work.

Step 5. Briefly describe how you will introduce the lesson. Often the sharing of a story or a poem, a song, or film may be used here. Time to discuss, brainstorm, and plan should be built into the time allowance for the entire lesson, and this is particularly true as the lesson is introduced. Rushing this important step in order to get to the actual drama activities often reduces the overall quality of the drama experience.

Step 6. *Warm-ups.* These are the short activities described earlier in chapter 3. They should fit thematically and skills-wise with the main section of the lesson as well as flow from the introduction.

Step 7. *Main drama activities.* Describe the main drama work to be covered in the lesson. Students in grades 4-6 are often working on pieces of work complex enough that they cannot be completed in one session. Note this in the plan. (When additional periods are required, it may help to begin subsequent sessions with a very brief review and a short warm-up to refresh memories and heighten motivation.)

Step 8. *Cool-downs.* Although these are always useful after physically involving work, often drama with later elementary students is more verbal than physical. Adapt to fit what has gone before. Cool-downs should always continue the content of the lesson.

Step 9. *Debriefing and assessing.* This is important if learning and progress in drama is to be accomplished. The lesson plan may include several sample questions that could be used to evoke and facilitate a lively discussion of what has happened, both in terms of the content and the drama processes used. See the Questioning Strategies section of chapter 2.

Step 10. *Evaluation.* Note anything pertinent to assessing and evaluating the work, including individual and group efforts.

The plan may also suggest a variety of follow-up activities, generally in other areas of curriculum, based on the drama experiences. Writing, library research, oral reports, art projects, special work in music, and science experiments are all examples of other content work that may extend from the drama lesson. Follow-up activities are especially important when drama tends to be regularly integrated with other content areas, including the other art forms.

Sample lesson plan for sixth-graders

Topic: Using Our Heads

Teaching Goals: To use several types of creative work to experientially explore different ways that we "use our heads" to process information, solve problems, accomplish tasks, to challenge students to think about how people think.

Student Objectives: Given the opportunity to engage in various drama activities, students will be able to:

1. compare and contrast different modes of thought.
2. describe different thinking strategies.
3. demonstrate through creative drama the application of different problem-solving strategies.
4. evaluate how well different strategies work for different kinds of tasks.

Introduction: Discover what the class knows about how people think—particularly how we use our brain to learn, to process information, and to think through solutions to problems. Use an overhead projector to show a line drawing of the human brain. (It is easy to make such a line drawing inasmuch as the brain looks very much like a large walnut with the two halves joined by the corpus callosum.) Discuss how each hemisphere has special functions to perform: producing language, working with numbers, and logical (sequential) thinking in the left hemisphere; spatial perception, synthesizing (pulling lots of ideas together from various sources to create a new idea), imagining, visualizing, and intuiting in the right hemisphere. Emphasize, however, how both hemispheres work together to perform most tasks. Compare this to groups of individuals coming together to solve a problem or carry out a task with each person contributing her or his own special ways of looking at things, experiences, and interests. Talk about times when we want to be by ourselves to think in private; compare with other times when we want to seek the opinions of another or others.

Warm-up: Invite all students to close their eyes and use their imaginations to do the following short guided imagery.

Close your eyes and see yourself in your favorite thinking place. You have gone there to think. See what you are thinking about in your mind's eye. (Maybe you are studying for a test, trying to get an idea for an oral report; maybe you are trying to think of something to do for a friend for his or her birthday . . . something special; maybe you have a problem of a personal, private nature that you just want to think about by yourself.) Imagine what parts of your brain you are using as you do all of your thinking. Look inside and see how you are "using your own special brain." Be impressed with what a wonderful thing it is to be able to think! Open your eyes but keep thinking about how you think. Have your brain tell your right arm to stretch up over your head; now lower it. Have your brain tell your face to look happy, serious, sad, silly. Have your brain instruct your left hand to pretend to pick up an apple and take a bite. Notice how good and juicy that apple is. Set the rest of the apple on your desk.

Discuss: Divide the class into four groups of more or less equal size. Each group is to be a problem-solving group. Each will get a card with a special problem to work out. The problem situations and solutions will later be dramatized, shared, and discussed. For the scenes to share, each group will show the following: who they are, where and when their situation takes place, the introduction of the problem (conflict), and how the problem is resolved and the situation ended.

Group 1. Some friends have gone for a hike on a Saturday afternoon. When they left it was a beautiful day. They have lunches in their backpacks, a portable radio and tape player, some favorite music to play, and a canteen of lemonade. They find just the right place for their picnic when suddenly a strong wind begins to blow and a huge summer storm blows up. Decide how best to handle the situation. Plan your scene to dramatize and later share.

Group 2. It is the year 2020. The government is trying to establish a colony of families on a space station. The mothers and fathers will be employed in running the station and the children will go to school there. Someone calls on your family and invites them to join the experiment. It sounds exciting but .... As a group, plan how you will make your decision and what it is. Be prepared to dramatize your scene including your discussions that lead to your decisions. (Hint: weigh the pros and cons; maybe some members of the family are for going and others are against but you must function as a unit.)

Group 3. Some person or persons have been abusing school properties—library books, gym equipment, etc. The principal has asked a group of sixth-graders to come up with a plan for either catching the culprits or finding some way to convince everyone to take pride in their school. You are the group chosen to help solve the problem. You feel honored but also nervous about your task. Plan how you will deal with your job and be prepared to dramatize the situation and solution.

Group 4. A group of friends plan to go together on a special school outing. They have been looking forward to this for several weeks. One friend accidentally discovers that one member of the group can't afford to go but is too proud and

embarrassed to say anything. The others want to help but
aren't sure how to go about it. Plan how you will solve the
problem. Rehearse and be prepared to share your situation
and solution.

After all groups have had sufficient time to analyze their
problems, decide on a solution, and rehearse their scenes,
each will be shared.

Debriefing and assessing should follow the sharing. Discussion should deal with the following questions:

Debriefing: Was it easy or hard to show how you set about
solving your problem? Describe how you functioned. What
role did nonverbal communication play in communicating
your ideas? Was it hard to put some of your ideas into words?

Discussion of the content: What was the nature of the problem
in each group? Which problems seemed most easily solved by
using very logical step-by-step thinking? Discuss.

Which required the problem solvers to use their imaginations, maybe to visualize pictures in your minds? Did some
problems seem to benefit from also using your intuition
(deep-down feelings) and/or trying to put yourself in someone else's place? Did some solutions involve several different
kinds of thinking? Which ones? Discuss.

Make three lists on the board. Label them this way: Logical
Thought, Imaginative Thought, and Both. Have the class
brainstorm different kinds of problems that seem best solved
using each approach. Evaluate the various choices and make
adjustments. Discuss the results.

Materials needed: Overhead or opaque projector. Line
drawing of the human brain or a picture from a science book.
Several books in which children solve problems: *My Side of the
Mountain* (George, 1959), *Hill's End* and *Ash Road* (Southall,
1963, 1966), *The Robbers* (Bawden, 1979), *Carry On, Mr. Bow-
ditch* (Latham, 1956) are all excellent examples.

EVALUATING DRAMA WORK

Your work does not end with the debriefing or getting
students involved with follow-up assignments. When drama

has become an integral part of the curriculum, you will also have to keep track of each student's progress and growth in drama, just as you do in art, music, and physical education. This requires some ways to evaluate and keep records that are not overly burdensome yet are sufficiently informative so as to be useful.

■ USING GOALS/OBJECTIVES FOR ASSESSMENT

Assessment and evaluation procedures are easier to set up and maintain when teaching goals and student objectives have been clearly determined and stated in the planning. A rather comprehensive list of verbs that are useful in writing student objectives in drama are included at the end of this chapter. These are not only useful when writing plans but in thinking about ways to assess learning. Many of the verbs used in writing objectives will need additional clarification; for example, "demonstrate an ability to analyze dramatic structure by creating a scene with a beginning, middle, climax, and ending that includes the introduction of a conflict and appropriate resolution." This communicates a great deal more than simply, "students will be able to analyze the dramatic structure of a scene." Well-written goals and objectives make the often difficult job of assessing work in drama less ambiguous. However, evaluating the quality of the work, once minimum criteria are met, is often quite subjective and challenging. Later elementary students should have a considerable amount of input into their own evaluation, both group evaluation of group efforts and self-evaluation of individual work.

■ DESIGNING EVALUATION INSTRUMENTS

Paper-and-pencil tests in drama are generally useless, although you might gain insights into what a student has derived from the drama experience through a story or some other mode of creative expression following the drama. However, the quality of the follow-up work would be evaluated against separate criteria and still would not give you a basis for assessing the drama work itself. The most commonly used assessment and reporting is done by giving feedback to the group and to individuals during or immediately following the lesson. It is useful to keep the goals and objectives clearly in mind so that feedback can be specific.

For example, one student objective reads: "Given the opportunity to explore an environment with a variety of topographic features, students will demonstrate with appropriate movement and facial expression how they would move through the various features of the environment." You would watch for movement and pantomime that suggests that the explorers are adjusting their movements to the different topographies (for example, "deep sand, tall weeds, sharp rocks, etc.") You would note several individual efforts as well as the general abilities of the group to move in convincing ways. Often you can give immediate feedback to several individuals, praising their efforts or suggesting that "it is difficult to see that you are climbing over sharp rocks; show me how sharp they are and how hard it is to climb over them." The debriefing session is a good time to give feedback as it describes the overall efforts of the group, but you can also praise some outstanding individual efforts as well. You would also guide the group in self-evaluation and provide a sensitive but helpful model for them to emulate.

Long-range progress is probably best handled by keeping a one-page "Drama Progress Chart" for each child, consisting of a checklist of items based on the long-range goals and objectives. Such a chart contains items associated with specific skills (such as progress in movement and pantomime work, increased ability to show appropriate emotional responses through facial and body expression, etc.). You may wish to create your own chart, or other evaluation instruments could be cooperatively developed by grade level for the entire school system. Some state boards of education offer guidelines for assessing drama work according to statewide performance objectives in drama. The scope and sequence chart at the beginning of this book could be used as the basis for designing a student progress form for a specific group.

CREATIVE DRAMA PROGRESS CHART (4th. grade)

NAME _____ Period Beginning _____ Ending _____

FOCUS: _____

(I - lowest; 5 - highest)

	First Observation	Second	Third
Able to use body effectively to show ideas, feelings, imitative actions.	1 2 3 4 5	1 2 3 4 5	1 2 3 4 5
Uses sensory recall to guide pantomime	1 2 3 4 5	1 2 3 4 5	1 2 3 4 5
Demonstrates understanding of spatial perception in			
(1) self-space	1 2 3 4 5	1 2 3 4 5	1 2 3 4 5
(2) shared space	1 2 3 4 5	1 2 3 4 5	1 2 3 4 5
(3) larger space	1 2 3 4 5	1 2 3 4 5	1 2 3 4 5
Can control body movement in terms of:			
(1) tempo (fast, med. slow)	1 2 3 4 5	1 2 3 4 5	1 2 3 4 5
(2) energy levels	1 2 3 4 5	1 2 3 4 5	1 2 3 4 5
Uses facial expression and gesture to demonstrate:			
(1) ideas	1 2 3 4 5	1 2 3 4 5	1 2 3 4 5
(2) feelings	1 2 3 4 5	1 2 3 4 5	1 2 3 4 5
(3) roles	1 2 3 4 5	1 2 3 4 5	1 2 3 4 5
Listens to:			
(1) follow directions	1 2 3 4 5	1 2 3 4 5	1 2 3 4 5
(2) show respect	1 2 3 4 5	1 2 3 4 5	1 2 3 4 5
Willing to try new things	1 2 3 4 5	1 2 3 4 5	1 2 3 4 5
Shows original thought and imaginative expression	1 2 3 4 5	1 2 3 4 5	1 2 3 4 5

Comments: (note areas of most improvement or greatest strengths and any problem areas)

Whatever the source, the progress report should also contain items that relate to each student's development as a risk-taker (willing to try new things), ability to function cooperatively in the group, ability to think and express imaginatively, ability to listen and follow directions, and growth in self-confidence as a participator in drama. Scoring may be done using a number scale from zero (low performance) to five (high performance), or using semantic differentials such as "seldom, occasionally, almost always." There should also be room on each report for individual comments. The total number of checklist items should be limited to no more than eight to ten, probably less when the chart is to cover a specific area of focus (such as characterization or pantomime) for a limited span of time. It is most useful to look at each child's progress in terms of the child's own growth rather than compared to peers even as we take note of how well the child meets our goals and objectives.

■ SCHEDULING INDIVIDUAL ASSESSMENTS

It is both impossible and unnecessary to assess each individual student during every drama experience. It is important to take note of each student's work regularly and often enough that progress can be noted. Unusual abilities or difficulties should be noted, especially if difficulties seem persistent and are impeding the student's normal progress and/or interfering with the work of the group. However, everyone has a bad day from time to time, so do not generalize from isolated instances that blow things out of proportion. To avoid this requires that you observe every student quite often, and on a regular basis, so that rare incidents do not get reported as usual behavior. You can set guidelines for yourself. This might involve determining that each student will be assessed for progress at least three times within a marking period. (This would be in addition to observing for special needs, problems, and aptitudes.) It is especially important to notice and make record of individual triumphs such as the student who has been apprehensive and self-conscious and then contributes with poise. Nothing is more motivating and facilitating than when you "catch 'em being great!"

■ REPORTING DRAMA EVALUATIONS

If your school system uses letter or number grades for most evaluation, you will want to find an alternative way of reporting progress in drama. A grade of "A" or "C" would not communicate much to parents, nor would simply noting "pass" or "fail," but comments that describe specific behaviors would. For example, "Maria is putting her whole body into the pantomime work in contrast to the half-hearted participation earlier observed"; or "Bill's eagerness to get into the action often results in only partial listening to instructions or group discussion. He is working on more active listening, but he needs to be reminded from time to time."

Upper elementary children should be encouraged to take increased interest in their own evaluation. Teacher feedback and self-evaluation can be shared through brief exchanges or formal conferences between marking periods. Such person-to-person sharing helps the student to better understand the formal evaluation as provided on grade reports. Helping students to become self-evaluative in drama can provide a format for self-assessment in other subject areas as well.

Because you can learn so much about a student through drama, comments from the progress chart could make a valuable basis for discussion during a parent-teacher conference or special visitation. When drama is included in the curriculum, parents or others responsible for the student should be informed about drama: what it is and is not, how it is used in the classroom and for what purposes. Teachers who include drama should be prepared to discuss the role and rationale for drama education in the classroom and in the school curriculum. When parents understand something about this art and its value for their children, they are generally interested, supportive and eager for their children to regularly engage in drama experiences. Because parents and guardians generally want to know as much as possible about the progress of their children, they expect to receive feedback on drama just as they would for the other arts. This is only possible when progress is systematically noted and evaluated.

THE SPECIAL DRAMA EVENT

In grades 4-6, students often spend blocks of time developing rather complex dramatizations, either based on a favorite piece of literature of built from original ideas. They may wish to enhance their drama with music, dance, bits of scenery and costuming, and other special effects. Some students may take a special interest in the technical areas of theatre arts and be eager to get involved with producing sound tapes, a musical score to accompany a play, or unusual lighting or multi-media effects. Whether suggested by the teacher or by the group, this level of enthusiasm often prompts someone to suggest that a particular work should be polished, show-cased, and shared with others. Sometimes the special drama work can be integrated with a larger program of some kind: a school assembly, a community celebration or festival, a holi-day event. Whether a modest production for another class or on a much grander scale as part of a school or community program, the special drama event takes time, planning, and commitment.

As in all work in creative drama, each student should be involved in a special drama presentation in important ways. Even a polished ready-to-be-shared creative drama produc-tion should remain student-centered and process-oriented. Every student should feel an integral and necessary part of it all. Ideally, every student is *in* the presentation, and everyone shares in the applause at the end. But there is much to do to take a classroom exercise in drama and ready it for guests.

■ ORGANIZING A SPECIAL DRAMA EVENT

Time must be devoted to careful planning and organizing. In addition to the program—the play or collection of scenes, "vignettes," etc.—there are a myriad of other tasks. Small committees, task forces, and crews will be required before "curtain time."

First, the class will need to decide just what they have been working on that they wish to polish and share. It generally helps to begin with something already in progress. Next, they need to decide when, where, and for whom they will present their show. Once a general plan has evolved, another planning session is in order to identify all of the jobs to be done. If the program is to be held in a special room in order to accommodate an audience, appropriate space must be found and scheduled as early as possible so that the players will have a chance to practice in the facility.

■ ASSIGNING RESPONSIBILITIES

One committee might be in charge of overseeing the scheduling of the facility for rehearsals and checking to be sure it has sufficient outlets for audio-visual equipment, adequate space for audience, convenient ways to enter and exit, etc.

Another group will take care of arrangements for guests. If other classes are to be invited, it is necessary to check their schedules before making other arrangements for the production. When parents and guests from outside the school are to be invited, notices or invitations should be sent out well in advance and should provide all necessary information as to time, place, etc. On the day of the show, students who are not in the opening segment should be assigned to front-of-the-house responsibilities—seating guests, handing out programs, making everyone comfortable and welcome. Playbills take extra time to prepare, but it is fun for the players and their guests to see their names in the program. A poster outside the room announcing the title of the show, date(s), time(s), etc. adds a professional touch.

A crew will be needed to take charge of preparing or acquiring any audiovisual materials—music on records or tapes, sound effects, slides for background if incorporated in the play, etc. If the multimedia effects become quite elaborate, those chores may need to be divided among two or more special crews.

If there is to be some costuming (and students often feel this is very important), another committee should be responsible for all costumes well before the show date. Elaborate costuming should be gently but firmly discouraged; generally, it is best to limit costuming to only a few articles that "suggest" the entire clothing of each character. The same is true of other properties; keep the emphasis on creative drama with everyone, players and audience, encouraged to use her or his imagination to furnish scenery, sets, etc. Makeup should be treated in the same conservative manner. Often just a few lines and a bit of rouge adds a great deal of excitement for the cast but does not require much in the way of materials or time to apply. It is helpful to have a parent or someone from the high school theatre class help with any makeup work.

■ POLISHING TO SHARE

Even though the players are not working from a memorized script, the cast will want to rehearse until the entire production goes smoothly from beginning to end. Then, when final decisions have been made, the product should be practiced with all of the extra embellishments that are to be used during performance. There may even need to be one technical rehearsal with an emphasis on getting all of the mechanics of working with the equipment ironed out and accurately cued. This might be combined with a dress rehearsal using all of the costuming and properties. If the program is planned for parents and other outside guests, students may wish to invite a group of peers (or younger children) to their final rehearsal. This gives them a chance to work with an audience.

On the day of the program, it is useful to have the services of a *few* parents to provide light refreshments for everyone after the show. If another facility was used for the program, the classroom may serve as the "greenroom" (the lounge where actors wait offstage) where players and guests can

VERBS FOR WRITING
STUDENT OBJECTIVES IN DRAMA

accept	display	leave	rearrange
add	do	lift	regroup
analyze	eliminate	limit	rephrase
apply	emit	locate	report
appraise	end	make	retell
arrange	enter	modify	revise
articulate	evaluate	move	sequence
attend	expand	narrate	show
be	express	negotiate	simplify
become	extend	offer	solve
begin	finish	omit	specify
bend	float	open	stand
carry	follow	order	start
choose	form	operate	step
communicate	formulate	organize	stretch
compare	generate	pantomime	swing
compose	give	paraphrase	synthesize
construct	go	participate	take
contrast	handle	pass	tell
contribute	help	perform	throw
cooperate	hold	pick	toss
create	identify	place	touch
critique	illustrate	position	try
cross	include	praise	turn
dance	indicate	predict	use
decide	inform	prepare	vary
defend	interact	present	verbalize
define	interpret	proceed	verify
demonstrate by	invent	produce	walk
describe	invite	project	whisper
develop	join	provide	write
differentiate	keep	question	
discuss	lead	react	

mingle. This is an excellent time to informally educate parents and others about creative drama. Guests are often surprised to discover that the play they have just enjoyed was done improvisationally and that every student had a role. A well-done piece of creative drama can catch and hold an audience as surely as a formal play.

The magic can be as powerful, the success as sweet, and the efforts as rewarding. Every special drama event should include some bit of audience participation, some moments when everyone is a player. For this is theatre of the imagination where a classroom can become another world, students are transformed into every sort and kind of creature, and adults can rediscover their own "child" within.

Creative Drama Resources for the Classroom Teacher

Burger, Isabel B. *Creative Play Acting*. New York: Ronald Press, 1966.
The second part of the book gives special attention to more formal play production.

Cottrell, June S. *Teaching with Creative Dramatics*. Lincolnwood, Ill., National Textbook Company, 1984.
A basic test for the use of creative drama in the classroom.

Courtney, Richard. *Play, Drama and Thought*. New York: Drama Book Specialists, revised 1974.
A comprehensive book on play, drama, psychodrama, social origins, thought and language.

Furness, Pauline. *Role-Play in the Elementary School*. New York: Hart Publishing, 1976.
A handbook for teachers with an emphasis on situational role-playing for problem solving.

Haggerty, Joan. *Please, Can I Play God?* New York: Bobbs-Merrill, 1966.
A firsthand account with which beginning teachers can identify.

Heinig, Ruth Beall, and Lyda Stillwell. *Creative Drama for the Classroom Teacher*. 2nd ed. Englewood Cliffs, N.J.: Prentice-Hall, 1981.
An easy-to-follow, carefully developed approach to creative drama.

Koste, Virginia G. *Dramatic Play in Childhood: rehearsal for life*. New Orleans: Anchorage Press, 1978.
Presents an enthusiastic advocacy for the value of drama for all children.

McCaslin, Nellie, *Creative Drama in the Classroom*. 3rd ed., New York: Longman, 1980.
A practical text written especially for the classroom teacher. A collection of readings representative of creative drama in Great Britain and the United States.

McIntyre, Barbara M. *Creative Drama in the Elementary School* (Language Arts for Children Series). Itasca, Ill: Peacock, 1974.
Emphasizes creative drama as part of the language arts program.

Siks, Geraldine B. *Drama with Children*. New York: Harper and Row, 1983.
Shares, in narrative form, eight drama workshops with children. Includes ideas for drama for people of all ages.

Slade, Peter. *Introduction to Child Drama*. London: University of London Press, 1958.
A useful condensation of Slade's earlier classic, *Child Drama*. Explains the philosophical and theoretical approach by this pioneer in Britain.

Spolin, Viola. *Improvisation for the Theatre*. Evanston, Ill: Northwestern Press, 1963.
Author's own approaches for teaching drama through theatre games are designed for people of all ages. Selected chapters are useful for work with elementary children.

Tyas, Billi. *Child Drama in Action*. New York: Drama Book Specialists, 1969.
Drama experiences are described in terms of teacher purposes. Narrates teacher/child interactions.

Wagner, Betty Jane. *Dorothy Heathcote: Drama as a Learning Medium*. Washington, D.C.: National Education Association, 1976.
An American educator presents the highly acclaimed work of an outstanding drama educator from Britain.

Ward, Winifred. *Playmaking with Children*. 2nd ed. New York: Appleton-Century-Crofts, 1957.
A widely used text by a pioneer in creative dramatics in the United States.

Way, Brian. *Development through Drama*. London: Longmans, Green and Company, 1967.
Discusses the relationship between drama and the development of the child.

Additional Related Resources for the Classroom Teacher

Allen, R.R., Kenneth L. Brown, and Joanne Yatvin. *Learning Language Through Communication*. Belmont, Calif: Wadsworth, 1986.

Ashton-Warner, Sylvia. *Spearpoint; Teacher in America*. New York: Knopf, 1972.

Berger, Terry. *I Have Feelings*. New York: Behavioral Publications, 1971.

Borton, Terry. *Reach, Touch and Teach*. New York: McGraw-Hill, 1970.

Bruner, Jerome S. *Toward a Theory of Instruction*. Cambridge: Belknap Press, 1966.

Charren, Peggy and Martin W. Sandler. *Changing Channels Living (sensibly) with Television*. Reading, Mass: Addison-Wesley, 1983.

Collum, Albert. *Push Back the Desks*. New York: Citation Press, 1967.

DeHaven, Edna. *Teaching and Learning the Language Arts*. Boston: Little Brown, 1979.

Dunn, Rita and Kenneth Dunn. *Teaching Students Through Their Individual Learning Styles*. Reston, Va: Reston Publishing Co., 1978.

Greenbert, Herbert M. *Teaching With Feeling*. New York: The Macmillan Company, 1969.

Hartley, Ruth E., Lawrence K. Frank, and Robert M. Goldenson. *Understanding Children's Play*. New York and London: Columbia University Press, 1952.

Jones, Richard M. *Fantasy and Feeling in Education*. New York: New York University Press, 1968.

Lukens, Rebecca J. *A Critical Handbook of Children's Literature*, 2nd ed. Glenview, Ill: Scott, Foresman and Company, 1982.

Maslow, Abraham. *Toward a Psychology of Being*. Princeton: D. Van Nostrand Company, 1967.

McLellan, Joyce. *The Question of Play*. Oxford, New York: Pergamon Press, 1970.

Mearns, Hughes. *Creative Power*. New York: Dover Press, 1958.

Samples, Bob. *The Metaphoric Mind*. Reading, Mass: Addison-Wesley, 1978.

Seiler, Wm., David L. Schuelke, and Barbara Lieb-Brilhart. *Communication for the Contemporary Classroom*. New York: Holt, Rinehart, Winston, 1984.

Singer, Dorothy, Jerome L. Singer, and Diana M. Zuckerman. *Getting the Most Out of TV*. Santa Monica, Calif: Goodyear Publishing Co., 1981.

Stewig, John Warren. *Children and Literature*. Chicago: Rand McNally College Publishing Company, 1980.

Taylor, Calvin W. Climate for Creativity. New York: Pergamon Press, 1972.

Willbrand, Mary Louise, and Richard D. Rieke. *Teaching Oral Communication in Elementary Schools*. New York: Macmillan, 1983.

Yardley, Alice. *Discovering the Physical World*. New York: Citation Press, 1973.

———. *Reaching Out*. New York: Citation Press, 1973.

———. *Senses and Sensitivity*. New York: Citation Press, 1973.

RESOURCE BOOKS FOR PUPPETRY

Gardner, Richard. *101 Hand Puppets*. New York: David McKay Co., 1962.

Jagendorf, Moritz. *Puppets for Beginners*. Boston: Plays, Inc. n.d.

Luckin, Joyce. *Easy-to-Make Puppets*. Boston: Plays, Inc. n.d.

Mahlmann, Lewis and David Cadwalader Jones. *Folk Tale Plays for Puppets*. (Royalty-free for school use.) Boston: Plays, Inc., 1980. Thirteen one-act scripts of familiar folk tales from around the world.

———. *Puppet Plays for Young Players and Puppet Plays from Favorite Stories*. (Royalty-free for school use.) Boston: Plays, Inc., n.d. More folk and fairy tales and plays based on familiar stories.

Merten, George. *Plays for Puppet Performance*. Boston: Plays, Inc., 1979. Includes several original plays by George and Elizabeth Merten. Excellent production notes included with each play.

Ross, K. *Hand Puppets*. New York: Lothrop, Lee and Shepard, 1969.

Rountree, Gorden, *et al. Creative Teaching with Puppets*. The Learning Line, University of Alabama, 1981. A comprehensive book in puppetry: how to make them; how to use them.

Zavatsky, Bill and Ron Padgette (eds.). *The Whole World Catalogue 2*. New York: McGraw-Hill Paperbacks, 1977. Gives directions for different kinds of puppets including life-size theatre dolls.

Films for
Use in Creative Drama

The following list of films is representative of the kinds that are useful in creative drama. They are arranged alphabetically by title, and for each there is a brief description that shows how the film can relate to the development and classroom use of creative drama. Where there are two names listed following the description, the first is the producer and second, the film distributor.

ABC of Puppet-Making–Part one
A ten-minute color film that illustrates ways to make and dress simple hand puppets. Bailey Films, 1955.

ABC of Puppet-Making–Part two
Shows how to make and use puppets with molded heads. Bailey Films, 1955.

Adventures of Baby Fox
A delightful film that uses music and rhyme to tell about the habits of a baby fox. Good portrayal of a young animal and nice sensory stimulation. Thirteen minutes long. Encyclopedia Britannica films, Encyclopedia Britannica Educational Corporation, 1955.

Animals at Work in Nature
Ten-minute color film that shows close-ups of animals at work. Encyclopedia Britannica Films, Encyclopedia Britannica Educational Corporation, 1956.

Arrow to the Sun
An animated tale of a Pueblo Indian boy who has an exciting adventure while looking for his father. Excellent for use in drama work on American Indians; the colors and designs can be used to stimulate the imagination. Texture Films, 1973.

Big Green Caterpillar
A color film showing the life of a caterpillar from birth to maturity. Excellent for insect movement and to illustrate growth. 11 minutes. Stanton, 1962.

Children Discover the World, The Time of Discovery
A 21-minute, color film showing children from three to twelve from the Idyllwild School of Music and the Arts exploring the use of various art forms for self-expression. Idyllwild Arts Foundation, 1967.

Children in Winter
Fun to use with Ezra Jack Keats book *The Snowy Day*. Shows children playing in the snow. Especially useful in climates where children rarely see snow or have an opportunity to experience it. Encyclopedia Britannica Films, Encyclopedia Britannica Educational Corporation, 1957.

Fable
A beautiful color film starring Marcel Marceau. Excellent example of the art of mime done by a master. Photographed in an Italian village, the cast includes several children. Xerox, 1973.

Fantasy of Feet
Delightful film showing feet doing a variety of movements and wearing many kinds of shoes and no shoes at all. Good to stimulate the imagination and creative movement. Encyclopedia Britannica Films, Encyclopedia Britannica Educational Corporation, 1972.

Follow Me
A five-minute film of children playing follow-the-leader along the streets of their neighborhood and through a playground. Useful for stimulating story ideas or to use with movement activities. Encyclopedia Britannica Films, Encyclopedia Britannica Educational Corporation, 1969.

Grand Canyon
A feast for the eyes and ears. There is no narration, just beautiful scenes of the Grand Canyon during all seasons set to Ferde Grofes' "Grand Canyon Suite." Walt Disney Productions, 1961.

I Have an Egg
Blind children discover all about an egg through their sense of touch. Celebrity Holdings, Inc., McGraw-Hill Text Films, 1969.

Impressions of a City
A 15-minute tour of London which reveals the contrasts of a big city. Excellent for story ideas and sensory stimulation. G.B. Instructional Films, 1965.

Incredible Wilderness
Short color film showing the remote areas of Olympic National Park. Beautiful vistas and close-ups to stimulate the imagination. Harper's Ferry Historical Association (no date).

Land of the Long Day
Gives children an excellent introduction to the land and life of the Eskimos. In color, 38 minutes. Suggests several ideas creating im-

provisational scenes. Encyclopedia Britannica Films, Encyclopedia Britannica Educational Corporation, 1952.

Learning through Movement

An excellent film for preservice and inservice teachers on teaching through creative movement. S-L Film, 1968.

Lion Has Escaped, The

A delightful film with the animation created from children's drawings. Featurette Film Studio, Poland, McGraw-Hill Text Films, 1972.

Little Red Hen

Live animals are used to tell this old favorite story. Many uses in the language arts program, and especially fun for young children to dramatize. Coronet Films, 1950.

Medieval Manor

The setting is a 13th-century castle in France. The story contrasts the lives of those who live in the manor with one of the serf families. Provides good background for drama work placed in that period. Encyclopedia Britannica Films, Encyclopedia Britannica Educational Corporation, 1956.

Mr. Shepard and Mr. Milne

A film visit with the creators of Christopher Robin and Winnie-the-Pooh. A treat for teachers and children who love the Pooh stories. Weston Wood, 1972.

Movement Exploration

Demonstrates a wide variety of movement activities for children K-6. 22 minutes, in color. Documentary Films, 1967.

Movement in Time and Space

Using drama, dance, dialogue and characterization, children explore through fantasy to make intellectual discoveries. 30 minutes, color. BBC Television, Time-Life, 1967.

Organizing Free Play

Of special value to nursery and kindergarten teachers, the film deals with the use and organization of free play in early childhood education. U.S. Office of Education, U.S. National Audiovisual Center (no date)

Pioneer Home

A ten-minute film for elementary children that offers a visual introduction to the life and environment of a pioneer family. Can provide a useful background for drama activities related to pioneer times. Coronet Films, 1948.

Puss-in-Boots

The well-known fairy tale told with animated puppets. A delightful film which may be used to stimulate language activities and an interest in puppetry. Encyclopedia Britannica Films, Encyclopedia Britannica Educational Corporation, 1951.

Rainshower

The changing moods of a day are captured with sight and sound. A photographer takes his camera to farm and city on a rainy day. A 15-minute color film that brings to the classroom a rich experience in listening and looking. Dimension Films, Churchill Films, 1964.

Red Balloon, The

A lovely fantasy about a boy and his red balloon. The film offers children a visual introduction to Paris. An excellent film for stimulating story ideas for dramatization or creative writing. Albert Lamorisse, Com Films, Inc., 1956.

Rock-A-Bye Baby

An examination of mothering practices around the world with an emphasis on the need of children to be touched and held. 30 minutes, color. Time-Life, 1971.

Searching Eye, The

A ten-year-old boy's visual adventures at the beach can stimulate looking activities for children. 18-minute color film. Saul Bass and Associates, 1964.

Show Me

The film shows children with physical impairments participating in a variety of movement activities developed for such purposes as body image, coordination and partner work. This is of particular value to the teacher of special children. Bowling Green State University, Universal Education and Visual Arts, 1967.

Stone Soup

Uses the illustrations from Marcia Brown's book, *Stone Soup*. Story is an excellent one to use for small group pantomime and improvisational work. Weston-Studios, 1955.

Study in Wet

A seven-minute color film all about water. The sound track is entirely created from water sounds. A fine film for looking and listening activities to stimulate the imagination. Groening, 1964.

Textures of the Great Lakes

A six-minute color film showing the textural qualities inherent in the waters, beaches, dune, and land areas around the Great Lakes. The visual images are accompanied by a beautiful score done on the harp. Karl B. Lohman Jr., Thorne, 1966.

Toes Tell

Another excellent film dealing with textures and movement. Encyclopedia Britannica Films, Encyclopedia Britannica Educational Corporation, 1972.

Up is Down

A film for older boys and girls done in both animation and with actual film clips. A little boy who walks on his hands see things differently than they really are. Morton Goldscholl Design Association, Inc., Pyramid Film Producers, 1970.

What's in a Play

A 17-minute color film that analyzes a simple scene, showing conflict, beginning, climaxes, and ending. Film Associates, 1967.

What's in a Story

Using James Thurber's *The Unicorn in the Garden,* the film explores the structure of a story. Film Associates of California, 1963.

Zoo, The

Presents a film "field trip" to the Brookfield Zoo. Provides an excellent background for drama activities about animals, their habits and characteristics. Encyclopedia Britannica Films, Encyclopedia Britannica Educational Corporation, 1961.

Collections and Anthologies: Traditional Stories

Andersen, Hans Christian. Several excellent volumes of Andersen's Fairy Tales are available (in translation). Two rather recent ones are *Fairy Tales* (trans. by L.W. Kingsland. New York: Henry Z. Walck, 1962) and *Seven Tales* (trans. from the Danish by Eva Le Gallienne, illustrated by Maurice Sendak. New York: Harper & Row, 1959).

Arbuthnot, May Hill. *The Arbuthnot Anthology.* Glenview, Illinois: Scott, Foresman, 1961.

Johnson, Edna, Evelyn R. Sickels, Frances Clarke Sayers. *Anthology of Children's Literature.* Boston: Houghton Mifflin, ed. 5, 1977.

Kipling, Rudyard. *Just So Stories.* Garden City, New York: Doubleday, 1912.

Ross, Eulalie Steinmetz, ed. *The Lost Half-Hour: A Collection of Stories with a Chapter on How to Tell a Story.* New York: Harcourt, Brace and World, 1963.

Saltman, Judith. *The Riverside Anthology of Children's Literature.* New York: Houghton Mifflin Co., 1985.
An excellent collection of all genres of literature.

Sandberg, Carl, illustrated by Maud and Miska Petersham. *Rootabaga Stories.* New York: Harcourt, Brace, 1936.

Siks, Geraldine Brain. *Children's Literature for Dramatization.* New York: Harper & Row, 1964.

Thorne-Thomsen, Gudrun, ed. *East o' the Sun and West o' the Moon and Other Norwegian Folk Takes,* rev. ed., New York: Harper & Row, 1946.

Uchida, Yoshiko. *The Magic Listening Cap.* New York: Harcourt, Brace and Company, 1955.

Ward, Winifred. *Stories to Dramatize.* Anchorage, Kentucky: The Children's Theatre Press, 1952.

Poetry for Use in Creative Drama

Baring-Gould, William S. and Ceil Baring-Gould. *The Annotated Mother Goose*. New York: Bramhall House, 1962.

Baron, Virginia, ed. *Here I Am! An Anthology of Poems Written by Young People in Some of America's Minority Groups*, illus. by Emily Arnold McCully. New York: E. P. Dutton, 1969.

The title of this outstanding collection of poetry written by children is self-explanatory. The range of offerings is remarkable.

Brooks, Gwendolyn. *Bronzeville Boys and Girls*, illus. by Ronni Solbert. New York: Harper & Row, 1956.

Children relate to the work of this outstanding contemporary black poet; she creates pictures with which they can identify.

Caudill, Rebecca. *Come Along!*, illus. by Ellen Raskin. New York: Holt, Reinhart & Winston, 1969.

Sensory imagery is easy to do in response to these Haiku poems about the year's cycle.

Clymer, Theodore, ed. *Four Corners of the Sky: Poems, Chants, and Oratory*, illus. by Marc Brown. Boston: Little, Brown & Co., 1975.

These poems of Native American cultures are full of imagery. The chants are especially delightful for choric work.

Cole, William, comp. *Poems of Magic and Spells*, illus. by Peggy Bacon. Cleveland: World, 1960.

Poems about all kinds of magical creatures; great for visualization work and fun for encouraging vocal exploration.

Dunning, Steven, et al. *Reflections on a Gift of Watermelon Pickle*. Glenview, Ill: Scott, Foresman, 1966.

Fleming, Alice, comp. *America Is Not All Traffic Lights: Poems of the Midwest*, illus. with photos. Boston: Little, Brown, 1976.

Excellent for imaging scenes of small towns and rural America.

Koch, Kenneth. *Wishes, Lies, and Dreams: Teaching Children to Write Poetry*. New York: Random House, 1970.

Larrick, Nancy, ed. *On City Streets*, illus. with photos by David Sagarin. New York: M. Evans, 1974.

An outstanding collection of poems about city life.

_____ , ed. *Piping Down the Valleys Wild,* illus. by Ellen Raskin. New York: Dell Publishing, 1973.
An eclectic collection of poetry with an emphasis on places and events in the natural world.
_____ , comp. *Room for Me and a Mountain Lion: Poetry of Open Space.* New York: M. Evans, 1974.
O'Neill, Mary. *Hailstones and Halibut Bones,* illus. by Leonard Weisgard. New York: Doubleday Publishing, 1961.
Each poem celebrates a color; outstanding for visualization work to recreate colors in the mind's eye. (There is an excellent film of this poetry but use the book for guiding imagery experiences.)
Plotz, Helen, comp. *Imagination's Other Place: Poems of Science and Mathematics,* illus. by Clare Leighton. New York: Thomas Crowell Co., 1955.
Visualization is also critical to creativity in the sciences; wonderful materials to integrate with drama/science lessons.
Prelutsky, Jack. *A Gopher in the Garden.* New York: Macmillan, 1967.
_____ . *Nightmares: Poems to Trouble Your Sleep.* illus. by Arnold Lobel. New York: Greenwillow Books, 1976.
Prelutsky uses words to paint wonderfully terrible images so enjoyed by many children.
Saunders, Dennis, comp. *Magic Lights and Streets of Shining Jet,* illus. with photos. New York: Greenwillow Books, 1978.
More poems about natural things, some by well-known poets and others by children.
Silverstein, Shel. *Where the Sidewalk Ends.* New York: Harper & Row, 1974.
_____ . *A Light in the Attic.* New York: Harper & Row, 1978.

Stories to Dramatize

Individual students and specific groups of students vary widely in maturity, needs, and interests. Students may feel most comfortable and free to experiment when working with thoroughly familiar materials. This is often true for older students who have had little previous experience in creative dramatics.

Stories on the following list have been selected to represent the most useful types of literature for dramatization and to expose students to ideas, traditions, and environments that may be new to them.

Aesop. *The Fables of Aesop,* retold by Joseph Jacobs. New York: Macmillan, 1964.
An excellent retelling of the famous fables of Aesop. Strong characters, conflict, and the brevity of the tales make them particularly suitable for small-group improvisation, with or without dialogue.

Alexander, Lloyd. *The Book of Three.* New York: Holt, Rinehart & Winston, 1964. Also: *The Black Cauldron* (1965), *The Castle of Llyr* (1966), *Taran Wanderer* (1967), and *The High King* (1968).
These five books, set in an imaginary land of Prydain, have been evolved by the author from a wealth of Welsh legends and mythology.

Anderson, Joan. *The First Thanksgiving Feast.* New York: Clarion Books, 1984.
Illustrated with black and white photos of the historical buildings at Plymouth Plantation, this is the pilgrim's story told in documentary style. The story unfolds through interviews with the Pilgrims. Excellent for integration of drama and history as children conduct their own interviews.

Aruego, Jose and Ariana Aruego. *A Crocodile's Tale.* New York: Charles Scribner's Sons, 1972.
Delightful story to play with improvised dialogue. Juan saves an

ungrateful crocodile who sees his rescuer as his next meal. In turn, a clever monkey saves Juan.

Bang, Molly. *The Grey Lady and the Strawberry Snatcher.* New York: Four Winds Press, 1980.

This wordless picture book about two strawberry lovers provides a visual feast full of surprises. Children of all ages will enjoy inventing the dialogue for the magnificent illustrations.

Bishop, Claire Hutchet, *Twenty and Ten.* illus. William Pene DuBois. New York: Viking Press, 1953.

Twenty French children help hide ten Jewish children from Nazi soldiers who have come to their mountain retreat in search of Jews.

Bonham, Frank. *Mystery of the Fat Cat.* New York: E. P. Dutton, 1968.

Members of a Boys Club suspect a caretaker of a cat of fraud in order to keep his job. The group sets forth to solve the puzzle. Includes a retarded child who makes a special contribution to the resolution of the story. Several exciting scenes to play with action and dialogue.

Brown, Marcia. *Dick Whittington and His Cat.* New York: Charles Scribner's Sons, 1950.

Poor Dick Whittington must part with his only possession, a cat named Puss, when his master insists that all of the servants must send something to be traded during a voyage of the master's ship. Later the cat is sold to a King of Barbary for a handsome price and Dick becomes a wealthy man. An old tale retold in words and prints by a superb storyteller.

Buck, Pearl S. *The Big Wave.* New York: John Day Company, 1948.

A story of Japan told by a woman who lived there for many years. Young boys who live in a fishing village show great courage and compassion when a great tidal wave radically changes their lives. The book is illustrated with beautiful 18th-century Japanese prints.

Buff, Mary. *The Apple and the Arrow.* illus. Conrad Buff. Boston: Houghton Mifflin, 1951.

An exceptionally well-told and -illustrated story of the Swiss hero William Tell.

Byars, Betsy. *The Summer of the Swans.* New York: Viking Press, 1970.

Older elementary students will relate to the ambivalent feelings associated with growing up as these are revealed through Sara and her friends. Also includes a sensitive portrayal of a retarded younger brother. Basis for situational role-playing dealing with a breadth of topics.

―――― . *The TV Kid.* illus. Richard Cuffari. New York: Viking Press, 1976.

Many students will relate to a young boy who is addicted to television. Students may brainstorm many ideas for what to do when confined to bed. Excellent for small group problem-solving and improvisation.

Chang, Isabelle C. *Tales from Old China*. New York: Random House, 1969.

Traditional Chinese folk tales, fairy tales, and fables. For group pantomime or for puppet or shadow plays.

Cleary, Beverly. *Dear Mr. Henshaw*. New York: Wm. Morrow, 1983.

Ten-year-old Leigh finds his own way in the world after the divorce of his parents. Situational role-playing for older children. (Newbery Award).

Clemens, Samuel L. (pseud., Mark Twain). *The Adventures of Huckleberry Finn*. illus. Norman Rockwell. New York: Heritage Press, 1940.

_____. *The Adventures of Tom Sawyer*. New York: Dodd, Mead, 1958.

Biographical information and drawings from early editions. Many scenes from both of these beloved books are fun to dramatize. Excellent for small group work.

Clymer, Eleanor. *How I Went Shopping and What I Got*. New York: Holt, Rinehart & Winston, 1972.

Thirteen-year-old Debbie feels left out in her family. She disobeys her mother and follows the advice of some friends instead and takes her little sister Judy shopping. Judy gets lost and Debbie must muster all of her courage to handle the problem.

Dahl, Roald. *Dirty Beasts*. illus. Rosemary Fawcett. New York: Farrar Straus Giroux, 1983.

Wonderfully illustrated, each poem details an animal's revenge on an unsuspecting human. Somewhat bizarre humor; full of action and personified animals to play.

_____. *James and the Giant Peach*. New York: Alfred A. Knopf, 1961.

When young James is suddenly orphaned, he goes to live with two dreadful aunts. He escapes from their tyrannical rule when he enters a giant peach and shares an amazing flight across the Atlantic with several supersized insects.

Dalgliesh, Alice. *The Courage of Sarah Noble*. New York: Charles Scribner's Sons, 1954.

Set in the Connecticut territory of the early 1700s, this true story shows how little girls can cope with danger with resolution and courage.

DeJong, Meindart. *The House of Sixty Fathers*. illus. Maurice Sendak. New York: Harper, 1956.

A young Chinese boy becomes separated from his family and finds himself stranded in Japanese-occupied China.

Dodge, Mary Mapes. *Hans Brinker*. New York: Charles Scribner's Sons, 1915.

A story full of suspense, human dilemmas, and action; particularly fun to use during the ice-skating season or with a unit on the Netherlands. Many fine scenes to dramatize.

Forbes, Esther. *Johnny Tremain.* Boston: Houghton Mifflin, 1943.

The setting is prerevolution Boston. Johnny Tremain yearns to become a fine silversmith, but an accident to his hand forces him to leave his apprenticeship. Later, as a messenger for the Sons of Liberty, he becomes deeply involved in the colonies' fight for freedom. (Newbery Award).

Hamilton, Virginia, *Zeely.* New York: Macmillan, 1967.

On her way to spend the summer with her Uncle Ross on his farm, Elizabeth Perry decides that for the vacation she will be a girl named Geeder. Her fantasizing takes on new dimensions when she meets Zeely Tayber who is six-and-a-half feet tall and the color of ebony. Geeder decides Zeely is really a Watusi queen.

Held, Kurt. *The Outsiders of Uskoken Castle.* trans Lynn Aubry. Garden City, N.Y.: Doubleday, 1967.

The story is set in the ruins of an old castle on the Adriatic coast in Yugoslavia where a group of children without homes have taken refuge. Their leader is a spirited red-haired girl named Zora, and the gang's exploits are based on fact. There is lots of action in the tradition of Robin Hood.

Isadora, Rachel. *Opening Night.* New York: Greenwillow Books, 1984.

A story about a young dancer's opening night. Girls, especially, would enjoy dramatizing scenes from this story.

Lloyd, David. *Air.* New York: Dial Press, 1982.

Interesting illustrations and easy to follow text. Useful when integrating creative movement and pantomime with a science lesson on the properties and behaviors of air or ecology scenes.

Konigsburg, E. L. *From the Mixed-Up Files of Mrs. Basil E. Frankweiler.* New York: Atheneum, 1967.

Claudia and Jamie run away from home and hide in the New York Metropolitan Museum of Art. They have many adventures and solve a mystery. Many excellent scenes to dramatize, several especially suitable for work in pairs. (Newbery Award).

Krumgold, Joseph. *And Now Miguel.* New York: Thomas Y. Crowell, 1954.

Miguel finally is old enough to help with the summer pasturing of the family sheep high in the mountain meadows. Several scenes to play about the trials and triumphs of growing up. (Newbery Award).

Lawson, Robert. *Ben and Me.* Boston: Little, Brown, 1939.

The story of Benjamin Franklin told by a very talented and self-important mouse. Fun to dramatize some of the famous discoveries and inventions.

_____ . *Rabbit Hill.* New York: Viking Press, 1944.

The "natives" of Rabbit Hill are worried when new folks move into the people house. Animal characters that are best played with strong human qualities. (Newbery Award).

Lewis, C. S. *The Magician's Nephew* (1955); *The Lion, the Witch and the Wardrobe* (1950); *The Horse and His Boy* (1954); *Prince Caspian* (1951); *The Voyage of the Dawntreader* (1952); *The Silver Chair* (1953); *The Last Battle* (1956). The seven books known as "The Chronicles of Narnia." New York: Macmillan.

A master writer of fantasy created these books for all lovers of "other world" stories; they are full of fantastic characters, both human and nonhuman caught in moments of great conflict. This list is arranged in the order recommended by the author and can provide months of fantasy reading and dramatizing.

Malory, Sir Thomas. *King Arthur,* retold by Mary MacLeod. New York: Macmillan, 1963.

All of the favorite adventures of King Arthur and his knights and ladies.

McCloskey, Robert. *Homer Price.* New York: Viking Press, 1943.

When young Homer helps out in the doughnut shop, he is plagued by near disaster from a lost diamond and a contrary machine that will not quit making doughnuts. Great fun to build machines with body movements and sounds.

NicLeodhas, Sorche. *Always Room For One More.* New York: Holt, Rinehart & Winston, 1965.

The good-natured Lachie MacLachlan invites every traveler who passes on a stormy night to share his "wee house in the heather" with his wife and ten children. A wonder assortment of characters to develop. Find some bagpipe music to use with this. Easy to adapt for sequential pantomime.

Norton, Mary. *The Borrowers* (and subsequent adventures of the borrowers) New York: Harcourt, Brace, 1953.

Children delight in the adventures of the tiny folk who live parallel lives to full-sized humans but do so tucked away in the recesses of old houses and rely on what can be "borrowed."

O'Brien, Robert. *Mrs. Frisby and the Rats of NIMH.* New York: Antheneum Pub., 1971.

A group of rats escape from an experimental laboratory using their newly acquired literacy. The story details their struggles to found their own society. Exciting scenes to dramatize, especially the many narrow escapes and the building of their colony. Also suitable for a readers theatre adaptation. (Newbery Award).

Pearce, Phillipa. *The Shadow Cage.* New York: Thomas Y. Crowell, 1977.

A splendid collection of short tales of the supernatural. Several work well for small group improvisations.

————. *Tom's Midnight Garden.* illus. Susan Einzig. New York: Oxford University Press, 1959.

When an ancient clock strikes thirteen, young Tom is transported to an enchanted garden where he plays with a child from the past. Excellent characters to portray, especially in pairs. A pure imagination tale, drama work can lead into imaginative creative writing. (Carnegie Medal).

Raskin, Ellen. *The Westing Game.* New York: E. P. Dutton, 1978.

A wonderful puzzle mystery full of clues and unique characters both young and old. Fun for students to predict what happens next and to use as inspiration for creating their own puzzle mystery scenes to play. (Newbery Award).

Rostron, Richard. *The Sorcerer's Apprentice.* New York: Wm. Morrow, 1941.

A contemporary version of an old tale about a sorcerer's apprentice who discovers that a little knowledge is truly a dangerous thing. Doubly exciting when played with the Paul Dukas music of the same name.

Seredy, Kate. *The Good Master.* New York: Viking Press, 1935.

An autobiographical story of life in Hungary prior to World War I. The round-up scene is exciting to play, particularly for children who only equate stampedes and round-ups with the American West.

Sherlock, Philip M. *Anansi, The Spider Man: Jamaican Folk Tales.* New York: Thomas Y. Crowell, 1954.

Folk tales of the West Indies based on older African stories. The animal characters are especially intriguing to play.

Speare, Elizabeth George. *The Witch of Blackbird Pond.* Boston: Houghton Mifflin, 1958.

An historical novel for young people about a young girl who leaves her home and comes to the Connecticut colony where she is confronted with attitudes and beliefs new to her. Like the old woman of Blackbird Pond who becomes her friend, young Kit Tyler is accused of witchcraft. (Newbery Award).

White, E. B. *Charlotte's Web.* New York: Harper, 1952.

A favorite story about a spider and her friends, especially Wilbur the pig. The story deals sensitively with death, and there are many fine scenes to dramatize.

Wilder, Laura Ingalls. *Little House in the Big Woods, Little House on the Prairie* (and others). New York: Harper, 1953.

The author tells of her own childhood and growing-up years which began just after the Civil War. She has described everyday events with such clarity that contemporary children can identify with the Ingalls family and its way of life.

Wormser, Richard. *The Black Mustanger,* illus. Don Bolognese. New York: Wm. Morrow, 1971.
Set in Texas after the Civil War, the story of a heart-warming relationship between a white boy and a half black, half Apache cowboy. Action scenes but also useful for character development and situational role-playing.

HISPANIC AND ASIAN STORIES TO DRAMATIZE

Andrews, Roy Chapman. *Quest of the Snow Leopard.* Illustrations, Kurt Wiese. New York: Viking Press, 1955. A fictional account of a 1916-1917 expedition by the author to Yunnan in Southwest China and Tibet. Many scenes to dramatize.

Behn, Harry. *The Two Uncles of Pablo.* Illustrations, Mel Silverman. New York: Harcourt, Brace, 1959. In his quest to learn to read, young Pablo learns much about himself and others. Several sensitive scenes to play.

Carpenter, Frances. *The Elephant's Bathtub: Wonder Tales from the Far East.* Illustrations, Hans Guggenheim. New York: Doubleday and Company, Inc., 1962. Excellent collection for more mature players. Stories from Vietnam, Burma, Cambodia and other Far Eastern lands.

Carter, Dorothy Sharp, ad. *The Enchanted Orchard: And Other Folktales of Central America.* Illustrations, W. T. Mars. New York: Harcourt, 1973. Variety of folktales for dramatization. Several would make wonderful puppet plays.

Goodwin, Murray. *Alonzo and the Army of Ants.* Illustrations, Kiyo Komada. New York: Harper and Row, 1966. Alonzo the Anteater is the only one who can save the lovely village of Paz from killer ants. Wonderful animals to play.

Kimishima, Hisako. *The Princess of the Rice Fields.* New York: Walker-Weatherill, 1970. An Indonesian folktale for dramatization. Beautifully illustrated by Sumiko Mizushi.

Lampman, Evelyn Sibley. *The Tilted Sombrero.* Illustrations, Ray Cruz. Garden City, N.Y.: Doubleday and Company, Inc., 1966. The spoiled son of a Mexican plantation owner suddenly finds himself penniless and thrown into a life of adventure.

Lewis, Thomas P. *Hill of Fire.* Pictures by Joan Sandin. New York: Harper and Row, 1983. An easy-to-read account of the birth of the volcano *Paricutin* in the field of a poor Mexican farmer. This true story is exciting to dramatize, especially if accompanied by music and sound effects.

INDEX OF ACTIVITIES AND IDEAS

DRAMATIZATION—WITH ACTION AND SPEECH

EXPLORING DRAMATIC STRUCTURE

MOVEMENT AND PANTOMIME

Creative movement and pantomime games

Sequential pantomime

Other creative movement and pantomime activities

Sequential listening game

INDEX